time of grace

time of grace

Thoughts on Nature, Family, and
the Politics of Crime and Punishment

Ken Lamberton

The University of Arizona Press   Tucson

The University of Arizona Press
© 2007 by Ken Lamberton

Library of Congress Cataloging-in-Publication Data
Lamberton, Ken, 1958–
Time of grace : thoughts on nature, family, and the
politics of crime and punishment / Ken Lamberton.
p. cm.
Includes bibliographical references.
ISBN 978-0-8165-2570-6 (pbk. : alk. paper)
1. Prisons—Arizona—Tucson. 2. Prisoners—Arizona
—Tucson—Biography. 3. Criminals—Rehabilitation—
Arizona—Tucson. 4. Natural history—Arizona—Tucson.
I. Title.
HV9481.T83L358 2007
365'.9791776092—dc22
[B]   2007007623

This book was supported in part by a grant from the Soros Justice
Fellowship Program of the Open Society Institute.

Manufactured in the United States of America on acid-free,
archival-quality paper containing a minimum of 50% post-
consumer waste and processed chlorine free.

12   11   10   09   08   07   6   5   4   3   2   1

For Dick and Lois

Contents

author's note

The poet Charles Simic says that "Long drawn-out works conflict with the fragmentariness of our consciousness. What is recorded in a notebook is the sense of the unique and unrepeatable experience of those rare moments of clarity."

These words of Simic's gave me the idea for this book. There's nothing more fragmented than my consciousness, than my life in prison. I lifted the first draft of this book—originally a 450-page tome—from the journals of my last years in prison where I had scribbled page after page of eclectic thoughts and wild rants to record my experiences and feelings about the place. After my release in 2000, I began revising this material to its present form, holding to the basic chronology of events over the passing seasons but also peeling away the skin and shapeless fat of my verbiage to expose and preserve what lay beneath. I am no literary Gunther von Hagens (although I may be as controversial as his "Body Worlds" exhibitions). But I hoped to uncover a raw and impenitent nature behind fences, meshed with the naked essence of my marriage and family, crime and punishment—my words and sketches and random thoughts, sights and experiences, articulated into a few isolated moments of clarity.

The book is not a story about a crime of passion, the events of which occurred more than ten years previous to this writing. Distance had cooled those emotions, and I had no desire to return to them, although I cannot deny that they occasionally still rise to the surface in my words. Nor is it an exploration of the reasons behind my crime. My journals reflect little of these issues, mostly because I made choices not to chronically sift through my past but instead to accept it as part of my character and focus more on dealing with its consequences. This is what my last prison journals show, not the personal breast-beating of guilt and remorse (I have already accomplished that in my earlier writing) but the broader effects of my crime, the slow erosion of lives ground down by years of prison's glacial ice.

I do, however, understand the importance of context, and so I include the following for the benefit of those unfamiliar with my story.

In 1986 I was Teacher of the Year. It was an honor awarded to me by the school district in my fifth year of teaching science, an honor I didn't deserve, for in the summer of that same year I became involved with one of my students. The crime would send me to prison for twelve years.

I had been married for five years. My wife and I were raising two young daughters, and Karen was pregnant with our third. We lived in east Mesa, Arizona, a few miles from the school in a modest tract home where we kept an organic garden, a yellow tabby, and a Harris's hawk. Each summer at the end of the school year, we took the cat and the bird, and our girls, as they arrived, to a youth camp near Oracle, Arizona, where Karen and I had worked since meeting and marrying there. The summer of 1986 was no different, except that I had released my bird and invited one of my students to join us.

When she first walked into my classroom, everyone noticed her. She had a presence, a way of carrying herself, that was unlike any student I had taught. Later, people would comment on how much she looked like my wife, tall and thin and blond, but I don't remember consciously recognizing her resemblance to Karen. As the school year progressed, she joined an inner circle of boys and girls whom I considered friends more than students. They were the center of, and the force behind, my reasons for teaching. They called me "Ken."

Occasionally, these kids would baby-sit for me, but by the end of that first semester she had taken over the job. Then, in December, she joined

Karen and me for a week of Christmas camp, singing at campfires, acting in skits, discovering her hair slick with mud while spelunking. She was the first student to cross the gulf between seeing me as a teacher and seeing who I became at camp.

At the end of the school year in 1986, I returned to camp for the summer and soon found a way for us to be together there. The infatuation we had encouraged now metastasized into secret letters and clandestine meetings. The forbidden nature of our romance energized us. We didn't need to eat or sleep, which would only steal time from us. Instead, we watched moonlight spread across the desert like the rumors of our affair. What I felt inside me had brought dimension to my life in the same way that shadows give form and depth to featureless things. But the shadows were more than love and infatuation. They also held desperation, and a fear that had curled itself around my chest.

She and I wouldn't finish the camp season, deciding instead to pursue our illicit relationship and run away together. Our romance burned to ash two weeks later when police discovered us in Aspen, Colorado, walking hand in hand while window-shopping. I was twenty-seven years old. She was fourteen.

This is *what* happened. Explaining *why* it happened is much harder to write about, on several levels, ethical and legal concerns for myself, my family, and my victim among them.

My first therapist believed my crime grew out of two events from my childhood—the death of my father when I was nine and a first love that ended badly when I was fourteen—that arrested my emotional development. In other words, I never grew up. Judge Minker, who reviewed my petition for postconviction relief and released me from prison in 1994, seemed to agree, saying that I had behaved like an even younger adolescent than my victim. Dr. Jennifer Schneider, a physician and expert on addiction, says that I became an "emotional addict," suffering from a form of addiction whereby powerful chemicals like adrenaline and endorphins produced in the body in response to, in my case, intense feelings, create a druglike state. Essentially, my victim was my drug of choice.

Richard Shelton, my close friend and writing mentor, says I simply fell in love, a romantic and forbidden Romeo-and-Juliet kind of love, which he describes in my first book as "disastrous, misplaced, and foolish—but love nonetheless." Karen agrees, although she prefers "stupid" over "foolish."

A newspaper reporter once contacted me about a breaking story the details of which I cannot remember except to say that it was similar to mine. The accused had claimed to be in love with his victim, and the reporter wanted to know from me how this could happen between two people of such different ages. I answered him with a cliché. I said, "Because love knows no bounds, including those of age."

People have asked me, "What were you thinking?" I tell them they're asking the wrong question. I wasn't thinking. I was feeling. If I had been thinking I wouldn't have fallen for someone half my age. But this still sounds like an excuse. Was I immature? Yes. Was I in love? Absolutely. The kind of star-crossed Romeo-and-Juliet love that is often held to be the highest form of love—but also necessarily ends tragically. Unfortunately, my love story isn't fiction. And, unlike most fiction, it's choked with messy incoherencies and loose ends. Instead of finishing with a tearful death scene, the plot lingers, becoming a dull clinging presence like an ugly and painful but nevertheless benign sore. Even now, after more than two decades have passed, there is no closure. But why should there be? In the real world, we may find a way to go on with our lives, but I've learned that finding closure is a myth. We all drag the baggage of our past behind us as we limp through our remaining days.

We live and move by parting our days as a ship parts water. The Lebanese poet-philosopher Kahlil Gibran writes that reason is the rudder while passion is the wind that fills the sails. After meeting her, my ship became a rudderless wreckage as it was swept into the hurricane.

Maybe there simply isn't a reason why I committed my crime—beyond a seriously flawed character. Possibly it is voiced between the lines of my words, and it will take a mind greater than mine to discover it. When you consider human frailty, maybe there doesn't *need* to be a reason. Those who ask "why?" are either marked by prurient curiosity or have never acknowledged their own darkness within.

The truth is, I can't justify or explain away what I did. I'm guilty. If it were in my power to do so, I would shred the fabric of all I am today, giving up anything "good" I've gained from the experience—including my deeper, more profound relationship with my wife—to return to 1986 and take another path. But this is just another fantasy, one I visit far too often. And so, tucked inside the baggage of my past, I carry the wisdom of regret.

In my first book, *Wilderness and Razor Wire: A Naturalist's Observations from Prison*, I discovered intimate connections between myself and the nature that came to me behind fences. In a sense, nature laid me bare. In my next book, *Beyond Desert Walls: Essays from Prison*, my own writing exposed me, revealing a deeper understanding of myself. Now, with *Time of Grace*, my third book in this "prison trilogy," nature and prison become a lens through which I see beyond myself and my immediate world to the larger issues of family and community.

For example, this lens has shown me how oblivious I've been about the law and the politics of crime and punishment. Like many people, I believed the justice system was a vehicle for truth. I discovered that truth is irrelevant and politics is not, that our adversarial system favors the affluent, that judges have become redundant, that a plea bargain is not a compromise but a surrender. That justice is a contest with winners and losers, and the winners are those with the deepest bench. I also discovered that prison is a society with a caste system based on the types of crimes committed and that those ranked at the top—murderers, drug offenders, gang members—prey on those at the bottom . . . and I was at the bottom.

Ken Lamberton #61728

time of grace

fall 1997

Prison, Primordial Soup, and the Effect of Edges

From this upper bunk where I write, an open plywood door allows me a view of the desert outside my canvas prison. Beyond the twin rows of tents and the nearby housing units, beyond the chain-link fence and razor wire, the sand traps and the scraped ground, a swath of creosote and cholla cacti lays siege to this twenty-acre encampment called Echo Unit. This September afternoon, heavy with humidity and sweat, ravens post themselves on power poles and security lights, and wait, holding their tongues. The huge black scavengers, overflow from a nearby city landfill, have the patience of the dead.

Echo Unit is a minimum-custody prison and part of the Tucson complex, a square-mile prison city that comprises six other units of higher-custody levels: Cimarron, Santa Rita, Rincon, Winchester, Manzanita (a women's facility), and the Central Detention Unit (CDU). Arizona incarcerates forty-five hundred men and women inside this fenced section of desert, home to the largest concentration of African Americans in southern Arizona. At Echo, 450 or so men live in housing units and dormitories, recycled trailers used during construction of the Alaska pipeline, and military-style twelve-man tents in a "tent city." The yard has a library and education center, a chapel and dining area. Men play basketball on painted courts and volleyball and softball on grassy fields. Unlike the other units at Tucson complex, Echo is an open yard: we have the "freedom" to move about most of the day, walking to work assignments, meals, and recreation unescorted. Echo is a place of grass and trees and sidewalks lined with rose bushes. An exercise track traces its perimeter. Here, teenage boys strum guitars under cottonwoods while old men with doves on their shoulders sit on park benches and feed rabbits. I think of Echo more as a monastery than a prison, although I'm certainly no monk.

Two months have passed since I arrived at Echo, my minimum-custody eligibility finally coming after nine years in prison, three years before my release date set for September 2000. Because "controlled movement" (prisoners are allowed out of their cells less than two hours a day) affects all medium-security prisons now, my move to Echo was like gaining my freedom. I can't shrug off the premonition that my placement here is tenuous, but this evening I walk the fence line simply because I can. Jupiter hangs in the east; but the rising moon demands center stage where it breaches the Rincon Mountains to accompany a sunburst of lavender rays reaching halfway to zenith. To actually feel the sky cover me, to step crisply along wet pavement smelling of oil and dust while catapulting bats and hawk-moths infiltrate the perimeter—it's a penetration. Scott Russell Sanders says, "We can study wilderness, harness it, worship or waste it, but we cannot create it; nor can we extinguish it, in spite of our worst efforts." While prison, this cordoned backlot of desert and humanity, may or may not extinguish me, even here wildness invades. I've seen it in the wings of a mallard duck curling over the razor wire.

TODAY, I returned to Echo Unit after two weeks inside a maximum-security lockdown unit at the Yuma prison because of an administrative mistake. I'm back, after two weeks with three other men in a concrete prefab cell where we had to ask permission from an occasional guard to get the toilet flushed. Two weeks ago the prison administration transferred more than a hundred men from Echo and other units to higher custody due to a sudden change in the law. This was the sexual predator law, Arizona's version of Megan's Law, whereby the state could hold certain prisoners

beyond their release dates, committing them to a mental hospital indefinitely. Our arrival at the Cheyenne Unit had made the local news, and men
were getting hurt. Yuma inmates watching television saw us coming. Sex
offenders. It took two weeks for the department to find an alternative plan,
an alternative unit. Two weeks of bloodied faces and cracked skulls and
investigative lockdowns. Most of us, those not escorted to the hospital,
ended up in the Central Detention Unit, four men to a cell. Prison inside
a prison. Then my wife and lawyers discovered an error in my prison classification—an anonymous staff person had recorded that I was a repeat
offender and targeted me as a sexual predator. As the department relocated
us from Yuma to Florence, Cook Unit, a captain of security separated me
from the group, removed my leg shackles, and put me in a van bound for
Tucson. I was the only one to return to Echo.

So on this October evening I walk the edges of this marginal place and
rejoice. To see the constellations again, Cassiopeia and Cygnus, to smell the
grass, to watch nighthawks flutter like great white moths and pipistrelles
thump the air in ragged spirals—I feel as though I've been released from
prison. If life is the most abundant and adaptable at the margins, as ecolo-
gists say it is, then prison is primordial soup: a place where something new
might evolve out of the muck.

I'VE RETURNED TO L TENT with Mike and Zeno and Hung, men who've
become friends. I also have my job back, working as an education aide for
Albert Benz, the Correctional Education Program Teacher (CEPT), and
I've regained my original position on the movement list for a single cell.
Instead of 200 men, there are 160 in front of me. Most of my personal
property is still missing, but things are settling down again.

I walk in my own sunset. A cochineal sky suffuses the landscape, which
seemed to grip the color, holding it in stasis, as if the quartz- and mica-
laden substrate both focuses and reflects the sky, mimicking it, a competi-

tion of earth and atmosphere. The day has been strangely fall-like. The first cold front from the Pacific Northwest has arrived, and summer's bright sun-wash is gone and the weight of heat with it. Urgency replaced lethargy: The Brewer's blackbirds have returned and established a presence. Monarch butterflies and pinacate beetles suddenly have destinations elsewhere. The trackside tarantula has boarded up her entrance with a plug of dirt and tucked herself inside, and the coyotes have found their voices. Something nears an end. I can feel it.

Walking the exercise track is a constancy I can draw strength from. The plodding tempo of my mind and steps loosens the burden of this place, and I begin to notice things unhindered by fences. Things like toads. At the Indian sweat lodge, in a ditch adjacent to my path, a huge Sonoran Desert toad squats loosely in its skin, unmoving, unblinking. The toad seems dazed, as if it were a new arrival just like me.

After lights-out, I write in my journal from my top bunk under the yellow glow of the security light, dressed in sweats and covered with two thin woolen blankets. Vapor rises from my coffee cup (instant Folgers and hot tap water from the shower trailer). The page is cold, stiff; even my pen runs sluggish. My tent mates have stopped slapping dominoes, a rare treat after lights-out, and I listen to the weather. Rain, like falling grains of sand, taps quietly on the fabric inches above my head, while sporadic gusts of wind inflate, then deflate, the tent. Hanging shirts and towels sway like pendulums, synchronized by pulsing air: inhale, exhale. I sleep inside a giant canvas lung, camping in the desert.

I PASS on Monday's dinner of nasty baked chicken, which the kitchen workers insist our private food service delivers to us in boxes marked "Not for Human Consumption." Instead, I keep to my blankets, alone in the tent. I'm thinking that living in this tent "city" is not so bad. Unlike many of the two hundred or so tent dwellers here, I can't complain; I have the broad perspective of Yuma prison lockdown. Crouched in a low area, a "flood-plain" for storm runoff and overflow sewage at the far west end of Echo Unit, our "city" comprises sixteen army-style tents (each holding twelve or fourteen bunks and wooden lockers), two television tents, and two shower trailers. The Arizona Department of Corrections (ADC) has it worked out mathematically that for every ten men there should be one shower, one toilet, and one sink. My tent (L), a twelve-man variety, rests on a fifteen-by-thirty-foot plywood platform. A frame of two-by-fours supports the canvas, which has been coated with white elastic roofing paint to slow leaks. In summer, we have evaporative cooling. In winter, portable electric heaters (which haven't arrived yet) and a third blanket keep off some of the chill. An insulating lining just under the canvas is supposed to offer weather protection also, but ours hangs in tatters from the two-by-fours. The torn lining, however, does create convenient pocket shelves overhead, and I've stuffed mine with books, magazines, pads of paper, eyeglasses, and other luxuries.

Outside, men crunch on gravel, coming back from dinner or heading for the shower trailers. The sound of footfalls is cold, nerve-grating, like chewing on ice. I should take a shower, too, but dread peeling off blankets and clothes, baring skin to night air. Maybe next spring.

IN THE MORNING I sit outside my tent drinking coffee and looking west, toward the Tucson Mountains, toward my family. My girls will be rising now for school; Kasondra, always the earliest, will be up and dressed already, making herself cinnamon toast—lightly buttered—for breakfast.

Prison makes me feel so helpless, isolated, fermented by emotions—like I'm the subject of an Edvard Munch painting. The anxiety and despair hang on, sapping my capacity for peace of mind; I become an ocotillo in drought, dropping leaves and bearing thorns. I need to find a sense of place, even in this place, to find a sense of time. I need to mark my landscape with more than images of concrete and steel, to mark my year with more than discarded calendar pages. For now, all I have is this place. But prisons do exist at the margins, those in-between places where life comes together, adjusts, and teems—even at the desert margins near here, there is a species of grassland whiptail lizard, a race of females, that reproduces without sex. Despite the limitation of gender, despite even the limitations of razor wire and chain link, there are no *real* borders, only the effect of edges.

After work and the afternoon mandatory lockdown and count, I walk the track, making perimeter circuits six-tenths of a mile per lap along the edge of my world. Somewhere, a Say's phoebe calls inconsolably. I'm look-ing for the bird when a sudden flush of feathers startles me. Wings in my face—two pairs of wings. A dove hits the fence with a metallic ring and then drops to the ground, its breast torn and red and heaving. Last week, a disturbance of birds alerted me to the presence of a Cooper's hawk here, an immature female by her brown-streaked breast and size, the first I'd seen at Echo Unit. The small, noisy flock of blackbirds chased the hawk, *check-checking* in alarm at the short-winged predator. The hawk shot, spun, and then alighted awkwardly on the perimeter fence to turn and confront its accusers. And just yesterday I watched the same hawk chase down a mourning dove and then miss it at the last instant. She perched on one of the light poles, bobbing her head, staring intently in the direction of her lost quarry, and remained there until I walked up directly beneath her. This afternoon she's made a kill—or had, until I blundered onto the scene. Now, she's atop the same light pole and staring at me. I back away and wait. Nothing. The dove lies motionless but alive. The hawk watches it. I make two more laps and nothing changes. Then, as I finish the third, I see her, flying low to the ground outside the perimeter fence, the dove facing for-ward and tucked calmly into her talons as if only going for a ride. I think: *This is one way out.* I follow the pair with my eyes until the two are part of the landscape. My own bit of mystery with feathers and claws. An edge-effect that raises my spirits. It's not Dickinson's "thing with feathers / That perches in the soul." But it's close.

TODAY, November 8, 1997, is my thirty-ninth birthday, my tenth birthday in prison. While waiting for my family to visit—it's also a quarterly food visitation day—I read the Psalms, words of encouragement that have become like One-A-Day vitamins to me. At Psalm 23, I pause at Melissa's name, the signature of my youngest daughter, printed in the margin when she was ten with an arrow pointing to the first verse: "The Lord is my Shepherd, I shall not want." Her handwriting, particularly the way her e's seem to smile, is as familiar to me as my own, each letter spelling so much more than a name.

It was Karen's idea to send me back to prison with a new Bible, favorite verses annotated by family and friends, words between the lines to remind me that people care about me. At the bottom of Melissa's page, a friend from church writes: "Dear Ken, may God be with you in your troubles and tribulations and hope. I pray to see you soon." I flip pages, trying to recall the place Kasondra wrote her name. I find it in Isaiah, her signature with a small heart, next to the words, "All your children shall be taught by the Lord, and great shall be the peace of your children." Jessica, my oldest daughter, who had just turned thirteen, chose a passage from Judges that I used to narrate to her during visitation hours, "Dad," she writes, "for all your Gideon stories." My wife, as I would expect, found a place in Hosea, the book she went to in the beginning to find direction concerning my unfaithfulness. Above the passage where God instructs Hosea to return and love Gomer, his adulterous wife, Karen writes, "My husband you shall be and I your wife—this I covenant with you." The first time I turned to her words shortly after my return to prison, I was shocked. Karen had kept her marriage vows and paid tragically for her faithfulness to me by becoming what she calls an "inmate wife." I never believed she would add to her vows, or confirm them this way. Many times I have turned to this place in my Bible, to her promise to me, and found consolation here. I know I don't deserve even this; Karen's words are so unlike the words I've spoken.

At ten thirty I walk up to East Gate to watch for the arrival of my family. Soon, I recognize my wife's Toyota Camry decelerating along the access road to the prison's parking lot. They leave the car together, each carrying packages, four blond girls. When I join them in the visitation area at one of the outdoor tables, a place is already set for me: a single plain-white paper plate. I sit down, and Kasondra says, "Happy birthday, Dad. We brought you something special." Then, she drops a can of Vienna sausages on the plate. They laugh. They know I hate Vienna sausages.

The real meal they bring is a favorite. We start with green corn tamales, sour cream enchiladas, and carne seca chimichangas with guacamole and work up to chicken fajitas, grilling the chicken breast with green chilies over a mesquite fire just like I would do on the weekends at home without the fences. My mom had baked our dessert, a recipe spiced with memories from my childhood: pecan pie. I never realized until I came to prison how much history she folded into those twelve-inch crusts cooling on her butcher block every fall. Visitation normally is an escape from prison, a few hours of forgetfulness when the razor wire is not quite so sharp in the mind. But homemade tamales and pecan pie places me in another time altogether, making visitation a release.

ON SUNDAY, the barn swallows, those seasonal visitors I mark the time with, have migrated south. The birds touch me in their gaping absence.

I walk perimeter circuits "listening for the eruptions of grace into one's life," as Kathleen Norris says. The writer and poet speaks about being tuned to those moments when words and images converge and being prepared to record them. Tonight, I'm graced by a night sky unfenced. Jupiter and Venus are bright flecks in the south and southwest. Cygnus is overhead. Orion, my winter indicator, mounts the east horizon. Planets, stars, constellations, the blackness of space. It's the one direction out of this place that has no edges—light-years of unobstructed line of sight. Ageless photons for my finite retinas only. "But if a man would be alone, let him look at the stars." I, like Emerson, used to stare at the night sky and feel my own insignificance. But here, where I'm hardly even a number, the stars make me feel differently. Someone once said that the secrets of the universe are uncovered by those willing to get down on their hands and knees. Perhaps. This evening, however, I'm looking up.

NO MORE TENTS. After nearly four months in those canvas cells, I move "up the hill" to a dorm, Housing Unit Four, and come to within a month or so of being assigned to one of the coveted single "rooms." The dorm houses thirty-six inmates, each one of us having our own five-by-ten semiprivate cubicle with a bed, closet, chest of drawers (two), shelf, bulletin board, and space. My own space. Finally, a place to put my feet on the floor. Nobody sleeps beneath me. This is more important to me than getting my television back from property storage. I also recover my boxes of books and writing files, which I slip neatly beneath my bunk. My reading lamp and the power converter to my typewriter are missing, however, lost in transit, probably somewhere between Yuma and Tucson. It's not the first time. I've learned to accept these "losses." In prison, it's permissible for staff to lie, steal, even abuse inmates, the attitude being that they're doing it to liars, thieves, and drug pushers. The attitude reaches far into law enforcement, court systems, and legislatures. Consider the irony of this argument from proponents of the death penalty: "We kill killers to show that killing is wrong."

VETERANS DAY. No work. I stay indoors all day, writing and enjoying the quiet. No card games. No dominoes. Many of the men in the dorm watch television with headphones or sleep. Everyone gets the day off, a holiday for war veterans in prison, the only veterans I know. At the Santa Rita Unit, they had a staff-sponsored Veterans Club, an organization that raised money by digging through the garbage for empty soda cans and, among other things, purchased Christmas gifts for the children of inmates. The club, which the department has now disbanded, had a large contingent of Vietnam veterans, men older than their years who could no longer deal with freedom after fighting so hard for it. Alcoholism, drugs, mental illness, violence are only acceptable in the war zone. What's most affecting here is the patriotism of these prisoners: their Fourth of July celebrations with ice cream for everyone. Their American flags. Their memorials. The men still honor their country, a country that has used and then discarded them and now requires them to serve another kind of tour, a country that honors them in return by locking them up.

Pete was one of the veterans I knew at Santa Rita. He lived on the tier above me on Yard Two, and I remember the time he told me he had recently lost his family to a divorce. We had just returned from church service and were standing on the run outside his cell. In his rough Hispanic accent, he quoted a line from Psalms: "The Lord has chastened me severely, but He has not given me over to death." This was his way of adjusting to the pain, of surviving. That night was one of the rare occasions when he spoke about his experiences in Vietnam. He said, "Ken, I'd never been so afraid in my life. We did terrible things." Pete's crime involved drugs, armor he'd learned to wear overseas while fighting a foreign war. I last heard from him after his transfer to minimum custody. He was driving a shuttle bus for the prison complex. Now, whenever I read that particular verse in Psalms, I hear it in Pete's voice.

SEVEN FIFTY-TWO AM. Forty-seven degrees. It's quiet and dark. Except for the sleepers, I'm alone in the dorm. Most of the men, those who work on the road crews for the Department of Transportation (ADOT), left hours ago. My job in the classroom begins later. Echo Unit is a work camp, and, except for those inmates with medical reasons, everyone has a job, many of them off-unit. During the day you'd never know nearly five hundred men inhabited this twenty-acre impoundment.

Last night I called Karen to wish her a happy birthday, her thirty-sixth. With work and kids and her master's program, she's too busy to enjoy anything. These days she doesn't much celebrate birthdays or holidays and only looks forward to taking vacations out of the state. She tells me she just feels old. Eleven years ago, when she was a more energetic twenty-five—even eight months pregnant with Melissa—Karen's youth began to end after I abandoned her for someone else. Most women would have divorced me, or simply collapsed altogether and killed me outright, then pled temporary insanity (justifiably so). But Karen has always striven for control. If our marriage needed repair, she would seek counseling. If I were in trouble with the law, she would study criminal justice. If prison were unavoidable, she would familiarize herself with corrections, its policies and its officials. When we were dating, she once showed up at my university dorm room with greasy hands and smelling like gasoline. We had plans for dinner, but the carburetor on her VW bug had come loose on the way to pick me up and she had to replace it. When our first child was born, Karen insisted on a natural birth. No stirrups, no needles, no drugs. In the delivery room the nurses kept referring to her as "the one without the IVs." Karen could have managed the two-hour drive to the hospital herself, fully dilated, stopping for gas on the way. But she allowed me to come along so I would make certain the doctors followed her requests.

It's understandable to me why Karen couldn't discard our marriage so easily, and that she would find something salvageable in me, even though she was alone in her thinking and would continue to be so for a long time. Family and friends urged her to leave me, sometimes verbally, sometimes in their silence. The unwanted advice was no comfort. Even her friends at church questioned her marriage, taking her side when she hadn't taken sides herself. They reveled in empty platitudes, lifting words from Bible pages to absolve themselves of really doing anything, to keep difficult people at arm's length. Christians so readily turn truth into cliché, reducing statements like "Trust God," or "God is bigger than your problem," or "God works all things for good to those who love Him" to glib remarks in the face of tragedy, as if people's problems were that simple. Nothing in Karen's life would ever again be simple. She must have known this, which is why she ignored the counsel of people and looked elsewhere for direction. It was the beginning of a hard road, much more pitted and rutted than divorce or separation, and one that posted no promises of anything good to come.

"WE LIVE ON one layer of the earth at a time," says writer Christine Colasurdo. It just happens that my one layer has razor wire horizons. Tonight, our one desert broom parachutes a fine, downy furze to the fence line. The western pipistrelles no longer come in the evenings. It's cold enough now for their "profound hibernation," a neat drop in body temperature, heart rate, and other processes to get them through the months when insects are scarce. Somewhere the winged mammals have located a cozy niche for cold storage.

I hole up in my own cozy cubicle and write, considering ways to make the approaching Thanksgiving holiday not just another day in this place. In prison, hope faces east; time is measured in wake-ups.

Two years ago, I learned I would be going back to prison. Three justices on the appellate court made their decision just before five o'clock on the eve of Thanksgiving Day, my first Thanksgiving since my release from prison the previous December, Thanksgiving 1995. The news was a gut-punch, the timing a kick to the groin. The broken ribs and head lacerations waiting for me upon my return to prison wouldn't match this pain. I've been assaulted twice in my life, both times by three men I never saw.

There was never supposed to be an appeal, not by either party. When my attorneys first approached Bill Perry, the Pinal County prosecutor, with my postconviction relief package, this was part of the prehearing agreement we sought. In return, we would be sensitive to the victim concerning making a public record of personal documents and psychological evaluations. We wanted to keep the case simple, to avoid hearings and arguments and the media attention these would generate. We hoped to explain our position to a judge and allow him to decide whether or not it was valid according to some recent changes in the law regarding cases similar to mine. We would set no record for an appeal on the likelihood he decided against us. We had bought a lottery ticket, probably the reason Bill Perry was so agreeable in the beginning. But as it looked more and more like Judge Minker was favoring our petition, the prosecutor grew increasingly hostile. My case, in terms of paperwork, hearings, and news media, rapidly escalated, although my wife and attorneys strove to keep our part of the original agreement.

Karen knew my release couldn't last on the day my judge ordered it. Today, she regrets the whole thing. "I should have told Judge Minker to keep you in prison if Perry was going to appeal the decision," she repeats often. We had focused on telling the whole story to my judge, a story the appellate court judges would never fully hear. One essential element of our case was a videotaped testimony taken by two of the state's detectives (who both had reservations about my long sentence and who testified as such on my behalf) on the day of my arrest in Aspen, Colorado. On it, my victim spoke of our love and her willingness to run away together and start a new life. The videotape had a visible effect on Judge Minker, who watched it with his head in his hands.

After that Thanksgiving two years ago when the appellate court reversed my judgment, reinstating my original twelve-year sentence and ordering me back to prison to serve the outstanding four-plus years, we turned to the Supreme Court of Arizona for relief. The order would not be enforced until we had heard its decision. It was during this interim that Karen and

I made our own decision. The media attention, my probation conditions, and responding to reams of petitions from the state and a second "Attorney for the Victim" had worn us down. We never wanted my case to go this far, much less to the federal courts. And there were finances to consider. We had played too long on the sympathies of the Sherick Law Firm. Karen and I decided we would not pursue an action beyond Arizona's Supreme Court. Its ruling would end this; if required, I would give up the time.

On the fifth of July, 1996, the state supreme court chose not to make a decision. The order of the appellate court would stand. I had less than two weeks left with my wife and children.

ON THE TRACK this evening I find the napless hide of a toad, skinned and stretched by the tires of a golf cart, no doubt. The cops should walk, lose some weight, spare the toads.

The past few days the sky has been overcast with light intermittent rain. The desert willow trees have been shedding their thready leaves, the dried castoffs corkscrewing across the ground when the wind shifts, rattling like lizard bones. The cottonwoods, however, hold tight to their greenery, reluctant to give up a possible few more days of sugar-making. Although thinned out somewhat, the leaves have been a vibrant, dimensional contrast against a flat aluminum sky.

The clouds have been obscuring an uncommon planetary conjunction that won't happen again for another hundred years: eight planets arcing across the sky, five of them visible without a telescope. Last night, I stood on the steps to the dorm with Mike, my friend from L tent, and shivered in my sweatshirt, waiting for a breach in the sky that would allow us a view of the event. When it came, we got only a peek at the brightest planet, Venus, and then Mars, a red period next to a crescent moon.

Tonight, however, the evening sky is dustless. The Santa Rita Mountains are cutouts pinned to the horizon, the planets, knots of light on a tether. I see five of them plainly: Mercury, farthest to the southwest, is a sand ruby, clear, unblinking, and as red as Mars, its nearest neighbor in the sky. Bright Venus dangles beneath the moon's eggshell, Jupiter follows next on the ecliptic, and then, high in the southeast, Saturn, both paling nearby stars. Uranus and Neptune are there also, I understand, somewhere between Venus and Jupiter but too dim for common eyes. Pluto, our system's rogue planet, is in the ballpark. It's in the same quadrant, only hidden from sight below the grenadine-colored rim of Earth.

Eight planets in the same sky and I'm standing on the ninth. I feel their pull in the liquid of my cells, competing with other gravities for attention. The sun, the moon, the earth, this place—I try to fathom the geometry of it all, settling the lights in their orbital planes, lining up the more distant planets with the inner ones in relation to where I stand. My attention? The spheres have all three dimensions of my mind.

THREE DAYS OF WINTER WEATHER and the ground is sodden. There's a snow advisory for the mountains above seven thousand feet. Rain has been falling since noon, when a reef of low dark clouds rose in the northeast, sweeping banded layers of dust before it. We're expecting the first hard freeze of the year this week, but I'm unconcerned. The cold again chafes my sleep, but I refuse to pick up a jacket from property because I hate the blanket-lined denim homeless-wear. I'll survive the season with thermals and sweatshirt.

Meteorologists are saying we may see the worst El Niño on record, worse than 1983. "Worse" must depend on your point of view. Certainly, the floods and drought, the loss of life and property associated with the cyclic storms are an unfortunate consequence. But, as Jonathan Weiner writes in his Pulitzer prize-winning book about natural selection research on the Galapagos Islands, "There is a special providence in the fall of a sparrow. Even drought bears fruit. Even death is a seed." El Niño is the kind agent that drives life, change, evolution. It is the rough beast slouching toward Bethlehem that, once born, adjusts even the beaks of Darwin's finches. El Niño carries margins with it; for me the storms are a penetration.

I've slept the last two nights back in the tents, cold, frustrated, curled into a fetal shape. On Wednesday afternoon, Officer Chad found me at the dorm and told me to roll up. The department was transferring me to A-14, Cook Unit, Florence. Medium custody. I felt the blood drain from my perimeter. It couldn't be happening again. Chad believed me when I told him it must be a mistake. He allowed me to call home and leave a message for my wife. That done, I went to the Service Center to see my counselor. CO IV Stanley Miller was no help. "If you check the movement screen on me," I suggested, "you'll see my placement here is per Director Terry Stewart." This certainly annoyed Miller. Inmates don't have access to information on the AIMS computer. I had learned about my status after the Yuma fiasco from my lawyers, who had connections in the department. Miller wouldn't tell me what he read on the computer; he asked me instead to step out of his office. Outside his door, I could hear him on the phone. He was confused. Apparently, the computer showed my transfer to Florence on one screen and my placement at Echo Unit by order of the director on another. "You'll cover me on this?" I overheard Miller say. When he called me back into his office, he gave me the news. There was nothing he could do.

I had seen Cook Unit the previous October after I got caught up in the sex offender reclassification and relocation to higher custody because of Arizona's new sexual predator law. Violence at the Yuma prison made the move there a failure. The department had to transfer more than a hundred men to another unit, Cook, a duplicate of many of the newest prisons: all dormitories and controlled movement. Concrete walls and steel fences. No trees, no birds, no weeds. There, even the inmates are lifeless. I never got beyond Cook's sally port before the director corrected the mistake (I didn't fit the criteria of a predator) and ordered me back to Echo. Now, however, it seemed someone had decided to delete that order.

Wednesday evening I packed my property, Officer Chad reluctantly marking off the inventory. He knew something but wouldn't share it. The men in the dorm were quietly watching. Friends expressed concern; some of them had seen this before. My neighbor asked, "Are they messing with you again, Ken?" When I called my wife later that night, she had spoken with the warden. "He called me at work," she said, "and asked me not to be upset. He had canceled the move." I said, "So why did they still roll me up?"

I lay on my bunk all night in my clothes, having stored my property at East Gate. I couldn't sleep, anyway. In the morning nothing changed. At 7:00 AM an officer at East Gate began paging me. Again, I located a counselor, this time Davidson, explaining to her the situation, and that I knew my transfer had been canceled. She stood on the steps of the Service Center, smoking slowly, waiting for me to finish my tale. "You have to go to East Gate," she said, blowing out a gray plume. The officer at the gate said he was unaware of my status change but told me I could return to the Service Center and ask my counselor about it. This time, Miller ordered me to report to East Gate. I didn't. Instead, I went to work, hiding in the education building and hoping the error would soon rise to the surface.

By now, I felt more powerless than usual. I wore my fear like a strait-jacket. The wheels of some great machine had been set in motion, and my counselors insisted on shoving me between its cogs. One phone call, a simple check on the AIMS computer, would have verified what I already knew, what I had been telling anyone who would listen to me. My next trip to East Gate was under escort. I was in trouble. Sergeant Gregory, a short, bald-headed cop with an attitude, wouldn't make a phone call for me, but he would make the effort to write me up for a major rule violation. "We've been through this before, Lamberton," he said, referring to my Yuma transfer and the similar objections I voiced then. I wanted to tell him, "Yeah, and I was right that time too. I'm still here." But I kept my mouth shut. He wasn't capable of reasoning with me. His message was clear. "You're on report for disobeying a direct order," he shouted. After more than a decade in prison, it was the first time I'd heard those words.

I waited in the East Gate holding cage with my property until a transportation officer arrived to take me to Complex Intake and Processing (CIP). "What were you thinking?" the officer asked. "You could hide and we'd forget about you?" At CIP, I loaded my boxes into the back of a property trailer. Pulling the trailer, a van filled with other inmates waited for me. As I collected my last box, I recognized an officer from Santa Rita. "I know this move has been canceled," I told him. "Is there any way you can check on it for me?" I pushed the box into the trailer and took a chance on one more trip into the building. Through the office window, I could see the officer on a phone. He looked up, saw me standing there, and gave me a thumbs-up.

So now I'm back in tent city. The accountability officer said I had to spend a few days in the tents until the next dorm opening. I don't care. Roll-up threats and major write-ups tend to diminish things like crowded conditions and cold nights. A major write-up could send me to Cook Unit as easily as an administrative mistake. Echo in a tent is better than any other unit, regardless of the housing situation. Family is here. Some of the prison staff think I have a yo-yo string dangling from my back. Karen believes someone in the department feels the need to personally punish me, someone with computer access codes to movement screens.

MELISSA IS ELEVEN TODAY, the 18th of December. Karen and the girls travel tonight to Kohl's Ranch near Payson, Arizona. Cabins and snow. Kohl's Ranch, and particularly the areas around Tonto Creek and Horton Springs, is one of our favorite places to camp, hike, fish. Several summers ago, while I was home on my temporary release, Melissa caught her first fish there, a milestone that was as important to me as it was to her. During my earlier incarceration I often thought about taking my daughters fishing. (Karen eventually taught them how—although she wouldn't allow them the benefit of hooks.) I'd always wanted to share my special places with them: East Fork of the Black River and Horton Springs. A first rainbow trout is something fathers do with daughters, and now our letters and phone calls to each other recall the event. Melissa caught hers at Tonto Creek with Fireballs and a #12 snelled.

I flip back through the pages of my journal to that date: June 21, 1995, Wednesday. It was the first day of a family retreat Karen and I had organized as a Father's Day event, and we had arrived at Kohl's Ranch a day early to reserve the upper campground. It had been more than eight years since my last visit there, and I remember how excited I was to make this trip. My probation officer had rejected my request for travel because he thought I shouldn't be camping in public. But then, he also objected to me living with my own children. But my judge overruled him and gave me permission—on both counts.

My notes show my proclivity toward cataloging things and recording obscure details. I list ponderosa pine, Douglas fir, white pine, New Mexican locust, sycamore, walnut, alder, willow, box elder, cottonwood, canyon grape, yellow columbine, fleabane, skyrocket Gilia, wild rose, lupine, aster, among others I first learned to identify from books I read in prison. (I've dug deep holes in my field guides, rubbing my fingers through their print, lifting out their illustrations.) I write, "Dark-eyed juncos in campsite, tilting their heads at the kids' handmade birdfeeders (pinecones smeared with peanut butter and rolled in birdseed). Emory oak have fresh, green galls at the bases of many leaves—inside looks like an empty eggshell with a pinhead-size white capsule and a tiny red mite." These words, written in pencil on unlined paper and bordering sketches of leaves and flowers, carry an emotional weight for me. They are impressions held on pages stained with sweat and pollen and bug sap, actual pages from a history beyond this time and place. The poet Charles Simic says that what is recorded in a notebook is "the sense of the unique and unrepeatable experience of those rare moments of clarity." My notebook is a work of consciousness, of eclectic thoughts, facts, opinions concerning the mundane and, occasionally, the significant. In my Kohl's Ranch entry, I don't find any rare moments of clarity, just the simple poignancy of a notation for eight small rainbow trout, one of them Melissa's first.

ON THE AFTERNOON of the winter solstice, a long, slow cloud pour drums its fingers on the windows and walls of the dorm. I'm reading Barbara Kingsolver's *High Tide in Tucson*, munching peanut M&M's, sipping hot coffee, listening to the rain. It's a perfect day to be locked up. The planet has begun leaning in its orbit toward longer days and summer. It's psychosomatic, but knowing we've slid past another solstice loosens something inside me. My present isn't perennial; it's annual. I live in a present of repetition, of cycles, rather than one that's linear like beaded days on a string.

They paged a long list of names for disciplinary "court" this morning. My name wasn't called. I don't know what happened to my write-up from last week's roll-up and transfer incident; I should have heard from Sergeant Abt, the disciplinary coordinator, by now and received my summary punishment: loss of privileges (no commissary shopping for a month), extra duty (cigarette-butt patrol), or even reclassification to a higher institutional risk score (and placement at a higher-custody unit). The hearing is perfunctory, a formality. There is no real defense. You say you're not guilty. The sergeant says you are. The write-up is proof of your guilt, making it automatic.

Besides being transferred away from my family, my concern about a major write-up for disobeying a direct order (by not reporting to East

Gate when paged) stems from what will happen to my community risk score when I'm evaluated prior to my release. A major write-up equals six points, effectively doubling my present score. This means I'm a greater danger to the public and, upon my release, the police department must notify the media and deliver neighborhood fliers. In the ten years of my incarceration, I've never received any disciplinary action. My public and institutional risk scores have steadily dropped. One write-up now, however, since Arizona's new law concerning sex offenders, would classify me as a predator. One write-up could lock me up in the state hospital indefinitely upon my release from prison.

LAST NIGHT while walking laps I spotted a pair of coyotes on the perimeter. The recent mange epidemic must be over: these animals had thick brown coats. The two trotted across open ground toward the desert scrub between Manzanita Unit (the woman's prison) and Echo. When I barked at them, one stopped to stare at me. Its partner, after continuing on and fading into the desert, started yipping—its voice full of authority and rebuke, as N. Scott Momaday says. The desert in winter requires coyote song.

This morning there's snow at Oracle, and Mount Lemmon has forty inches on the ground. It may snow in Tucson tonight, a white cactus Christmas. At Echo, there's rime on the benches and frozen skin on the puddles, and I'm moving into a single "room." Housing Unit Two, Charlie run. "Condo" number thirty-three. My Christmas gift courtesy of ADC. The room is square, eight by eight, with a large closet filling one corner. Shelves extend from one wall—all the walls are paneled—and a bulletin board hangs on the opposite. A two-drawer file cabinet sits next to my cot, and a large mirror hangs next to the door. A window, shuttered with a venetian blind, opens nearly a third of the wall alongside my bed. It's a window *I* can open. I have a picture-window view of the tents and the cloud-masked Santa Rita Mountains beyond them.

THE NEW YEAR BEGINS with an interview for the Sex Offender Treatment Program (SOTP). I have serious reservations about it; in fact, my lawyers have told me to have nothing to do with the program. There's a dilemma here, however. By not "volunteering" to participate, I risk being transferred off the yard. My counselor has already threatened to send me to Globe, Arizona, more than three hours away from my family, for not signing up for the "treatment." I also risk a raised community risk score. If I do join, I must agree to participate in all aspects of the program: group sessions, smelling-salt therapy (how Pavlovian!), polygraphs, plethysmographs. It's medieval. Smelling salts, lie detectors, and genital monitors? It reminds me of shock therapy and lobotomy, treatment tools used during the dark ages of psychotherapy. A husband and wife without a PhD between them developed the program. Most therapists follow the addiction model for treating sex offenders. Not Steve ("Doctor Steve," he calls himself) and Sandy Gray. Addiction is just another excuse to them. Since 1990, I've been meeting with a therapist and addiction specialist who disagrees with the Grays' philosophy and methodology. Dr. Jennifer Schneider, MD, practices internal medicine in Tucson, publishes books about sexual addiction, and lectures nationally. Once a month or so, she visits me and we talk about twelve-step programs that she says are best suited for promoting recovery. But my private counselor matters little to ADC. I must sign up for treatment. Never mind the lack of confidentiality, that my program reports and evaluations will become state record and available for review, that my "counseling" can be used against me if the state decides to pursue civil commitment. My lawyers convince me to refuse the program, even if it means a transfer to another unit.

The public's fear concerning sex crimes only grows. Now, a candidate for Arizona attorney general wants to sponsor a law allowing the death penalty for sex offenders. This kind of sensationalism might just get him elected. Strike the emotional nerve; reason is unnecessary. He says that the death penalty won't increase the likelihood that suspects will kill their victims because "these kinds of criminals don't think rationally." I guess if deterrence won't work for the irrational then we should simply kill them off. Arizona already executes the mentally ill.

The problem is how broadly we define "sex crime." When I was young, television programs treated trenchcoat-wearing exhibitionist "flashers" as hilarious jokes. Today, we call them sexual predators. Violent acts against innocent victims are one thing, and should be prosecuted severely, but some sexual behaviors seem to have become more like crimes against our present culture rather than crimes against nature. Take Sam Hughes as an extreme example. The Welsh immigrant, now called the "father of Tucson," arrived in our city in 1858 and soon took a twelve-year-old (or possibly eleven-year-old) Mexican girl as his bride. He was thirty-two. If Hughes rode into town today, we'd post warning fliers in our neighborhoods and grade schools instead of naming them after him.

ON OUR SEVENTEENTH WEDDING ANNIVERSARY, Karen visits for two hours—all she can handle of this place at one time. Today, however, she seems less upset. Rarely does she preen before coming out, but she's freshly showered, and I enjoy the herbal fragrance of her hair as we sit side by side at one of the picnic tables, our fingers locked together. At one point, for a moment, our eyes meet and I tell her she looks good in her size three black denims, but she turns away, saying, "You're just desperate." This is her standard response to my amorous advances. Karen's defensive strategy of projecting unavailability—the way she deals with being "single" by appearances—extends even to me. Being affectionate here is dangerous for her in her state of forced celibacy. "It wouldn't be very smart of you," she says, waving her free hand, "to charge me up and then send me away into a world of free males." She isn't kidding.

After Karen leaves, I remove my clothes in the visitation strip room, thinking, *Here's one way to calm pent up nerves.* Officer Chad puts me through the visual inspection routine, and then as I dress, tells me he wrote a letter to Central Office criticizing the handling of my roll-up last month. At first, I'm not sure I'm hearing him right. "They sent my letter to the counselors," he explains. "They're all mad at me, but I don't care. They messed up." Chad says it was a computer problem the counselors should have corrected, as I suspected. Now I understand why Miller was apologetic last week, and why Davidson, after another counselor paged me to the Service Center, answered my knock with "What do *you* want?"

ONE REASON southern Arizona is the prison of my choice: we've had a week of pleasant midseventies weather. Last night, I walked laps in my T-shirt. In January! White and yellow irises unfold from tentative spikes in Cottonwood Park, more than a month earlier than last year's blooms at Santa Rita.

At lunch, the officer taking count said Sergeant Abt wanted to see me at the disciplinary office. I quickly lost my appetite. The vegetable soup seemed more watery, leftover peas and carrots in warm dishwater. When I got to the sergeant's office, he said I wasn't in trouble, "If that's what you're thinking." Abt explained that during a recent security audit the captain had found a map in my work area. I have priors with maps, which the department considers escape paraphernalia, although phone books and *National Geographic* magazines have always been available to us. He then pulled out of his desk a page I recognized immediately, a flier my wife had sent me advertising her dad's annual New Year's Day football party. The map filled one corner, a business card with cross-street directions to his house. "We wondered about the inmates in the photos, how you got them," Abt said. I was perplexed. Inmates? My father-in-law? My brothers-in-law? Abt cut the map out and handed me the flier, telling me I shouldn't hang personal material above my work desk. I didn't ask him if he had seen my name on any write-ups.

WE'VE HAD TWO DAYS of heavy, ground-saturating, El Niño rain, which began yesterday evening with twenty-five mile per hour gusts that rattled the whole trailer and forced fine sand to beach on my windowsill. Then, all night, drizzling and thunder and downpours and more wind. Today, I stay inside. No walking laps. But before the clouds homogenized from white to gray to black at sundown's darkness, I glimpsed snow, flat-lined halfway down the Catalina and Rincon Mountains. It is a moment I still hold like a flower, by its stem.

I received a Valentine's Day card from Karen today. On the cover it has a sketch of a starry-eyed couple under bedsheets and reads: "90 percent of people get laid on Valentine's Day." Inside are the words: "The other 10 percent get a greeting card."

My wife's humor: dry, sarcastic, on-the-edge, survival humor. I laugh, and then hope that my negligence in sending her a card doesn't mean she's among the 90 percent.

spring 1998

Gifts of Grace, Polyps of Inhumanity

I wear shirtsleeves on a warm March morning with smudges of green filaree starred with pink blooms at my feet. It's my first, and sometimes only, indication of the wildflower season, other than outside news reports. Besides a rare desert chicory, filaree is the winter annual of this place—my signal species.

Twelve years ago, in another life, I climbed with my wife to the wind cave in Usery Mountain Park near our home in Mesa, Arizona. It was our intention to share together a fine wildflower season, to celebrate spring with a short day hike among the poppies and lupines coloring the desert around "Scarface," a local name for the rocky outcrop. Karen had packed a lunch, and we had left our two small girls with the baby-sitter, one of my eighth-grade students whom I'd just begun to notice was unlike any of my other students.

It was Karen's idea for the Saturday outing. She had concerns about me, about our relationship, because of changes she had started to see in me. Over the past few months I had grown distant, temperamental, preoccupied with my teaching. I was spending more time at school, even filling up the weekends with science trips and other activities. It had been months since we'd set aside a day just for us. Even so, I was reluctant about the day hike, about being alone with Karen. I didn't know what I wanted. Emotionally, I was having doubts. I was in trouble.

Karen walked ahead of me, stretching out her smooth legs and the tight fabric of her shorts. We passed people on the trail, a few winter visitors out to experience the flowers, but no one was around when we arrived at the wind cave. Karen laid out lunch—bagels and cream cheese, vegetable sticks, fruit, and juice—while I explored the area. I'd never hiked this far up Usery Mountain, and in the shaded, wet recesses of the wind cave I found beds of mosses and hanging gardens of star ferns among the boulder-tossed ledge. The place was idyllic and unexpected, a pleasant surprise after a hot morning climb. The whole desert, in fact, I began to notice, was verdant and alive.

After lunch, Karen fed me grapes, one at a time, her long fingers lingering at my lips. She felt it, too, this desert fecundity. I didn't resist her advances, the weight of her body on mine. I neither wanted to nor could. Weeks later, when the bouts of morning sickness began, we would learn just how fertile Karen was. In December, Melissa, our third daughter, would be born, and I would be on my way to prison.

TODAY I WALK in steady circles, pacing my perimeter, my mood more elevated than usual. My corrugated horizon, the mountain ring of the Catalinas, Rincons, and Santa Ritas, still has an obvious trace of snow. It's a comfortable place to rest my eyes, something distant enough that the fences lose focus. In front of the library, a Say's phoebe waits in a shrub for an insect passerby. A roadside line of irises has begun to bloom, the plants pushing up olive spears tipped with yellow or white. It's almost as beautiful as the news that Mercury House wants to publish my first book, *Wilderness and Razor Wire*.

A PACIFIC COLD FRONT has dragged its heels across the Southwest, bringing cool temperatures and rain. Thunder woke me at 6:30 AM, just before sunrise. Winter continues to make demands as we approach the equinox.

I've discovered a hedge of rosemary at the eastern limit of the unit. A clump of pungent sprigs dries on my windowsill, refreshing the air and reminding me of my childhood home in north Tucson. In a few days I'll pack the herb into a clean peanut butter jar and use it to spice all the pasta on our menu. If I can only find some basil and oregano—or better yet, some cilantro.

I stay in my "room," under self-imposed lockdown, drinking Folgers instant, reading and writing. I had a honey bun for breakfast and a peanut butter sandwich for lunch and dinner. It rained off and on all day, strafing my window with each assault. All week we've had highs in the eighties, prompting the maintenance crews to refit the air conditioners. I wished I had some heat to go with my pair of blankets.

More thunder. A soft white hail coats the ground, the roofs of the housing units, and the tents with what looks like Styrofoam packing material. It's not sleet or frozen rain but an imitation of snow, which somehow seems appropriate for this place. Prison doesn't rate the real thing.

I open my window and extend my sweat-shirted arm. Hail bounces off my sleeve and sticks in the wrinkles of the fabric, collecting there in bloodless veins. More falls, and more. It's the softest hail I've ever seen. It makes cotton ball impacts, sparkling over the ground and among the fences and razor wire with incandescent flashes before dissolving into dirty gray. It's desperate snow, wannabe snow, but it smoothes over the hard edges of this place.

OSCAR is a Mexican national I teach basic literacy skills to during the morning class, although he often shows up for the afternoon class as well. He's from Hermosillo, Sonora, and he's serving three years for drug sales. Months ago, when I told him what I was in prison for, he said, "You know, Ken, in the old days I would hurt you for what you did. But I'm a changed person. It don't matter as long as you feel sorry for it." I told him my regrets reach beyond my ability to form the words. My first impression of him made me cautious. Like other *vatos*, he combs his black hair straight back and buttons his chambray shirt all the way up to his neck. But on his right wrist Oscar wears a black-and-white band with the initials WWJD. "What Would Jesus Do?" Oscar's a changed person because he found Jesus in prison. I believe he's sincere, that he's not using religion to make points with the parole board as some do, that it's not a game with him. Oscar is a missionary to other Mexican nationals, particularly those who can't speak English. He leads Spanish-speaking Bible studies and church services most weeknights, and he translates the chaplain's sermons on weekends. He has assisted more than a few men with changing their own lives.

Today, before class begins, Oscar wants to show me something outside the education building. He's excited about it, but he won't tell me anything. "Just come outside," he says in his heavy accent. Around the corner and next to the building he points at the ground where a small dark animal is pulling itself under the trailer. "See?" he asks me. I kneel close just as it slips through the heavy grill access panel and escapes out of reach. I watch it crawl around beneath the trailer for a few moments, planting each folded wing in turn and dragging its hind quarters like a legless man on a dolly. "Mexican freetail," I tell Oscar when I notice the bat's long, naked mouse tail.

I occasionally find western pipistrelles here, usually stuck to a building like a dollop of mud. This is the first time I've seen a Mexican freetail up close. Oscar has given me a bit of grace, a real gift, and I tune my senses to the tiny package, knowing in a moment it will be gone. The bat is all membrane: skin tucked into wings, spread between feet; even its head is wrinkled tissue. Above its shar-pei nose, twin ears frame its head like facial wings, seraphim wings: "with two he covered his face, with two he covered his feet, and with two he flew." Not the image of an angelic being you'd expect to find in the Sistine Chapel.

Oscar says there are more and takes me to the corner of the building. "It fell from there," he says, indicating a space in the eaves above us. "Listen."

Oscar makes a noise through his teeth and immediately there's a response from the shadowed seam, a quadraphonic response of high-pitched hisses. Inside the seam I can just make out the darker bodies of a dozen or so bats, huddled together in one leathery-winged mass. It's a small colony of freetails, right outside the education building, a science lesson come to the classroom, a teachable moment come by grace. I can't wait to show my other students, to share the gift.

After sundown I walk laps against a dusky sky. The first bats of the season screen the evening for insects. My trackside tarantula has opened up her hole in the ground, shoveling out the loose dirt with her heavy brown body. Spring cleaning. She looks somewhat leaner than last summer, but she's agile and healthy. I'm pleased to see her, to see that she has survived the winter. I thought she might have relocated after all the attention she got last year, the twig-poking, the pebbles dropped in her den, the beetle-feeding, the cigarette butts. (I saw a guard flick a lighted butt in her tunnel, whereupon the tarantula charged to the surface and chased the officer off the wall where he was sitting, the spider holding the smoldering obscenity between her fangs as if to brand him.) There's been no sign of her den entrance since last October, the area hard-packed and hoed smooth until recently. This evening, it's time to restock the larder. She's raked her perimeter sand traps and laid out her sensor net. She waits at the door, eight legs retracted against her body. I can feel the tension.

I once allowed a tarantula to climb up my face, a sensation I'll never forget (or repeat). I was working at a youth camp, leading a Sunday night campfire program for a hundred excited kids, many of them new to the camping experience. The impromptu was a standard of the program. Visiting toads, insects, a marauding bull snake invariably worked themselves into a song or skit. As emcee, I would sometimes place a tarantula on my shoulder off-stage, then pretend ignorance and play to the reaction of the crowd. Other times spiders might ride among the curls on my head—the one that crawled up my face found that perch on its own. It was a macho thing to do, but I was on stage and only twenty. I did it to impress the audience, particularly one young blond counselor watching me through curtains of mesquite smoke from her seat on the campfire logs.

One of Karen's friends, upon seeing me attempt to stuff an oversize toad into my mouth at one of these campfires, said to her: "And *you* want to kiss this guy?" I don't think Karen answered her. She did kiss me, however, often. We had met at the Triangle Y Ranch Camp near Oracle, Arizona, in the summer of 1979, both of us hired as counselors for the camp's back-packing program. A romance began, which we carried out under desert stars and moon glow, meeting after hours (or whenever we could get away from the campers) at trailside and hilltop to talk until the eastern horizon lit up. We didn't need sleep; we were in love. Eighteen months later we married in the camp chapel.

This summer, our eleven-year-old daughter Melissa will go to Y camp to spend a week with horses. Karen still can't go back there, not without wading through the residue of our years. There are ghosts there, she says with certainty, as if mentioning that corpses continue to grow hair in the grave, ghosts of herself living a life that's no longer possible. The camp was our life. I often joked that I taught school in the off-season as a sideline. We had grown from being a pair of naive, starry-eyed counselors to being program directors responsible for fifty staff, two hundred children. Now, Karen sees ghosts at the chapel, at trailside and hilltop, at the campfire circle. And I am one of those ghosts, I'm sure, a vague figure, leading songs with toads and tarantulas and mesquite smoke, trying to impress another young blond in the audience.

I HAVE ABUNDANT DISTRACTIONS along the exercise track: yellow Bahia sunflowers, blushing verbena, white-cupped euphorbia blooms. One taran-tula at the entrance to her hole, spring-loaded. One road-dizzy, dust-laden blister beetle. A pair of house finches (an elegant crimson-breasted male with his drab female "housewife"). On my first lap this morning an uncommon bird movement caught my eye. The quick wings, darting-then-hovering flight, registered as "flycatcher." As I approached it, a familiar outline appeared: erect body, heavy beak, crested head. The soft yellow underbelly clinched it. The western kingbirds have returned from Mexico.

My mind drifts from bird-watching to a bird-watching friend, Susan Tweit, who will visit me this weekend for the first time. I'm looking forward to seeing her again, although this time it isn't the best of circumstances. I first met her at the Haunted Bookshop in north Tucson where she was signing copies of her latest book. Karen had recently won my postconviction relief, and I was a few months into what I call my "temporary release." I knew Susan through her writing; I also knew her mother, although I hadn't yet made the connection. Her mother worked at the Tucson Audubon library, and we had been corresponding. Joan had graciously responded to my queries from prison concerning barn swallows and other birds I had encountered there. It was Joan who approached me at the bookstore. "Are you Ken Lamberton?" she asked, and then introduced herself. "Come. My daughter wants to meet you."

I have admired Susan's work since I began reading her books and essays in prison. We have similar backgrounds, biology, and so approach writing from the same science foundation. At the time of our meeting, she had just published a book about her home in the Chihuahuan Desert of southern New Mexico. I was writing about the Sonoran Desert. At the bookshop I bought *Barren, Wild, and Worthless* and she signed it: "For Ken with hopes that I'll be reading many of your stories in years to come. *¡Que le vaya bien!*"

Now she is coming to visit. Months ago, when Susan wrote and asked to see me, I was embarrassed to put her through the process. It would be a violation of her privacy: the forms requiring personal information; the

NCIC check, a nationwide computer search for criminal history; the subjection to possible search and seizure without cause or reason; the restrictions on clothing and jewelry, on what you can carry on your person and in your car. Without implying that she's unseemly, how do you tell a woman that her skirt can't rise more than six inches above her knees? That she must wear underclothing? I couldn't. Instead I asked her to join my wife before coming. Susan never indicated any hesitation, only amused interest in what the NCIC might find.

On Sunday, I wait near the east perimeter for the arrival of Susan and Karen. From my perch, I can see the visitor parking lot and the Wilmot Road turnoff that leads to the prison. After all these years at Santa Rita and Echo Unit, I'm still drawn to watching my wife going to and fro, shaking out her car keys, unlocking car doors, threading her vehicle along access roads. Fences are hardly barriers to anything, especially the mind. Prison is such an abstraction. Today, I live in an abstraction.

I see two women cross the distance from the parking area to East Gate. Sharply dressed, tall, long blond hair flying, they could be sisters. When they get to the gate I still don't recognize them. One waves her arms in conversation with the other. My wife? I'm not sure. Karen rarely dresses up to visit me, but the semaphore style of communication is familiar—it must be them.

"Who's that?" an inmate standing next to me wants to know. Walking through the visitation area, Karen and Susan have attracted the attention of the men watching beyond the fence for their own visitors. I smile but don't say anything. I don't have to. In a moment, the paging system announces my name.

I join the two women and we move outside to the covered tables where Karen continues talking with her hands. There's a connection here, I see right off, and I soon know one of the reasons why. Susan says: "I met the lizard." Karen adds: "I invited her in and introduced her to Pern." Pern is the green iguana I bought as a baby for my daughters before I came back to prison two years ago. Since then the "baby" iguana has outgrown three cages and now resides in the center of the living room in a six-foot-high wrought-iron aviary where she keeps a half-lidded eye on the whole house. Karen's introduction: "This is Pern—another small thing Ken left me with that grows up."

People don't always know how to take Karen's sarcasm, her humor. Susan, however, Karen tells me but won't elaborate, appreciates it.

Later, we find a table inside. Susan buys an orange soda and M&M's; Karen drinks her usual Pepsi. We talk about our books, and the "Insider's Report" profile of me *Writer's Market* is publishing. Susan says it is a big deal and the publicity will help the promotion of my book. Her enthusiasm raises my expectations and encourages me. Visitation usually releases me from this place, but Susan has me considering the virtue of even my return to prison, that this present fragmentation is a necessary part of my life.

When visitation closes, I walk with them to the exit. While the two collect their driver's licenses, I tell Karen I'll call later and then I thank Susan for coming. I don't know what else to say and feel awkward with the airport departure. Susan steps close, touches my arm, and looks me in the eyes. "Let me know if there's anything I can do for you," she says. Her words, her sensitivity, crush me, choke up my response. "Sure," is all I can manage to say.

THE SCENTS OF FLOWERS AND MOWN GRASS mix with a warm earth smell like struck flint this pleasant May evening. Cottonwoods flush in green. The sycamore dangles marble-sized seedballs. I make my circuits on the yard and notice that the blackbirds have already migrated north for the summer. Gone in one day. Can't handle the heat, I guess. Everywhere, however, movement covers their absence. Dozens of cottontail rabbits skitter over lawns and among shrubs. Baby cottontails I could hide in the palm of my hand are peeling grass stalks in Cottonwood Park. Carpenter bees, black and lumbering, orbit an old stump at the sweat lodge. A pair of king-birds has claimed a section of the southeast perimeter fence as a possible nest site and are busy strafing the area for flying insects. The grackles are courting. The males, glossy black and strutting, station themselves on posts and light poles and at the tops of trees, anywhere high and in plain sight, to squeal and display for arrays of disinterested females. Tails erect and flared, beaks thrust upward, the hormonally crazed birds stare at the sky in desperate supplication: "Please, God, please, make her notice me!" they seem to pray, over and over, while the females only pluck at the ground.

Outside the fences I hear voices. I've heard them all week, shouts of men in drill, the cadences of TSU, the prison's Tactical Support Unit. I think the noise is some kind of warning to us, like all the gunfire at the nearby weapons range is supposed to be. Like grackles squealing to be noticed, TSU even wears the same color—black—above their Desert Storm fatigues. Every day the unit parades around the facility. It must be Riot Prevention Week at the Tucson complex. Although in my ten years here there's never been a riot—unless you consider a thirty-minute protest march around the track at Santa Rita or a boycott of breakfast (bread and gravy) at Echo. The department considers any kind of disturbance a riot; there must be federal money involved in the reconstruction of damaged property. I suppose it doesn't hurt to be prepared. The unit does come in handy for the quarterly searches of our work areas, cells, and bodies, but I'm sure this is an insult to its real talents. And its people don't get to wear the fancy riot gear, the helmets and shields, batons and Kevlar vests for shakedowns.

I noticed at our last shakedown that TSU had recruited guards I've known from Echo and Santa Rita. One in particular, Sergeant Gregory, "Bam-Bam," as he likes to be called, is in his element, although the clothes look a bit tight on him. (One of the men wanted to know from what height he had to jump to get into his pants.) His pride in himself is clear, sparring with his comrades in mock bouts, acting loud and obnoxious. The Tactical Support Unit is perfect for him, perfect for all the short-of-stature, testosterone-impaired simpletons the department attracts. Why is it that these people always have attitudes inversely proportional to their height? They are humorless Danny DeVitos with badges. It's no revelation that TSU, the whole prison system, in fact, serves at least one purpose: employing the unemployable.

I'm being rude; I didn't always think this way. It took years for prison to teach me this lesson. There was a time, in the early years of my sentence, when both Karen and I approached this place with less gravity, with a willingness to give prison the benefit of inertness, not so much toward me but certainly toward my family. We were naive. Because we didn't want our children growing up disrespecting authority, we explained to them that the guards were here to help me, that I was sick and the guards were like nurses. This wasn't deception. My oldest daughter wasn't even four. Karen and I had already determined that we would answer the girls' questions about my crime and imprisonment truthfully, but at their level of understanding. We didn't anticipate, however, that our explanation of the guards' benevolent purpose would lead to their question: "When Daddy's better can he come home?"

Unfortunately, the prison staff quickly undermined our efforts to keep prison benign. We did encounter a few officers and administrators who treated people fairly and honestly. But they were European honeybees among the Africanized. And, as it happens, it's the sadistic officers, those polyps of inhumanity, who do the most damage, who darken your thinking. In my second year, when a sergeant ordered my visiting wife strip-searched, the system we cautiously thought professional betrayed us. In one malicious act, one that would require more than a year of counseling for my wife and oldest daughter to adjust to (all of my girls were present;

Jessica could never understand why people would hide things in their bodies), our attitudes began to shift, to smear toward bitterness.

It's an attitude I still fight this evening. It digs in its fingers and pulls me down along with the weight of my history. I don't want to grow bitter.

The voices stop after sundown, the men and the grackles. Overhead, the first nighthawk of the season paddles through the cottonwoods. The sky inclines to the color and hardness of azurite; it's huge, clear, so clear it's as if all the dust has gone looking for Bibles.

THE MEXICAN BIRD OF PARADISE SHRUBS have puckered and bloomed, their gaudy, yellow-lipped flowers with red tongues set on a heavy green backdrop. Red, yellow, and green—the colors of a Mexican festival, and right on time for our one Mexican celebration, Cinco de Mayo.

I run into Bruce, a young friend I've known since coming to Echo last summer. He's watching two newly fledged mourning doves, as fat and comfortable as squabs, huddled together on the bare ground under a peppertree. The birds ignore us as we share our observations of other local wildlife—the new kingbirds, the phoebes, the blackbird migration. Then Bruce asks, "Have you seen the mamma duck?"

I've seen a mallard pair here and have heard stories about the two nesting at Echo. For three years running the female has laid eggs in the same spot, and every spring at hatching she herds her brood across the yard, through the perimeter fence, and off toward the wastewater settling ponds.

Bruce takes me to the volleyball court and to an adjacent hedge of umbrella plants—and there she is, right at our feet, a brooding duck. My eyes won't adjust to the scene. It isn't her camouflage; it's her presence. In the meager cover of the plants, in the middle of a prison yard, a wild mallard incubates eggs settled into a nest of down and garden litter. My eyes have trouble with the incongruity. I kneel close and the bird only blinks. "She's been here about a week," Bruce says. "People have been watching out for her." There are pieces of bread scattered around, and someone has placed a torn cola can of water next to her. Bruce says she doesn't seem to mind all the attention, and I tell him I'm surprised she and her eggs haven't wound up in someone's hot pot.

I guess that the mallard continues to choose to nest here because the prison offers protection from the coyotes that patrol our desert border. Her challenge is to lead her young across the open ground between the prison and the sewer ponds. I'm trying to calculate the day of hatching as I pass the southeast lawn, and there in the middle of it is the male. He lifts off as I approach, splashing bright wings halfway across the wet grass to get airborne.

TODAY, my mailbox holds a letter from Susan Tweit. She's read through *Wilderness and Razor Wire* again and says she's awed by my ability to see the dimensions of the prison "ecosystem" so clearly. I'm thinking the "dimensions" aren't that great. Then she adds, "I was struck by your omission of any hint of feelings—remorse, love, anger, whatever—for the girl you ran off with. That seemed odd, given your openness in other ways." I want to tell Susan this omission is indicative of my present emotional condition: the opposite of love is indifference.

It took me a long time to get over her. For months after Melissa's birth and my decision to go back to my family, my emotions remained in upheaval. The fact that I was on my way to prison had nothing to do with the decision, which seems significant somehow in our punishment-driven society. I had to make choices independent of how I felt about the choices, an idea soon to become a revelation I would adopt as a way of life. Making right choices meant I learned to distrust my heart. Eventually, my feelings for the girl began to subside. My love for her cooled, as everyone said it would. There is no anger or bitterness to fill the gap, only relief. After all the emotional intensity of our relationship, indifference is a relief.

Besides, there are others to feel strongly about. I recently read an amazing essay in a three-year-old *Quarterly West* (number 40) called "The Wheel of Appetite." In it, John Davis writes that trust is a paper boat floated on an ocean. I was struck by the metaphor, which immediately made me think of my wife—although I know Karen would say she couldn't keep the ocean out, that her boat never survived its maiden voyage.

It's been hard for Karen to change faiths. The God she believed in all her life has turned false, a God she knew and trusted with the confidence of a child. Her faith was simple: As long as she did what was right, God would protect her from the dark underside of the world. It was what she calls a "belief system" grown out of a fundamentalist Christian heritage that teaches that evil is a result of sin.

Faith has a way of maturing. For Karen the changes came in excruciating increments—my betrayal, conviction, twelve-year sentence, imprisonment; her strip search, my return to prison and subsequent assault. In the beginning, the path seemed clear for her. I had sinned, repented, and suffered the consequences; she would stand with me.

Seven years later, after dozens of national and local television and radio broadcasts, speeches and newspaper interviews, after earning a paralegal degree and a bachelor of arts in political science, Karen won my release. Working for the Sherick Law Firm, who had hired her because of her research ability, Karen convinced a judge to take another look at my case. Judge Minker ordered a hearing, which lasted two days. Ninety days later, on December 8, 1994, he changed my sentence. It was time for all of us to go on with our lives, he said, and sent me home to my wife and children.

Karen's world was black and white, and in this world existed only goodness and evil, justice and mercy. I wish life were that simple. I wish God were that simple. Unfortunately, simplicity and mystery reside on opposite poles, often in alternate universes. All is not reasonable. Or understandable. The fact is that in this world we must accept "uncertainties, mysteries, doubts without any irritable reaching after fact or reason," what John Keats called "negative capability." Upon my release in 1994, the county prosecutor filed appeals against my judge's decision. Eighteen months later, the appellate court ordered me to serve the remaining four-plus years of my original twelve-year sentence. There was little we could do except prolong the inevitable, and we had had enough.

Today, Karen faces a God she doesn't know, one who's not in control or, if He is, one she's not sure she wants to know. Negative capability. Sometimes losing your faith is necessary before you can find it.

"WHAT A FOOLISH THING a man's heart is!" says Kenko, the fourteenth-century Japanese writer and Buddhist monk. "Though we realize, for example, that fragrances are short-lived and the scent burnt into clothes lingers but briefly, how our hearts always leap when we catch a whiff of an exquisite perfume!" I work with Barry in education where he is the clerk, a job that suits his demeanor. He likes to be in control of people around him, a dangerous personality quirk for a prisoner, and being in charge of the program, the payroll and supplies, adds a few mental inches to his short stature. He says he doesn't have a problem with his limitations, repeating this to me every time he wants me to twist open a bottle of Liquid Paper for him. In any other prison unit, he'd be abused by other inmates, but here, where people tend to avoid conflict as sentences shrink toward release dates, Barry is tolerated. Really tolerated. Everything about him is high profile, his crime, his attitude, even his appearance: black, greasy hair, dense glasses, dingy clothes. His ragged shirts and jeans droop from his frame, boxer shorts visible from behind.

Now, he feels the need to share his sexual orientation with me. He's not the first to do so; I have many friends who are gay. I admire his courage, and I want to know how he knows he's attracted to men rather than women, if it's a feeling he has or something deeper. My own experience has taught me that feelings should be questioned. Emotions are capricious, ephemeral. "He who trusts in his own heart is a fool," Solomon says. I've come to accept that wisdom must supersede emotion. This was my greatest failing, believing that my feelings were significant, that I should follow my heart above all else, above my mind and conscience. My heart misled me, deceived me. My heart made me a criminal.

Annie Dillard writes, "It would seem that emotions are the curse, not death—emotions that appear to have devolved upon a few freaks as a special curse from Malevolence." I'm one of those "freaks," although I do believe feelings have a place. For me, being creative means listening to my heart. I write as a safe expression of this emotional part of me, a kind of sublimation of energy rather than repression, following my heart with words only. My muse has limits: the perimeter of pages. In this, I'm not only safer, I have some wholeness in my life, a balance of unconscious and conscious, the emotional and rational.

foresummer 1998

Paper Boats Floating on Oceans

Foresummer, our eight-month-long incandescent period, makes winter an exception in this desert. Winter comes to us as leftovers, discarded and unwanted scraps from Alaska when the heat flies south with the swallows. For a time. But now there is heat upon the land. It rests on the ground, on the rocks and dust of this layer of earth I live on at present. Heat that seeps from the desert of my childhood, holding memories in its substance as it softens the amalgam in my teeth. Stone-heat of foresummer, cloud-heat of monsoon, wet, dry, dust- and wind-heat. It shapes even the thin shadows that lie beneath it. It speaks to the heat that is in me, the heat of metabolism, of muscle function, of blood flow and unrequited desire. It says, "I am the jalapeño, the chiltepine that soothes skin and tongue."

Wind flicks dust and pollen into my eyes, which collects under the rims of my contact lenses like the yellow powder that forms drifts along my windowsill. It's impossible to rub my eyes sufficiently, and I resign myself to an interminable, eye-watering itch.

I circle the prison yard, pulling on my eyelashes, when a cicada suddenly sounds off somewhere inside a desert willow. The insect is the first one I've heard this year. It punctuates the heat with its Skilsaw whine, scorching my nerve endings, giving me a kind of insect-driven tinnitus. But the sound stirs me, too, this song of desert summers from beyond my present, from beyond these fences. It touches places that rarely get touched anymore.

ON THE DAY we finally push one hundred degrees, the wind presses heat against the brittle parchment of my skin. There is no windchill, only a blowtorch. Outside the fences, cicadas sing at the desert's fringe. A flicker plucks at insects in the duff beneath a flowering bird of paradise. The acacia and paloverde are in heavy yellow flush, but in this midday sun, the color is anemic next to the sharpness of shadow and spine.

On every lap I can smell the sycamore. The tree is the only one of its kind here, and I see it's mostly regrown from a grievous cutting that years ago left it a stump. Now, its branches are thin and numerous, suckerlike, and its canopy crowded with applauding bright green hands. I breathe its scent. The sycamore's mossy breath is a riparian tonic for me, and it soaks through me like drawing ink soaks into the fibers of bristol board. The fragrance places me in Sabino Canyon, an oasis of algal mats and blood-warm pools that splits the front range of the Santa Catalina Mountains north of Tucson, where I once chased minnows and listened to passionate-voiced canyon treefrogs. This one sycamore ties me to that place emotionally. With the wind in its leaves, the tree mimics the sound of water pulsing through constrictions of rock. Here, where there is no creek, the sycamore makes up for its absence with the right sound, even the right smell, its best imitation of home. I marvel at this. It's what I'd do, misplaced in this place.

I break from my laps near the east perimeter to get in a set of push-ups, and just as I finish a cicada begins a serenade from a mesquite tree. I pick out its dark, fat body clinging to one of the upper branches. Local folklore says the cicada sings six weeks before the arrival of the monsoons. I've heard them for more than two weeks now, which means the first summer thunderstorms should douse us the second week of July, somewhat late this year for what I consider to be my desert epiphany.

The cicada continues its monotonous chorus. It's a male: I know this because only the male sings or, more precisely, beats his drum. Muscles at the base of his abdomen vibrate a thin membrane 200 to 500 times a second, and this creates high-frequency sound waves that resonate in acoustic chambers adjacent to the "drum." Scaled up, it's like snapping a sheet of metal to make thunder. My dull ears hear only a continuous drone. The female cicada, however, senses separate pulses of sound: the heartbeat of a lover. Who says prison is devoid of passion?

BARRY, my gay friend and coworker in education, is gone, rolled up and transferred out. He's near the end of his sentence—three more months, I believe—but his sudden departure yesterday was unexpected. I talked to him at the East Gate cages, where he waited for transfer to higher custody. "It's the evaluation," he said. "It will happen to all sex offenders before their release."

I call Karen in the evening to vent my fears about Barry, about what his roll-up means for me. I've already called her three times today; the fourth is my limit. Four fifteen-minute phone calls at a dollar fifty-five apiece for a local computer-controlled and recorded touch of real life, freedom. It's not always pleasant, but I call anyway, as often as Karen can afford, financially, emotionally.

My family leaves tonight for Texas, a two-week vacation to visit friends and spend some time, as Karen says, "as far away from Arizona as I can get." But there are problems with her thirteen-year-old Toyota Camry: a dead battery, leaking tire, faulty air conditioner, and a worn rack and pinion. Her car isn't subtle like me; it plainly doesn't want her to go.

My calls and concerns are inadequate and border on inconvenient. I'm frustrated but not half as much as Karen is. The last time I talked to her, she told me I'm a threat to her security, a cause of her unhappiness. "I had dreams once," she said, "but not anymore because you are in the picture."

It's been twelve years since I betrayed her, and still it's as fresh as that first summer. Prison does that, keeps emotions raw, picks at the scabs. Prison is an oozing reminder for both of us of what I did. My guilt makes me defenseless against her words. I have no argument; she's right. I am the source of her unhappiness, and this digs at my own emotional wounds. She feels caged, trapped in a troubling marriage as I am trapped within walls and fences. Prison marriages give new meaning to the idea of being committed to an institution. Karen would say we have no marriage, no relationship, no love, just commitment. Where is trust in this environment? If trust is a paper boat floated on an ocean, Karen's boat, I'm afraid, did indeed grow soggy and sink.

I understand some of what Karen's idea of marriage means. So it would be clear, she wanted me to read Gene Stratton-Porter's *The Harvester*, a romantic Victorian fantasy about a man's devotion to a woman he first falls in love with in a dream. What became clear was that I could never approach her ideal, that I had failed before I knew how to start. Karen wanted to be defined, sketched with detail, expertly, passionately. She wanted me to study her as Monet studied the Rouen Cathedral; instead, I pursued another. I know this now, but the damage is done. It's too late. By Karen's definition, a real man wouldn't do what I have already done. Karen won't give me a second chance because some things can't be forgotten. She has, however, allowed our relationship to continue, her version of forgiveness.

Her dissatisfaction with me grows with time as though time makes me a repeat offender. I have two more years until my release. It weighs heavy on her, on us. We haven't kissed each other since last October, the eleventh. When she visits me, and she does, every week, we hug. But it's perfunctory. Sometimes we hug and she pats me on the shoulder (no wonder the men think Karen's my sister). I feel her body, but nothing else. There are choices we make, some to love, some to forget. Karen has chosen to keep our marriage perfunctory, like our hugs.

It helps me to remember that the best kind of love, real love, is not an emotion but a behavior, and a choice. Emotion has its place: in the whimsical realm of ebb and flow. Behavior, however, is control. Romantic feelings? What's romance anyway but that worm—the bait that hooks you into doing something irrational, like getting married in the first place. Romance is nature's way of ensuring procreation, survival of a species.

I can dwell on these thoughts while she's staying away from Arizona. Sometimes I think I should allow myself not to care so much, not to miss her so desperately. But it frightens me, this detachment. I'm both frightened by and attracted to emotional numbness, to doing easy time.

MY OLDEST DAUGHTER, Jessica, turned fifteen yesterday. She was three when I came to prison—so many years I haven't been a parent, her father, years I can never recover despite all the letters I've written, the phone calls I've made. Despite the thin connections I have with her life.

We're on lockdown. (No doubt, some officer has discovered his own footprints in the sand traps, again.) Warden Hallahan has informed his staff that no one may refer to the East Gate detention cages as "cages" anymore. They are cubicles, he says, a more "politically correct" term. PC has infected ADC. This seems to me like an indication that something is wrong, that someone recognized this and doesn't like what he sees. Instead of correcting the problem, however, it gets a new label. We aren't confined to cell blocks; we're assigned to housing units, controlled not by guards but by corrections officers. I'm not locked in a cell. I live in a house, a "room." It's ridiculous. I suggest that from now on we call prisons "gated communities." Inmates should be "residents," no longer criminals but "judicially challenged." But can a new label hide what's behind it? A cube of galvanized chain-link fence, eight feet on a side, is a cage when you add a door and a lock. Shut a man inside, and he's not cubicled, he's caged.

Later, after the yard opens again, inexplicably as always, I find a sign of the approaching monsoons: my first toad of the season. A thin, skeletal Great Plains toad. I reach for it, wanting to make it real in my hands, but the amphibian outmaneuvers my grasp and escapes into some irises. All the same, my mood brightens. Humidity and dew point on the rise and now a toad confirmation. A change is coming.

At 3:00 PM clouds darken the southeast and I smell creosote and dust. Wind shoves against me as I walk to my mailbox. Huge, warm pellets spatter my shirt. Now, I hear thunder. A deep, throbbing, distant sound so new to me that it makes me believe I've never heard thunder before. As rain pelts my window in sloppy waves, I listen to the desert groan.

BARRY HAS GONE TO PROTECTIVE CUSTODY. I learn from the men in my writing workshop at Santa Rita that last week Barry received an anonymous note threatening his life. "I'm almost out and I'm not taking any chances," he explained on his way to tell the cops to roll him up. Now, I understand, he's in lockdown at the Cimarron Unit, maximum custody. The next time Barry sees the sky will be the day of his release.

In the late afternoon, another thunderstorm shakes this trailer of single cells, my wood-paneled room. I open my window, taste the wet air, and watch the sky. I remember Barry.

Earlier, I ate lunch with Keith, another friend I work with in education, another sex offender. Keith likes to talk, chatter in a seemingly endless trail of whatever he's conscious of at the moment. I tell him it's not necessary to vocalize all that comes to mind, that I have a tendency to ignore him when he begins frothing verbally. But it doesn't matter. Keith's in his fifties and reaching the end of his seven-year sentence. His security depends on his ability to communicate his needs, and I know that what has happened to our friend Barry concerns him as well.

I looked up from my taco mix when I heard him say suddenly, "I wouldn't stay in a relationship if I wasn't happy." The statement grabbed my attention. It demanded a response. "Even marriage? I can't believe you'd exchange a marriage for a feeling," I said, thinking that that's exactly what I tried to do. "What about obligation? Who says you should be happy at all costs?" It wasn't sinking in. Keith said, "I wouldn't want to remain married if it meant I had to be, grudgingly."

Divorce, I've come to believe, is a selfish act. What's wrong with integrity? What's wrong with remaining in a marriage because of promises made? If a marriage is based on obligation, emotions can have their part—all the wildest feelings of love and indifference, joy and spite—but the relationship stands firm. I should be happy my marriage is perfunctory. It's resting on cold, hard cement, but it's secure.

Keith says we are emotional creatures, and I agree with him. But we are also intelligent creatures. A fool vents all his feelings, Proverbs says, but a wise man holds them back. I'm not wise. But I know from experience that trouble comes when emotions rule. Much trouble.

There is, however, another proverb that says it is better to dwell in the wilderness than with a contentious and angry woman. The wisdom of Solomon: with over nine hundred wives and concubines, he should know. No special revelation there. I'm glad my wife and I have worked out some essential details of our relationship. Simplicity: When Karen asks me to do something that I want to, I respond, "Yes, Dear." If she asks me to do something that I don't want to, I say, "As you wish."

AT 9:20 PM the fire alarm suddenly blares away. The holiday cops insist that we have to leave the housing unit and line up outside. I learn that this has become a tradition at Echo. Every Fourth of July someone pulls the fire alarm after 9:00 PM, after our evening lockdown, so we can watch the fireworks at Sentinel Peak, "A" Mountain, west of Tucson. The cops are ignorant of this and tell us to stand on the softball field in the dark where we can't see anything. Maybe they aren't so ignorant. Several men begin slapping their bare legs. The crowd murmurs. There are ants crawling on us.

By the next morning, a steady rain has dropped two inches in Tucson.

Outside my window, the tents are flooding, but I'm secure in my little room. Today, the monsoons will become official, with three consecutive days of dew points about fifty-four degrees. It's been exactly six weeks since I heard my first cicada of the summer. The insects are more accurate than most meteorologists.

I walk my laps before work in a slow drizzle, thinking about what Alison Deming said in a recent *Bloomsbury Review* interview: "I disdain how easy we want life to be and the superficiality of American culture. We want things comfortable; we want to be entertained all the time. I think a lot of it is distracting ourselves from asking what it means to be a moral person, to understand the spiritual dimensions of existence, to pay attention to the fact that we've got a life and that it's a very small, narrow opportunity to have this experience of perception, of existence."

There are days when I want so badly to be free of this place, this existence. Prison functions best under the weight of fear and uncertainty, the way massive glaciers pound granite mountains into moraines, and I grow weary of the erosion. The steady, unrelenting pressure of ice. Prison and gravity shove me along the path of least resistance, the direction of emotionlessness. I want to be comfortable. I want to be home with my wife, to hold her, touch her skin without saying words, without being watched. I don't want to be absent in my children's lives anymore. This is my distraction, the desire of the unattainable and the pain it brings me. It does cause me to lose focus on the significance of my present experience. I refuse to be "warehoused." My life is not on hold; it's real and valuable, if only in small invisible ways. Rather than escape this place, emotionally or otherwise, what I have to do is embrace prison as part of my existence—and accept the fact that prison will be with me for the rest of my life.

Another critic of the human inclination to be superficial, the poet Charles Simic, says: "The world is always looking to reward conformity. Every age has its official line of what is real, what is good and what is bad.

A dish made up of dishonesty, ignorance, and cowardice served every evening with a serious mien and an air of highest integrity by the TV news is the ideal."

I wonder if in our drive to conform to the "official line," we aren't attempting to keep minorities in their place: poor, unmotivated, dependent, imprisoned. Today, blacks and Hispanics make up 47.9 percent of Arizona's prisoners, in a state where these minorities represent 21.6 percent of the population. The department's *Inmate Population Status Report* for December 1997 states that "African Americans tend to be over-represented in the prison population, 15 percent compared to 2.8 percent for the State's general population. In addition, Hispanics tend to be over-represented in the prison population, 32.9 percent compared to 18.8 percent for the state's general population."

In Arizona, the official line seems to say that minorities will go to prison. But even in prison, we write our own official lines to conform to. Official lines of separation. We celebrate—with special food and activities—holidays that reflect our three major ethnic groups: Cinco de Mayo (Hispanic), Juneteenth (black), and Fourth of July (white). We watch race-corresponding television: Telemundo, BET, and the Discovery Channel (which I'm told is the "white" station). Even this minor kind of separation favors the racial extremists who thrive on control. The prison administration knows this and quietly promotes it for the same control reasons. Mexican Mafia, Mau Maus, Aryan Brotherhood—these are racists who tell all of us whom we will cell with, exercise with, eat with. Even at Echo, a minimum-custody unit, our dining area is divided into sections for the brown-skinned, the black-skinned, and the white-skinned. Sitting in the wrong section risks either a disciplinary write-up for inciting a riot, whether or not it would cause one, or having someone threaten your health.

We all know our place: we make it ourselves.

THE LEAFCUTTER ANTS have finished their evening nuptials. After last night's thunderstorm, clouds of the reproductives (alates) hung low over the wet ground in a mating frenzy of wings, black bodies, and hormones. Now, the males are dying; the females search for ideal places to start new colonies. A slight breeze piles cellophane wings, now useless, into drifts.

It's been two years since I came back to prison. Two years since Karen dropped me off at Alhambra, ADC's reception and "treatment" center. My return hasn't been smooth or easy, but the time has passed quickly for me, if not for Karen and my daughters. I'm praying that the next two years pass as swiftly and without incident. I'm not a brave person. I want prison to be as simple and uneventful as this place allows, for me, for my family.

Last Sunday, my family visited after church, my three daughters in dresses and nylons and patent leather shoes. We talked for two hours about vacations and pet iguanas. After they left, I waited in line to be strip-searched and thought about how much I value our time together. There is only so much of it—a few hours on a visitation day, only so many visitation days, only so much life. Our time together is finite, and this raises its price. Like other precious commodities, one day it will all run out. I've wasted too much already, and I can't take for granted what little is left to me.

Today, Karen visits me by herself, and we hold hands the entire time. (I can smell her Lady Stetson on my hands as I write this.) She tells me she's thin and gaunt, but I say she looks great. There's a softness in her touch, in her eyes, that I don't often see in her in this place. Perhaps her guard is down, momentarily. When visitation is over, we kiss for the first time in more than nine months. A simple, awkward kiss. She says we've forgotten how.

monsoon summer 1998

The Price for Swallows and Sanity

Last night, a terrific thunderstorm swept through the prison. Now, I walk half-laps along the chip seal perimeter road to avoid the mud, my blue T-shirt a sticky second skin. Runoff has flooded the sweat lodge, spilling into the roadside ditch, and draining into the tent area to create a large brown lake. I look for leftover toads but find only floating debris, the flotsam of the dead and desiccated, beaten and broken. This is toad weather, toad heaven for breeding, but somehow they must know that the pools will shrink and dry to mud curls before a new generation can sprout legs and crawl out of the thickening syrup. Toad mathematicians: able to perform complex calculations through the pores of their skin.

At 3:00 PM another thunderstorm splits the desert, and the prison yard goes on lockdown, the lightning apparently affecting security systems. It's an afternoon to hole up and read.

The next morning is dark. Clouds with attitude approach from the southeast. I've finished my exercise laps, and it feels like I've just gotten out of a pool. Now the rain comes, a mist loosened from the sky.

The shadowed mountains beyond my perimeter draw my eyes. And the sky-bright pools within it. A brace of dragonflies dips into clouds. Then another. And another . . . all the dragonflies arrive in pairs this morning, clipped together like Day-Glo bobby pins. I wonder from what great distances these bubble-eyed insects can spot water on the desert. Do they look for bright reflected patterns of sky and cloud hugging the ground?

I walk my laps ignoring the humans. I'm not a people person. (I say this knowing I spend most of my days teaching men in prison.) There are about 450 men on this yard. Those who aren't at jobs off-unit work in the labor pool: raking lines in the pea gravel, hoeing weeds, mowing the grass, planting and pruning shrubs and flowers. Landscape crews. Others scour designated plots for cigarette butts, plastic bags tied to belt loops. But I avert my eyes. I won't see them. When I walk, I shy away from faces as if it were a question of modesty and focus on the habits of dragonflies.

I've been reading Richard Shelton's poem "Some Words" in *The Southern Anthology*, and I'm struck by his last thought: "loneliness / so absolute we cannot acknowledge it / except in the silence of our gaping sleep."

There is a loneliness here that comes from a need to be territorial. Twelve men may share a twenty-by-twenty tent, but each will carve out his own space. Shelves are cordoned off; a single locker becomes precious. Men argue over lower bunks. I've known those who forbid their cellmates to even *look* at their television, making its airspace off-limits. Territories, those physical, emotional, and racial—we make distinctions based on skin color, religion, even the type of crime one commits. Society is compressed in prison, concentrated, yet we remain separate and alone. What holds us together are the fences; without them there would be only distance between us.

AT TRACKSIDE, an Anna's hummingbird flicks itself among the bird of paradise. The hawkmoths by night trade off with hummingbirds by day. It's going to be a good summer for both, I think. The hummingbird darts from bloom to bloom, sampling each with its only body part that isn't blurred, touching tongues with flowers.

I'm searching for other hummingbirds shrub to shrub when movement in one of the shrinking runoff pools flags my attention. Wave circles. I stop, close in. Something dark and pea-sized kisses the surface and disappears into the muddy micro-depths. I'm thinking: diving beetles? Whirligigs?

Have some toad mathematicians made an error in their calculations? I can't believe I'm actually seeing tadpoles after ten summers of watching for them.

I return later with two empty Folgers coffee jars and collect thirty or so tadpoles to swim on my windowsill. Already the pool seems smaller.

By the next morning, the pool is mud, crisscrossed with the hieroglyphs of birds: the language of killdeer feet and beaks. Stranded tadpoles had gathered themselves into a small oval before their world imploded on them. All that's left now is a skillet of sautéed escargot.

The tadpoles I rescued swim the borders of their clear coffee-jar pond. My daughters say that tadpoles love cooked cabbage, so I feed them cole-slaw from my meal tray, which they nibble at in energetic lines. Their movements are soothing. It's like having my own aquarium and recipe for stress relief.

In the afternoon, I stop by the pool once more on my way to work and find another place where tadpoles have mixed into the mud. The spot seethes and bubbles with life drawn down to its edge; there's no dying here, only living, and surviving. I pour out my coffee, fill the cup with the mass, and carry it with me to the classroom where I find a large plastic container to hold the tadpoles.

My students tell me I'm crazy, but the tadpole aquarium stirs their interest in the amphibians. They say a sergeant is in the habit of mistreating a large Sonoran Desert toad, recently unearthed by the storms, that's visiting East Gate in the evenings. The officer amuses himself by tossing lighted cigarette butts to the amphibian, which promptly snatches them up. Sometimes the only difference between the guards and the inmates is the color of their clothes.

The men also talk about licking toads. One inmate offers this recipe: Squeeze the milky poison from the two large glands behind the toad's eyes and collect it on small squares of aluminum foil. Once the poison has dried, roll the foil into tight tubes and keep them in a plastic cigarette case. To get high, heat one of the "toad rollies" with a lighter and inhale the fumes.

The presence of hallucinogenic toads can't touch the drugs I've seen in prison, which are more abundant than the department wants to admit, I'm afraid. All of my knowledge about drugs has come from my experiences in this place. The accessibility still surprises me. I find toad venom, jimsonweed, and morning glory quaint and ironic by comparison. There's the approved drug source, the health unit, which hands out powerful psychoactive drugs to the "watch-swallows," a term that has become a euphemism for the mentally ill, crazed, and deranged. I remember the surprise of Richard Shelton, our writing workshop director, one Saturday morning when dozens of inmates suddenly funneled past him on their way to Santa Rita's health unit. "Where are they all running to?" he asked us. "Watch out," someone offered, "the crack house is open. Time for morning meds." Approved drugs are like television in prison: it's about control. Then, aside from what the medical personnel dispense, there's the unapproved (or less-approved) drug trafficking. I once believed the department's propaganda that most illegal substances got into prison through visitation. I was naive. Packing dope into body cavities is unnecessary when the right employee will sell you whatever you want. Guards like "Smitty," who kept rolls of cash in one sock and baggies of pot in the other. Or "Boss," who peddled Jack Daniels out of his lunch thermos. (The Roman Tacitus's query is still apt today: "Who will guard the guards?") A few years ago, the complex psychologist got mixed up with a random vehicle search, a program designed to catch weekend visitors with contraband. After pulling into the parking lot, she spotted the K-9 unit, turned around, and drove away. An alerted sheriff's deputy stopped her farther down the road. Officers found marijuana on her person, in her truck, and in her office; she was immediately suspended and later forced to resign. The last I heard, she's directing a drug rehab center in another city. One thing about prison employees and illegal activities: criminal proceedings are rare. The attention is too embarrassing for corrections officials, who prefer that the public thinks the only criminals here wear blue and remain inside the fences.

One of the men I teach is doing two years for his drug habit. Manny didn't get convicted for sales or possession, however, but for theft. It's common: strung-out addicts stealing property to sell for the next fix. I'm certain that if we legalized drugs, there'd be a 90 percent drop in property crimes. Manny's clean now, by choice. "Drugs will kill me next time," he says. He's a pleasant man with a permanent smile, dark skin of Hispanic origin, maybe thirty-five years old. I imagine he would wear a large-carat diamond on his left earlobe if prison allowed such jewelry. Today, he tells me about his former habit, the cocaine and methamphetamine, and how he turned his little brother on to drugs and got his older sister off coke by introducing her to meth. The horrible waste, I keep thinking, as he describes his life to me. Manny won't get help with his recovery in prison. The few programs here hardly approach anything substantial. He also won't have a job when he leaves, or any skills. He can't manage sixth grade reading or math. We are so misdirected, pouring our resources into drug laws, enforcement, and prisons. We should have learned something from Prohibition. More progressive countries focus on rehabilitation and treatment programs rather than incarceration. More progressive countries value life.

Our country, it seems, values only dollars and political clout. Arizona's former governor, the convicted felon Fife Symington, will be spending the holidays this year in Honduras. A federal judge has agreed to return his passport, allowing him to vacation with his family this December. Mr. "Tough-on-Crime" Symington received his felony convictions earlier this year while still governor of Arizona for fraud crimes related to his business dealings—the theft of millions of dollars in pension funds. Manny's thievery pales in comparison. I remember the reaction of many inmates when the judge sentenced Symington to less than two years. It wasn't disbelief. Everyone seemed to know he would get a light sentence; after all, he had money and influence. It was more like respect. He beat the system. One man told me he'd received fourteen years for the same crimes, federal time he'd already served. I'm thinking about all the rhetoric Symington spun while governor concerning his tough stance on crime and particularly his position that white-collar criminals not receive preferential treatment. Sure. Like traveling out of the country for Christmas instead of going to prison, I suppose. I don't know anyone who has managed to remain free after a conviction and sentencing just because he didn't like the ruling of the court. Normally, you work your appeals from behind bars.

When I returned to prison in 1996 after the appellate court overturned my release, people I'd never met wrote to me expressing their belief in the unfairness of the decision. Some had also written our governor. One woman from Phoenix, thinking she had found a solution for me, sent me a copy of Symington's response to her letter. In it, he thanked her for her concern with my case and then suggested that I should seek relief through the pardon process. The woman was excited about this. "You must start the paperwork right away," she wrote. What our governor failed to mention to her, however, was that by statute a pardon wasn't available to me. No commutation of sentence. No pardon. No passports. No vacations in Honduras.

ONE OF MY STUDENTS, a tall, muscular black man with a shaved head and hands for palming basketballs, has instigated a "Free Willy" campaign against me. Arvin's objecting to my plastic bucket of several hundred tadpoles. I assure him that the amphibians will go free as soon as they're not dependent upon my artificial puddle, those that survive the rampant cannibalism.

I'm wondering about the species of tadpoles. Of the four kinds of amphibians I've found here, one, the western spadefoot, has larvae that can develop into two forms, or "morphs," one growing slowly and feeding on algae and the other a quickly maturing carnivore. If my "willies" are western spadefoots, I'll be releasing only a few, but very fat, amphibians.

More likely the tadpoles are the strictly omnivorous larvae of the Couch's spadefoot, a thumb-sized bug-eyed "toad" I often see here in summer. Couch's spadefoots are record-holders for metamorphosis, just eight days when their pond isn't too crowded and food isn't too scarce. I can't do much about the space constraints (this *is* prison), but my salvaged charges don't have to worry about sprouting legs before their pond dries out. If the toads can do the math, we do have the time.

AT 4:00 PM a thunderstorm strikes. I slide my window open all the way and give my tadpoles a drink of rainwater, pummeling their liquid world, stirring them into crazed swimming. I've discovered that the tadpoles, now bean-sized with hindleg buds, love peanut butter. They swarm over the dab I've smeared on the side of their container at water level, their heads plowing and tails flagellating in a perfect picture of ovum conquest.

Later after dark, the storm subsides and it grows quiet outside. Or is it? Through my open window I hear something on the edge of a memory, a sound that registers first subconsciously, making me believe I'm missing something important. A lamb-bleat cry I haven't heard since that night three summers ago when I led my daughters to the arroyo behind our house following the sound of singing spadefoots. This time one of the men I teach joins me. Flat, brown water connects the tent area with the sweat lodge as a single large expanse. Amphibians call from all directions. It's a whole cantata. Matt, wearing shower shoes (a necessity for tent dwellers this time of year), steps into the water and sloshes out into the inundated roadway. "Easy," I say, "I want to find the toads." The Mexicans call him "Soapy" because he washes laundry for scores of men, charging them a dollar per load. His parents are raising his three-year-old daughter while he serves time for trespassing into his estranged girlfriend's apartment. He can't manage the fractions I teach him, but he's amazing at the game of chess.

We move toward the sweat lodge, tracking a single voice, but as we approach, the voice ducks into the water and won't resurface. We wait, and then turn toward the tents where another male is sounding off his intentions. At the ramada, a spadefoot holds onto a berm of mud and inflates its vocal sacs, blowing twin bubbles of translucent skin. Lamb impersonations from a balloon animal. Toad decibels. Matt and I stand in the water ten feet away from it and watch. A large Sonoran Desert toad appears on the right, paddles in the spadefoot's direction, and then passes by. The spadefoot sings and pivots to face the visitor, but there's no connection, no interest. A few minutes later, another spadefoot breaches at my feet and swims straight for him without hesitation. The two tumble together and instantly lock into amplexus, the mating embrace, the male gripping the back of his mate. A moment's rest and the pair leaps into the water and pushes away as one animal.

The next morning I search for toad eggs along the borders of shrinking pools, but I can't find anything, only one tiny toadlet breaststroking across open water. I'm surprised by the absence of egg masses. After last night's mating frenzy I expect more, but then, seeing breeding toads here in the first place seems an anomaly.

The appearance of spadefoots is nearly miraculous to begin with. That their eggs hatch within a day and their larvae grow from gilled wrigglers to lung-pumping quadrupeds in a week reflects the spontaneity of these desert amphibians. Adults emerge en masse at the onset of a gully-washing monsoon thunderstorm after being tucked underground, dormant all year and sometimes several years. The storm's low-frequency vibrations—a

cue that water will be present—awakens them, and, like seeds, the animals push their way to the surface. After a few nights' rehydration, sex,
and gorging on insects—spadefoots relish the calorie-rich termite reproductives that also swarm with the rains—they retreat once again below
ground, using the black, half-moon spades on their hind legs to corkscrew
themselves into the earth where their body becomes a living chamber and
the long period of rest begins. Estivation. Metabolism slows to that of a
walnut. Respiration, digestion, circulation all but cease. The amphibians
won't even excrete, and instead use their bladders as canteens to escape
mummification. Doing time on the cheap. The Department of Corrections
might learn something from the wisdom of toads.

For ten years I've watched for the nuptials of spadefoots in this place.
We've had the summer storms, the floods and their leftover pools, all the
prerequisites, including the adults themselves. At the Santa Rita Unit I
could crack my window just enough to hear them sing beyond the fences
on quiet monsoon evenings. But until last night, I'd never found a single
pair in amplexus. It was as if the animals understood that sex is forbidden
in prison, that sex is the anomaly.

I continue walking laps, sauna laps, in air that is so thick it clings to my
lungs and remains there. Near the east perimeter I pause at the pull-up
bars. I wait for three Aryans to finish working their legs. Squats: one man
rides the shoulders of another and holds onto the bars for support while
his partner tries to avoid a hernia. The three are shirtless, and it amuses
me to see that one of them, the overweight, bald one, is suffering from bad
sunburn. On Friday, the same trio had just started exercising here. I overheard one of them, a man with two full "sleeves" of black tattoos covering
each arm and the words, "Thank God I'm White," stenciled across his back,
criticize "Fester" about his complexion. "It's good to be white," he said, "but
Dude, you are too white." He looked Scandinavian. He would be blond if
he had hair. Like the other white boys who begin losing their hair, he had

shaved his whole head. It didn't help his appearance; his naked pate only makes him look more baby-faced.

After my turn at the pull-up bars, I finish one last lap and then scoop up a handful of algae-laden mud—all that's left of the storm runoff. The slime makes perfect fodder for tadpoles, which have grown into nothing more than tight coils of intestines with tails.

My fellow prisoners must think I'm nuts, tracking through pools to locate mating toads, gathering mud to feed tadpoles living on my window-sill. I'm sure the men in my housing unit know about my proclivities for collecting things—the toads and spiders, the cocoons and sycamore seed-balls, the dead hawkmoths. It's not voyeurism, this observation into my life; it's more knowledge by default. Living in close quarters with a group of men is an education. You learn personal things unintentionally, things you'd rather not know, things only a mother or wife would know. After only a few months here, I can identify the men who sleep or stay up late, the men who watch professional wrestling or enjoy the Discovery Channel, the men who use Irish Spring, Alberto VO5 shampoo, those who brush their teeth and those who soak their dentures. I know, unfortunately, every man on my run who doesn't wash his hands after using the toilet. I can't help but notice. (I no longer shake hands with anyone.) It's not only the nuances of nature that I see here. It's the shape of people's lives.

ALL THAT I AM comes to me by assimilation, not personal invention. I'm reading the poet Charles Simic, who quotes Thomas Aquinas: "Nothing is in the intellect which has not been previously in the senses." Twelve years ago yesterday, August 5, I left my pregnant wife and two small children and ran off with a girl half my age. It's impossible to ignore the cycles of emotions when the very aspect of this place keeps rubbing my face in the mess I've made. That one event has narrowed my life down to twenty acres—I can cross it in less than five minutes—but it's room enough to hurt.

There is a difference between being sensitive and being emotional. I prefer the former. Sensitive and perceptive. I want to notice things, both externally and internally. I need to see and hear and touch; but rather than allow my emotions to distract me from real meaning, I engage my mind. I wonder, explore, and muse my way to awareness of the connections between memory and present experience, between history and metaphor. I can't escape the emotions, the chemical storage in my head of what I did. This is part of me. Nor can I intellectualize the emotions. What I can do is accept them—and search for significance in the pain. Sometimes redemption, undeserved, is too costly. Like Tantalus, I can never quite taste what I need.

LAST NIGHT I released the last toadlet. I found it floating on the surface in the Folgers jar. The animal had miniature forelegs and hindlegs, a limp tail, and was about half the size of its previous tadpole form. It could comfortably crouch on the nail of my little finger.

The last time I raised spadefoot tadpoles was exactly three years ago. I collected the eggs with my daughters after a thunderstorm. That summer, my girls carried more than a hundred toadlets from an aquarium to an outdoor terrarium they had constructed for them and began feeding them blackworms by hand. Today, they still have two of the toads, Pin and Princess, living with a salamander in a glass tank atop their dresser drawers. I like to think that their pets remind them of the toad-finding adventure we had together that stormy night.

I'm missing the tadpoles on my windowsill. This morning, I'm not as relaxed as I have been. I have no swimmers to watch, no tadpoles circling endlessly clockwise as tails atrophy and leg-buds stretch into oars. I have no tadpole reminder of a past connection to my daughters.

ON MY EVENING WALK, hummingbirds and hawkmoths ravage every narrow flower requiring tongues: aloe, bird of paradise, desert willow. I mark them all, out of habit, out of survival, thinking I've only just begun to learn how to notice the obvious.

Charles Simic, my favorite poet lately, says, "Time exists only where counting exists and counting is an activity of a lonely soul." His words reach deep inside me. I count everything: insects and toads, the migrations of blackbirds and western kingbirds, the motions of constellations, the ebb and flow of renegade weeds. I've seen the courage of deciduous trees and listened to the hormonal persistence of grackles in their season. Nature promises nothing. In this time-stagnant place I make my own frame of reference, convincing myself that what the philosopher says is true: that the only certain thing is the passage of time. Prison wants me to doubt, so I accept loneliness as a price for the certainty of counting.

THE ARIZONA DEPARTMENT OF CORRECTIONS is constructing a new, 4,300-bed facility near Buckeye. Named after the former director, Sam Lewis, the prison is the largest in the state and will certainly relieve the depressed economy of the small farming community. Prisons do that. It's why we place them near struggling mining and agricultural towns like Douglas and Globe, Florence, Yuma, and Safford. The beauty of it is that prisons are a self-adjusting market, Arizona's "field of dreams." "You build it and they will come." "They" being inmates, not necessarily new officers. I recently read an essay in *Newsweek* about how our prisons are filling up as fast as we construct them, and how law enforcement and the courts increase arrests and warrants knowing when a new facility is coming on line. In Arizona, this is good business. Empty beds are wasted resources.

Construction has also begun where I live in Housing Unit One. The feds have ordered ADC to replace the floor tiles in all the units because of asbestos contamination. In a typical knee-jerk response, the department will remodel not only the floors but every room as well. No more closets. No more paneling. No more drawers, file cabinets, and desks. Someone has complained. Our rooms don't look enough like prison cells—stark and white—and we'll spend the money to correct the problem. It will be Christmas before they get to my run, the last, at which time the forty men living here will refamiliarize themselves with tent life.

The construction means I must find a detour for my exercise laps, and when I do, my new route allows me to discover the largest jimsonweed I've ever seen in prison. The plant is the size of a bushel basket and draped with a dozen florescent blooms in full display, with at least as many "thornapple" fruits. The plant stuns me, amuses me. It grows in a flower bed at the side of a dormitory adjacent to a well-traveled sidewalk, well traveled by officers, not just inmates. There's a man caring for it, an inmate landscaper, but he doesn't recognize it. "Sacred datura," I tell him when he notices that I'm staring at his husbandry. "Hallucinogenic jimsonweed." He says he'll try to keep the plant concealed among the other shrubs and flowers. I'm hoping it survives the notice of the men, thinking I'd like to visit it in the evening and watch the hawkmoths sip its nectar and spin away in drunken corkscrews.

But the next day the jimsonweed is gone. It was fine for my first few laps, and then Sergeant Spangler appeared. I passed him and said to some friends standing nearby, "'Spanky' is about fifteen feet away from a hallucinogenic plant. Do you think he'll notice?" On my next lap the plant was missing, a torn hole in the ground where it had sprawled.

I'm disappointed and anxious. Have I said too much, told too many people? Did word get around to the cops? I worry that the plant's caretaker might connect me with its discovery, a link that could be dangerous. He's a weight lifter-horticulturist, and the type of quiet, brutal man who defies prediction. The coincidence is hard for *me* to believe. Yesterday, I found someone's leafy drug stash. Today, Sergeants Spangler and Abt are driving around in a golf cart with a large jimsonweed wilting in the back.

Jimsonweed has a long "medicinal" history, possibly going back more than three thousand years. Southwestern tribes used the plant in religious ceremonies. Local folk wisdom claims that jimsonweed helps heal varicose veins. I'm interested in stories of how inmates use the plant—so far, no one I know is treating the blue veins in his legs.

A few days later I spot another plant on my morning rounds. The plant crouches low in the grass next to the volleyball court, its stems just putting out buds as they push along the ground. Someone has been pruning its leaves. I tear off one: it's a sticky cat's tongue between my fingers and smells like wet skunk. I clip a whole stem to sketch into my notebook.

Last summer some men living in the tents got the yard locked down after eating the seeds of jimsonweed. One tried climbing the fence, claiming his mother was on the other side. A friend tells me that he once brewed jimsonweed tea at the sweat lodge with his Native American friends. "We didn't know what we were doing but drank it anyway." Ralph, a former nurse with a prescription drug habit, says the concoction was oily brown and tasted bitter. "That night, I had trouble sleeping, even though I felt exhausted. I kept seeing flashing, colored lights on the ground. Another guy started licking rocks until his tongue bled. Another was urinating on people's bunks." The cops ordered them all to drop urine but found nothing. Apparently, there's no test for jimsonweed.

For the past few weeks one of the ADOT crews has been traveling to Kitt Peak to clear roadside brush charged by El Niño's pulses, plants like jimsonweed. Arvin, my student who led the "Free Willy" insurrection last month and who is in prison for selling drugs, tells me that the plants are nearly waist high, saturated with flowers, and impossible to rip out of the ground. He also tells me that an inmate had acquired a piece of the root and boiled it in his hot pot like a potato before drinking the liquid. His cellmate woke that night to find him wrapped around their porcelain toilet, stripped naked, hugging and kissing it while laughing and repeating, "Oh, Baby, I'm here! I'm right here!"

BARREL CACTI bloom in fiery orange eruptions as if there were no tomorrow. I've released about a dozen toadlets so far: twelve dark, wet, sticky watermelon seeds, perfect kernels of amphibian energy, the fortunate residue of a pool that has dried and cracked to pottery shards. I may be upsetting some kind of balance. Nature teaches me that too much can lead to too little: The more toads, the less insect forage, which in turn means fewer toads as the weakest starve. Population excess brings population crash. The truth is that bounty is an illusion, a delusion. You never have enough. My own poverty now has come from believing a lie, that I could have all I wanted and desired. Twelve years ago today, on August 19, I was arrested in Aspen, Colorado. As my wife and I again cycle emotionally through this time, I know that Karen has grown more distant. When I call, I hear the burden of our marriage in her voice. When I hug her in visitation, she says I'm holding her too tight. If I take a rare chance at kissing her, she ducks her head. It's the small daily rejections that hurt the most: fever blisters—those periodic and incurable manifestations of pain.

Today's Psalm reads: "Lord, why do you cast off my soul? Why do you hide your face from me? I have been afflicted and ready to die from my youth up; I suffer your terrors; I am distraught. . . . Loved one and friend you have put far from me, and my acquaintances into darkness."

It is best to live a life that is lean and hard and simple, yet productive. Not like the spadefoot, which puts all its energy into a single night of egg-laying and faith, faith in a long-lived pond or a miraculous rescue from prison. It's best to live a life more like the swallow, which focuses all its resources on *raising* the family.

TODAY WE'RE ON LOCKDOWN. No movement. No phone calls. No visits. No lunch either. There's a spatula missing from the kitchen, and the cops are searching for it. The brownshirts are angry; someone has spoiled their Sunday. It's the second shakedown in ten days and as much an inconvenience for the staff as for us.

This morning, I left the housing unit for my exercise laps and made it halfway around the yard before I noticed I was alone. Really alone. No one was within sight, officers or inmates, and I was walking the perimeter. Some officers had recently handcuffed and written up a friend of mine for mistakenly leaving his cell during a lockdown, citing him for possible attempted escape. He could receive more time. Like me, he hadn't heard the announcement over the paging system. But I was fortunate. No one had seen me. I quickly crossed the softball field and hurried past the yard office, checking for brown in all directions. All clear. As I ducked into House Two, a man appeared at the door and asked me if the yard was open. "I didn't know it was closed," I said. "Some security."

I'm still berating myself for my stupidity. Awareness is critical here; one mistake can change so much in a system that's less than forgiving. What I want most is invisibility, and today I tested it. I must have been thinking about Dave, a friend I've known for ten years who left Echo yesterday. His release date is in six months, and now he's in protective custody for an administrative evaluation. Dave is another sex offender nearing the end of his sentence. Ten years of prison, however, is not enough. The state, in typical retroactive thinking and decision making, requires more for those still locked up, but this is not double jeopardy the courts have declared.

On the morning of the lockdown ten days ago, two white transportation buses waited at East Gate. I knew something was coming. The ADOT crews hadn't gone out. The labor pool hadn't distributed tools. I completed one nervous circuit of the yard when I heard a man say, "The last time I saw those buses at the gate, I lost a lot of friends." He was referring to the predator roll-ups eleven months ago when more than a hundred men, I among them, were suddenly transferred to higher-custody units. As soon as he finished his sentence, the guards began shouting for us to return to our cells.

My journal entry for that date records my anxiety over the uncertainty of the lockdown. I had seen dozens of unfamiliar officers and several administrators moving about. The TSU (Tactical ["Testosterone"] Support Unit) was gearing up for action in black Kevlar and riot helmets. I felt sick to my stomach and feverish, remembering the similar incident last September. "We can't use the bathroom without escort," I write. "Never seen this before ... now we can't go at all. I urinate in an empty peanut butter container and toss the liquid out the window. Repeat three times. Nervous bladder. Cold hands." My thoughts also turn to my wife, whom I had tried to call the night before but couldn't get through to. "I should have called this morning, but she's been distant lately."

By late afternoon I knew it was a shakedown, not another major roll-up. I expressed my relief by writing about how violated I felt after the Tactical Support Unit ransacked my room, confiscating personal property that wasn't contraband, like my typewriter manual and drawing supplies, and rifled through my letters and files and books, dumping everything on the floor.

I did have one reason to be appreciative of the shakedown: finding a misplaced toothbrush. Several months previous, the department had collected all our toothbrushes, replacing the "weapons"—the staff decided we were all altering the long handles to use them as knives—with a three-inch, travel-type toothbrush. Using it requires the dexterity of an oral surgeon, and my rear molars have suffered a patina of plaque ever since. Twice, I nearly swallowed the thing. Keeping the regular-sized toothbrush meant I risked disciplinary action, but at least I could brush properly. Today, I still have the toothbrush, which I've been hiding in my closet inside some rolls of toilet paper. My teeth feel better for this luxury, slick to the tongue, polished like marble. What can I say? I'm a criminal.

Or am I? Last night during class, Oscar, my Mexican national friend, brought me a large male tarantula he found outside the building. "Ken, I have a present for you," he said, the unshaven (noncompliant) spider clinging to his arm with all the tensile passion of a year's sexual frustration. Oscar complained about an irritation on the inside of his forearm after I took the spider from him. "Tarantula hair," I said. "It's a defense, like the fine glochids of a beavertail cactus that can leave you scratching for days. You don't want to get them in your eyes." After an impromptu classroom show-and-tell, the spider quietly rode on my shoulder for the evening. I considered leaving it in my desk drawer for the night as a locked-and-loaded present for an officer who's been snooping around lately, but decided it wouldn't do to find him dead on the floor in the morning. My wife is right; I'm not devious enough to be a proper criminal. She says I'm misusing my knowledge about the nature of weeds and bugs, that I should be doing more. Like how two entomologist brothers, she says, both in separate prison camps, treated their captors during the Vietnam War with lice and assassin bugs, mites and ticks and fleas they collected and slipped into their clothing. "Their fellow prisoners thought they were crazy," she explains, "until they realized what the two were doing. Then everyone joined the bug hunting, and helping the guards with their jackets, shaking their hands." Karen would make a better criminal than me; she would do so much more than show-and-tell.

TROPICAL STORM ISIS arrives bringing steady rain and a plague of toads, hundreds of them, mostly the size of test-tube corks, popping wherever you step. Great Plains toads, Couch's spadefoots, western spadefoots,

Sonoran Desert toads—nightly they visit the area outside the education building. My students think I'm responsible, that by rearing a bucketload of tadpoles I've unnaturally overpopulated the prison.

This morning on my exercise circuits, I consider the words of Thoreau, deciding that I am not ready to leave father and mother, brother and sister, wife and children and friends, never to see them again. I have not paid my debts, made my will, nor settled my affairs. I am certainly not a free man— but I am ready for a walk. And I don't saunter! My steps have purpose. The turkey vultures are migrating, and I'm expecting something unusual. I'm always expecting something unusual.

Like today, I blister my mouth on pineapple. Skin peels away from my hard palate and I ignore it, savoring tongue eruptions of fresh blueberries and strawberries. This is the weekend of our quarterly food visit, and Karen and the girls bring barbecued ribs—precooked because the administration no longer allows us to grill food—with a fresh green salad. We sunburn within an hour, Melissa, the worst, her fair complexion now burnished like new copper. She smiles bravely, my poor wilted flower.

Where I have failed, my family has prevailed. My daughters are proof that I am worth salvaging—something I want other inmates to see, particularly those who would cause me trouble because of my crime. They should know how much pain it would bring my girls if I got hurt, a kind of child abuse already committed by the three men who attacked me at Meadows Unit. I remember losing my own father when I was nine and how I suffered after his fighter jet crashed on a training mission. His was an abandonment I've already passed on to my own children.

If my daughters spare me from being human waste, my wife grants me a mote of respectability. The fact that she remains married to me, as degrading as it is for her, demonstrates it. It doesn't come without cost to her, but Karen is my human credential. Her own personal integrity demands it. Like Jephthah, the Israelite commander who kept a promise to God and lost his only daughter as a result, Karen "swears to [her] own hurt and does not change."

I think it must be her father who taught her this. Retired now, he worked twenty years for the Tucson Fire Department and never made chief, although he was more than qualified. He had mastered the training, aced the exams, but year after year the department passed him up for promotion. Possibly, this was because he refused to join the firefighters' union. He couldn't support an organization that owned a local bar. He had principles, some relating to the drinking of alcohol, which he saw too often turn into blood on the streets during his shifts. Regardless of the consequences, he would hold to his principles without complaint, even to his own hurt.

That's the problem with integrity: handling its consequences. Karen speaks often about how careful she was not to harm anyone unnecessarily with my postconviction relief case, and how this played into the hands of the prosecutor. We had agreements—no appeals for one—that, as it turned out, only she remained committed to. Those commitments would eventually lead to my return to prison. Karen has regrets now, but I don't. We made these decisions together. Maybe we should have been more suspicious of the motives of the state, particularly the honesty of the prosecutor. Karen believes Bill Perry used her sensibilities to his own end—a personal affront that continues to shame and anger her. Bill Perry had a job to do—win at all costs. Justice is never about truth, only about winning convictions. I can accept this. I would rather have Karen's integrity than my own freedom.

ON MONDAY, a bit of the unusual: I encounter a juvenile diamondback rattlesnake on my second lap around the yard. My morning caffeine, as Ann Zwinger says. It's a gorgeous animal, fifteen inches, dark diagonal pattern the length of its back over a cool, gray canvas and a venetian blind underbelly in Navajo white. I try to convince the two men who actually found the snake that we should let it go at the perimeter fence. One of them, a Mexican national, only speaks two words, "Not good," over and over. He wants me to put the rattler down so he can kill it. I stall, but I'm in the minority. The Mexican cuts off its head with a shovel. He will clean and preserve the skin with the rattles (two beads) attached and stew the meat in his hot pot. He doesn't invite me to dinner.

It must be rattlesnake season. Some men at the tents killed two more juveniles last night, according to Colin. He tells me his calf still burns off and on from yesterday morning's scorpion attack. He's been sick to his stomach, too. Colin is living with forty other men in the temporary tents on the basketball court for a few weeks while construction crews remodel and paint his housing unit. (My turn will come soon enough.) Yesterday, after he slipped on his pants, he felt he wasn't alone in them. "I only noticed a burning sensation at first," he told me, handing me the six-inch, giant desert hairy scorpion, dead in a plastic bag. "I grabbed it through my jeans and crushed it. I was afraid to let go, and I couldn't get my pants down." I've known Colin since coming to Echo. He's what most refer to as a "youngster," raised by the state and now in his early twenties. He's been in prison since seventeen, a graduate of the juvenile system and, like many other teenagers finding themselves in adult prison, he's learned to fight to keep from being some lonely convict's "son." This has made Colin hard for his age, confrontational, isolated. The only thing youthful about him after seven or so years locked up is the Dutch-boy cut of his straight brown hair.

Colin's leg is still red and warm to the touch where the scorpion inserted its sting. He says the snakes and his scorpion visitation have everyone in the tents nervous. "The first thing you hear in the morning," he tells me, "is the sound of people shaking out their clothes."

THIS MORNING'S PSALM READS: "How long, Lord? Will you hide your-self forever? Will your wrath burn like fire? Remember how short my time is; for what futility have you created all the children of men?"

I discovered the Psalms in prison. The morning devotional has carried me through more than a decade of this place. We have Christian program-ming (Trinity Broadcasting Network) on television, but I'm put off by the plastic Christianity, the ultimate cliché of our commercialized American society. Do people really believe everything should be perfect? Even our hair? I prefer the psalms for their emotional honesty, the way the psalmist deals with pain and ecstasy, faith and doubt, life at its essence, peeled down to the bones and bloody marrow. Like the writer Kathleen Norris, I, too, identify with the psalms' "disruptive tone, their bold and incessant ques-tioning of God." Norris says, "You come to the Bible's great book of praises through all the moods and conditions of life, and while you may feel like hell, you sing anyway. To your surprise, you find that the psalms do not deny your true feelings but allow you to reflect on them, right in front of God and everyone." So, when I read, "You have put away my acquaintances far from me; you have made me an abomination to them; I am shut up, and I cannot get out," the psalmist's prayers are my own, a harmony of voices calling from prison and getting no answer—except, occasionally, a sense of peace in the common effort.

After my morning meditation, I notice that the prickly pear cacti have set their heavy purple fruits. Above me, the turkey vultures are migrating, their dark wings turning circles that lean toward Mexico. And the western kingbirds are absent, but Say's phoebes call from outside the fences, the first of the season. There's a change on the way. The autumnal equinox arrives at 10:37 PM local time.

In a recent *Bloomsbury Review* interview, Barry Lopez says, "To me, the way you introduce yourself to a landscape is the same way you intro-duce yourself to a person: a certain kind of wariness till you see where the boundaries are, and then increasingly making yourself more vulnerable, in an effort to achieve intimacy." Intimacy with place has never been a question for me, even if the place is prison. It happens precisely as Barry Lopez describes it: the more vulnerable I become here, the more intimate I get with its nature. I could remain in my cell, accomplish a daily routine of meals and television. I could allow events beyond my control to preoccupy my mind. (There are plenty of them: On Friday, the administration unexpectedly rolled up another friend and sent him to higher custody because he's a sex offender. There's a rumor that "counselor" Davidson is clearing her caseload of sex offenders by requesting the "evaluation" for each one.) But this kind of preoccupation is not vulnerability. I must see my boundaries, leave my cell, walk the yard, travel to the writing workshop and my job, teach the men what I know and learn from them, too. I have to accept that there will be questions about my crime, questions I must answer honestly, regardless of the ridicule that may come. For me, vulnerability means the possibility of confrontation, of rejection. I must face the fear of dangerous words, the shame of the stares and the spitting when I pass by. I must be willing, every moment, to take another beating. It is the price for intimacy with this place, the price for swallows and sanity.

THE AIR COOLS AND DRIES as we step into the aftersummer season following the monsoon, a time of year most of the country calls fall. The change is immediate and distinct. The sky means business, its normally bleached-out color seems revived, hardened. And sounds carry weight, too: aircraft engines roaring at Davis Monthan Air Force Base; diesel locomotives Dopplering along their tracks near I-10. The smell of cut wet rye hangs in the air where thin shadows freckle Cottonwood Park. The sunlight across my path, on the buildings and fences, has waned. It's a soft, melancholy wash that my pineal gland can't accept or adjust to. My whole body resists the diminished sun, leaving me dizzy and confused. A phoebe calls from somewhere, the hollow voice a lament of summer's passing.

The seasonal flex and flux of birds begins. But I feel ill prepared for change. Some people find the shift from summer to fall physically invigorating; the air seems charged with expectation. I sense only the charge of anxiety. Maybe it's because I have exactly two more years until my release. Two more winters, two more springs . . . Or maybe my lingering melancholy stems from the first anniversary date of my Yuma transfer as a result of the predator law. The lockdowns, the roll-ups, the cops walking the runs with their radios squealing—it all makes my heart pound. It could happen to me again. Nothing is certain.

I read an article in today's *Arizona Daily Star* about how the sexual predators are filling up the state hospital. The hospital director, who wants to construct another facility, admits that they have no sure way of determining whether or not an inmate will reoffend. His implication disturbs me; in fact, the whole article seems to have one overall glaring implication: no one is getting out.

In my mailbox today is a square slip of paper. It says I must report to the Service Center on Tuesday for reclassification. Failure to do so will result in "disciplinary action."

aftersummer 1998

The Permeability of Perimeters

Aftersummer scents of wet earth, mown grass, and second-growth green add garnish to this bright tangible morning of early October. The desert shrugs off the heat of summer, and there is a long, audible sigh in the air.

Judith Plant says bioregionalism means "learning to become native to a place, fitting ourselves to a particular place, not fitting a place to our predetermined tastes. It is living within the limits and gifts provided by a place, creating a way of life that can be passed on to future generations." I won't pass prison on to anyone, only, I hope, the way I fit my life within these fences, the way I survive them. Today, there are birds to meet my needs, and their presence is more than a distraction. The ubiquitous mourning doves rest in the grass like toadstools. A single yellow-headed blackbird communes with a flock of Brewer's blackbirds as if no one would notice. Say's phoebes have returned for the cooler months, a migratory habit that my notes are just beginning to bear out. Another seasonal occurrence: ravens collect in large spiraling thermal-groups, riding the updrafts like untethered bird shadows.

In a place where activity is mistaken for progress, where change is disguised as improvement, nature gives me faith in a larger picture, one where God resides in the details. Robert F. Kennedy Jr. once said that nature isn't God, that we shouldn't worship nature, but that nature is the way God communicates with us most forcefully. Right here, the birds remind me that there is purpose in everything. Birds and insects and trees. Nature is neither fragmented nor uncertain. It suffers no real separation but fosters a relatedness across boundaries, those among species and environments and ecosystems, between life and death. Nature connects it all, making even prison a permeable place, an ecotone where evolution leans from equilibrium toward punctuation.

These thoughts give me some perspective when events occur beyond my control. Yesterday, Keith, my coworker and friend, went to lockdown at the complex Central Detention Unit (CDU) for the predator evaluation. He is three months away from his release date—that is, if his evaluation is favorable, and he isn't committed to the state hospital. For now, he waits in maximum custody, dressed in an orange jumpsuit, his days regimented by mealtimes and television in a seven-by-ten concrete cell with a steel door. The department's method of rolling up these men unnerves me. It comes without warning—a page to East Gate from which you don't return. Guards box up your property. Sometimes it happens at your classification hearing. A new law or policy change and your numbers are too high. A "counselor" raises your score, calls for escort, and the cops lead you away in handcuffs. I've seen it happen, more than once. My own classification hearing this week lasted three minutes. Mr. Cornevaux, the reclassification coordinator, called me by my first name—a good sign. He recommended to Central Classification, those officials in Phoenix who have the final word, that I remain at Echo.

THIS EVENING, our former governor Fife Symington is a topic of discussion in class. He's in the news again: Attorney General Grant Woods is asking the U.S. Department of Justice to investigate his dealings with "Big Tobacco" while he was in office. Woods is accusing Symington of taking money from tobacco companies in exchange for his opposition to Arizona's $500 million tobacco lawsuit. Symington, responding from his vacation hacienda in Honduras, no doubt, says his opposition was based on principle. My students think his principle is colored green. One of his aides says Symington "sought a written commitment by the tobacco companies to provide him with a 'public relations fund' to help him battle any negative public opinion for his opposition to the lawsuit." Sounds green to me, too.

I expect more angry words from the men than I hear. They are frustrated, even bitter, but there also seems to be a general attitude of resignation. They've seen this kind of hypocrisy before: those with money and influence getting special consideration. Symington has become the epitome of what prisoners have believed all along: the rich and powerful don't go to prison.

At six thirty I take a break from teaching to watch the moon rise above the Rincon Mountains. I wait in front of the library while dozens of bats swarm over the black grass. Little jumpy western pipistrelles, Mexican freetails, big browns—it's a frenzy of ragged wings, dark corpuscles against my retinas. A lone nighthawk accompanies them, blinking on and off as it swoops in and out of webs of light.

Mark joins me as the moon lifts itself from the backglow of the Rincons, a motion that's barely discernible as one long pull, as if the moon were warm tallow lit from within. Mark (Marra, he insists) transferred from the Santa Rita Unit recently, and it had been more than a year since we celled together there. I noticed right away that he'd put on weight. His hair seemed thinner, too, though still dark and tied back into a ponytail that brushed down his spine. This feminine mane is all the hair he has. Under his blue ball cap he's mostly bald. I shared my "Queen" essay with him, and he was touched, readily supplying me with more details about his life as a "woman" in prison. "The cops discriminate against me, here," he told me. "I hate Echo. They've taken my makeup and panties." This evening, Mark hands me a story he's written about the events leading up to his accidental killing of his wife, a tragedy stemming from a drug-crazed, paranoid evening with loaded weapons. His wedding anniversary is October 10, and I remember Mark always celebrated the date by expressing the pain in the only way he knew how. "I wrote it as my atonement," he says of the story, "so I won't cut myself again this year."

Back in the classroom, Oscar stops by to inform me that he's found a bat clinging to the north side of Dorm Four under the second window. Oscar's new job as an inmate firefighter takes him to a variety of locations on the yard to monitor fire extinguishers, hydrants and hose storage, and test smoke detectors and alarms. A previous student of mine, before the department ordered us to stop teaching noncitizens, Oscar has found his niche. He tells me that after his release he would like to stay in Tucson and join the fire department. "No more selling drugs," he says. I'm wishing that he'd gotten his GED.

I find the bat, a western pipistrelle, where Oscar said it would be. I attempt to grab it by its wings, but the animal lunges at me and takes flight, fluttering mothlike and skimming the ground for several yards before clinging to another wall at knee level. Now, it gets the attention of three men standing nearby. One says, "A fruit bat," and looks at me. "Insectivorous, actually," I correct him, and when I see his question, I translate: "It eats bugs." We gather around the bat and it drops to the ground. It's jittery, lethargic, and someone suggests it needs a sugar fix. I scoop it into a Folgers jar.

"Bats, of course, are better than any piece of writing," says poet and author Luis Alberto Urrea. "I'd rather burn a book than a bat." I agree, and I take both, the book and the bat, to my class to arouse some interest in dry words and facts. "Smallest bat in United States," says James A. MacMahon. "Usually the first bat to appear in the evening, it often flies before dark and is even seen in broad daylight." The men ask questions: "What does it eat?" "Will it bite?" "Can you get rabies?" They definitely have an oral fixation. When we release it, the bat shoots away in a narrow ellipse and then lands on the wall of the building above our heads, where it remains.

The excitement of my "teachable moment" over, I spend the remainder of the evening teaching what I call "street math" to Arvin, the "Free Willy" tadpole lover. We work on fractions and percents, and the concepts finally begin to sink in as he connects them to his former experiences with the business of buying and selling drugs. We monopolize the chalkboard, inventing problems with metric conversions like how many ounces to a kilo, with fractions like how much vitamin B12 to cut into quantities of cocaine, and with multiplications like the street value of cut versus uncut dope. We come up with the idea of writing a textbook with exercises based on the practical application of math in the drug culture. The appendix would include metric conversion tables and feature the working elements of a triple-beam balance.

I have a new education motto: We turn dumb criminals into smart criminals.

ON MONDAY, Columbus Day, I sit in front of the library waiting for Karen. Small brown birds with zebra-striped caps sing a sad string of grassland notes that makes me think of Kansas summers.

White-crowned sparrows—a new species to add to my prison life list, another seasonal visitor to connect with, to pace myself with. I think about my encounters with all the unrepentant migrants of this place. The razor-winged barn swallows, bold western kingbirds, and secretive Say's phoebes. The Brewer's sparrows and blackbirds. The paddling nighthawks and soaring turkey vultures. They are the tidal motions of a feathered sea. I adjust my calendar to the metronome transgressions of birds. For now, they cue me to aftersummer's ebb: shorter days as the desert gradually cools and dries. Grasses beyond the perimeter fence bleach and go to seed under scattered cholla cacti, tiaras of light caught among their blond spines.

Sparrows cheep. Mourning doves coo. I relax. Ash and pine and desert willow shade the stone- and wood-buttressed terraces, which rise half a dozen feet above a manicured lawn. I wait on a bench of stonework nested among irises and rosebushes and various unfamiliar hedges. Where sunlight lies across them, railroad ties perfume the air with the nose-wrinkling oily smell of horse corrals and telephone poles, what people who live outside the desert call "creosote." Soon, I can see Karen in the parking lot, and I begin to feel my pulse in my throat as I watch her walk alone down the sidewalk to East Gate. She's beautiful at any distance.

AT 6:00 PM I write while sweating on my bunk and smudging the pages of my journal. My room must be a hundred degrees. The cooler is nonoperational, and the southern exposure of this trailer heats it up as if it were a solar collector. I'm finding it hard to believe this is the end of October. I'd open my window except for the hot, blowing dust.

An interesting note on CNN pulls me away from my page. Mary Kay Letourneau, the former teacher from Seattle who is serving seven years for her love affair with a thirteen-year-old student, has given birth to a girl, the second child from the relationship. The father, Vili Fualaau, who is now fifteen, is in Paris, France, promoting his book about the affair: *Un Seul Crime, L'Amour* (Only One Crime, Love). I've followed her case in the media for some time now. Oregon had originally given her probation, but she violated it by continuing to pursue the relationship with her student. The last incident, when police discovered the two in a parked vehicle, apparently preparing to flee the state together, sent her to prison. My heart breaks when I see those courtroom videos of her, her face, her eyes heavy with fear and confusion. I've been there, and I know prison will offer nothing to help her. She needs help. First to deal with her emotional obsession for the boy (what she feels for him is not love in the true sense); then to adjust to the emotional weight of prison. She's fortunate she doesn't live in Arizona. Here, you're offered psychological counseling after you've served most of a very long prison sentence, when the reason *why* you came to prison no longer matters, only *how* you survive prison.

ON THE MORNING OF Veterans Day, the yard opens after more than two days of lockdown, two days of escorts to meals, shakedowns and roll-ups, of television and sleep.

A few evenings ago, a commotion of shouts and banging started outside my window in the tent area. I thought I heard gunfire, too. A truck on the perimeter raced across the bare ground, spitting rocks and dust. I raised the blinds and saw the dark shapes of a dozen men moving around the east shower trailer. More shouts, and a vehicle stopped on the other side of the fence. An officer yelled, "Get down now!" and two shapes dropped to the ground. Two more trucks arrived, carrying officers with flashlights. Men in the tent area scattered, leaving an inmate hanging in the razor wire.

An hour later and little had changed. Two men still lay prone on the ground and another was stuck six feet in the air in the coils of razor wire while officers attempted to extract him. I heard voices but not words. Officers continued to search the area with flashlights. The men on my run were saying someone was stabbed.

At 3:30 AM noises awakened me: laughing in the hallway, boots thumping against the floor, doors slamming. Bright security lights pierced my room and my eyes. I grew conscious of the vocal posturings of the Tactical Support Unit. A figure in black walked past my door striking the floor tiles and walls with his baton. TSU proceeded to shake down the run, moving room to room, ordering men in boxer shorts and shower shoes to leave the housing unit and wait outside. I pulled on my sweatpants, shirt, and tennis shoes before a man in full riot gear banged on my door. He couldn't have been more than four feet tall, a midget storm trooper whose oversize helmet made him look like a mushroom, *phalloides* species. He complained about a smell. "What smell?" I asked, as if dozens of men packed like sardines were completely odorless. He demanded that I strip.

When I returned to my room, my bedding, clothes, and books were strewn on the floor, my property boxes spilled onto my bunk. The wooden bar in my closet where I had hung my shirts was missing—a potential weapon confiscated—but all my trash was still in the hallway. I retrieved it, along with my contraband Liquid Paper, glue stick, and standard-sized toothbrush.

At 6:00 AM we had a mandatory turnout for breakfast: undone potatoes and gravy, plastic sausage patty, coffee, and milk. In a show of force, officers paraded us to the dining area and pat-searched us coming and going. There were dozens of uniformed men and women, most of them unfamiliar to me, stationed singly or in pairs at various points along the way.

At breakfast I learned that the incident involved some Mexican nationals and African Americans, and that it had been brewing for weeks for reasons still unclear to me. The rumors say one man accused another of being a sex offender, that one of the nationals stabbed a black man three times, which then escalated to a conflict involving several dozen men. The inmate caught in the razor wire had been attempting to flee the tent area, not escape over the perimeter fence. The Mexicans had him cornered. The cops rolled up twenty-one men, three from my run. And there may be more movement to come.

At lunch I talked to Arvin, who was at my room just moments before the lockdown. As he filled me in on the details, he kept looking over my shoulder at a petite female officer standing at the door. "Ken," Arvin asked, "that woman, why she mad-doggin' me?" I didn't turn around. "What's her problem?" he said. "Must be us," I suggested. "I guess we're making her nervous, me being white and you black."

Arvin laughed. "What *she* gonna do?"

This morning, doves by the dozens huddle together on the razor wire, fluffed against the weather. A Say's phoebe chases insects from the sycamore, whose branches look weary, its leaves ragged and dull. It is the first tree to feel winter's sapping as the first Pacific cold fronts of the season sweep through.

When I'm finished walking, I stop at the sweat lodge to pick some mint growing near the border of the woodsy enclave. The commissary no longer sells tea bags; herbals are especially rare, it being two years since the last Christmas food package passed the prison gates. The cold and rain have started me fantasizing about mugs of hot mint tea with cinnamon, a spicy tonic to warm my hands and insides late in the evenings when blankets aren't enough. I have one more woody cinnamon stick, which from one end I burn for incense and from the other I scrape for the brown spice. The simplicity of cinnamon and fresh mint. It's nourishment for cold bones.

At noon back in the classroom, the chaplain says the security staff over-reacted to Sunday night's incident. The worst injury occurred because of the razor wire, a particularly vicious invention designed to slip under the skin and hold you in place. The black man was only stabbed in the butt. I tell the chaplain that TSU never has anything significant to do here, that the program is like training soldiers in peacetime: the smallest incident becomes an act of war.

A WEEK LATER, we're awakened again in the middle of the night (three thirty), this time for a fire evacuation. A guard asks me if I smell smoke, then he orders me to leave the building. Outside, it's cold in my T-shirt, but it's also dark without security lights and I'm treated to some gorgeous constellations. Ursa Major stands on its tail to the north: Alkaid, Mizar, Alioth, Megrez, Phecda, Merak, and Dubhe—I can still name the bear's seven major stars, stars I memorized to impress Karen the summer we met at the YMCA camp. (While holding her at night, I would whisper their names into her hair as though I was quoting poetry.) Leo, also rising on its haunches, dominates the southeastern sky with Regulus. High in the southwest and only 8.8 light-years distant, Sirius is planet-bright. And nearby, I see Orion for the first time this season. The star-girded hunter is my winter indicator and my favorite constellation. The red giant Betelgeuse on his right shoulder is four hundred times the diameter of our own sun and 270 light-years away. Blue Rigel at his left knee is twenty times the diameter of the sun and 650 light-years away. But we see these supergiants, and all the other lights in the constellation, as if closely connected with lines drawn in the sky. To see Orion is to look hundreds of years into the past, and more, to beginnings—not of time but of the stars themselves. There are star-seeds, appropriately so, in the nebulae of Orion's loins.

When a meteor lays a neon track across the blackness, I remember that tonight is one of the best nights of the Leonid meteor shower. I concentrate my viewing toward Leo, the constellation from which the meteors are supposed to originate, and they come. For forty-five minutes, while the inmate fire-response team gears up and drags hoses into the housing unit, I watch the sparks fall, one every few minutes. Some leave brilliant blue green trails in their wake that hold for seconds and then fade. The men see them, too; I hear their pleasure every time a particularly magnificent rock splashes into the atmosphere.

There is no fire, only smoke from a burned-out motor in a heating unit. In the morning I go to the phones to call home and Melissa says she also watched the meteor shower, waking alone and dressing in the middle of the night without the assistance of a fire alarm.

THIS MORNING carries with it a new bird voice, which I trace back to its source. The sharp twitter belongs to a small wren, probably a winter wren, perched atop the fence at the visitation area. It calls excitedly, *chirr, chirr,* in twin notes and bobs its head, watching me from its high, exposed position. I close some of the distance between us and wait. The bird bobs and calls, bobs and calls, and then finally flies off to a Mexican bird of paradise where it creeps around on the ground like a shrew. It's amazing how such a nondescript bird can take on such character.

The birds in this place resist being ciphers: this clear message to me from today's winter wren. The department would have it otherwise; it strives to depersonalize, dehumanize. There's a rumor that all inmates statewide will be clothed in orange "uniforms," orange T-shirts, jackets, hats, and socks, starting in January. No more blue jeans and chambray shirts. The department will replace even our personal sweatshirts and sweatpants with orange. When I came to prison in 1987, inmates wore their own personal clothing, within guidelines. Then, the state picked up our clothing bill, supplying us with "prison blues." Now, it seems, the state wants us all to dress in Day-Glo orange, one-size-fits-all jumpsuits, probably with "Property of ADC" stamped on the back and our numbers on the front. I wonder why the department didn't choose zebra stripes for us, like the outfits of the men in Sheriff Joe's Maricopa County Jail. I shouldn't be surprised. Prison depersonalizes even its buildings, painting them gray and numbering them as if they were inmates. Plant Operations: Building 10. HUB Programs: Building 8. They are all gray, ciphered blocks of concrete, faceless places.

ON THANKSGIVING DAY, I watch the Macy's parade on my television, sip caffe latte, eat fig bars, and think about what I'm thankful for: a marriage of eighteen years, three beautiful girls, friends, health and peace for the past year, a book publisher with a Lannan Foundation grant. My family sleeps in this morning, before preparing a simple turkey dinner. Our menu here includes pressed turkey loaf, stuffing, vegetable medley, dinner rolls, pumpkin pie and will be served at noon; a sack of bologna sandwiches will be handed to us at the exit door for dinner.

After the holiday, the remodeling of my housing unit begins. "A" run, one of three wings in the housing unit, moves out into the temporary tents, forty men dragging their bunks, filing cabinets, and property down the hallways and out to the basketball court like a nest of ants relocating its larval nursery. Then maintenance crews move in to strip the rooms of their closets and shelves while painters roll Navajo white over the wood paneling, making them cells. I figure it will be my run's turn in a couple of months; I can't wait for those cold nights of tent life.

On this morning's broadcast, CNN had a short segment about James Hamm, an acquaintance of mine from Santa Rita, who won his release in 1992. Arizona State University, where Jim is studying law, has hired him to teach classes in criminal justice. After explaining that Hamm served seventeen years in prison for murder, anchorman Bill Hemmer said, "We don't make this stuff up." Public criticism surrounding Hamm began when then-governor Rose Mofford granted him a commutation of his sentence and, reacting to sudden adverse attention and vocal complaints, immediately rescinded it. The federal courts later determined this illegal and finally ordered Hamm's release.

I know Jim, and his critics confuse me. While serving a life sentence for a 1974 shooting during a drug deal, he studied law, assisted other inmates with their cases, and, with his wife, founded the prison advocacy group Middle Ground. There are few men who are as gentle and quiet as Jim, and as intelligent. Prior to gaining his freedom, he scored in the ninety-eighth percentile on the LSAT. He had already earned a bachelor's degree in applied sociology at Northern Arizona University in 1983. Once he was free, the law school at Arizona State University accepted him, and he graduated with a Juris Doctor in 1997. I read the editorials in the papers when the news of his law school acceptance made headlines. Most were negative. One woman claimed that the "convicted murderer" had taken her place at law school, that he scored well on the entrance exam because taxpayers had funded his education and provided him with plenty of time to study. She herself had scored in the twentieth percentile. It wasn't fair. I would hear similar arguments from prison staff about Hamm's state-financed education and practical experience. He should have only received a GED, I guess, or maybe studied to be a truck driver. It's crazy. Jim Hamm is a success. He ought to be a poster child for the Arizona Department of Corrections: See what corrections in Arizona can do? We can turn a murderer into a law professor!

Our own Warden John Hallahan says 95 percent of all prisoners will be getting out over the next ten years. The public should hear these words. A convict will be someone's neighbor, and what kind of neighbor he becomes may depend on the kind of education he receives in prison.

Later, I read that James Hamm won't be teaching at ASU after all. His hiring "put the school on a hot seat," that the "debate surrounding Mr. Hamm's employment in the classroom at ASU would be too disruptive to the educational environment, as evidenced by the reaction to his hiring." Jim, still the man I remember, responded with disappointment and acceptance. He says, "I would prefer to teach but that's just not in the cards."

TWO DAYS OF FROST have knocked the first leaves off the sycamore, and they cling to the perimeter fence. The leaves are yellowing and age-spotted—geriatric hands climbing the chain link as if begging for release.

Karen and the girls began stringing up Christmas lights yesterday. I talked to them by phone after they returned from church. Karen said the chapel has a nativity scene and seasonal decorations and that people are in a festive mood. She's not, however. Christmas is rough on her, it being the time of year of my release . . . and the appellate court reversal. "God doesn't care," she repeats often. I tell her that she knows differently, that the way God cares for us isn't always clear, that our view of reality is narrow and finite, especially when we hurt . . . Pain has tunnel vision. But my words are shallow, comfortless. Karen needs more than words. I see how greatly her circumstances have crushed her faith when she shares her thoughts with me. Yesterday's nativity scene wasn't a symbol of hope and peace for her. Instead, she imagined an elaborate scheme by a pregnant fourteen-year-old to cover up her premarital indiscretion.

THIS MORNING, I'm reading Don Gayton's essay about Bragg Creek, Alberta, from the journal *Manoa*. He writes, "We humans tend naturally to be rather woolly thinkers, forever bringing things in from left field and cobbling them on to the issue at hand. . . . It is our nature to be free-form, hot-dog, and eclectic: we live in holism." I find this true in my own life and believe it's one reason why I've never been able to accept prison as simply a time of confinement, of warehousing. Even here, I'm constantly "cobbling" nature on to concrete and steel, focusing on the transgressions of birds and weeds and weather. I have one conviction, and multiple conflictions, contradictions. I have come to see prison as my wilderness, and what can be more "hot-dog" than that?

Recently, while I waited in line for my weekly commissary shopping, a brown pelican traced the northern perimeter fence. The bird was huge, prehistoric, reptilian, with bent wings that leaned into a Cretaceous sky as it drifted, circled, and slipped toward the sewer pond. It could have been an animal cobbled to my imagination, all gular pouch, crested head, and wing, but instead it was real.

I once used the wing of a pelican, stretched and preserved into a perfect avian airfoil, as a classroom model for Bernoulli's principle. It was as long as my arm, and it *was* an arm: a hand of stiff primary feathers with a thumb-alula, a forearm of broad secondaries, the short humerus-handle. Swinging it through the air produced a dramatic effect, raising your arm against gravity suddenly and forcefully. I could leave this place with pelican wings and a strong headwind.

In the evening, I return from the GED class under a dome of stars, many of them visible even through the security glare. I walk with my neck wrenched dorsally, eyes upward, a habit I can't break even if I wanted to. It's as if the stars draw my attention, and I rest my mind on those lights most constant and familiar: Sirius, Betelgeuse, and the Pleiades.

At Housing Unit Two, a statuette of an owl posts itself on the lip of the rooftop. The burrowing owl is motionless except for its head, which swivels left then right, left, right. "Look," one of the men watching it with me says, "it's tweaking. Just like I used to do on crystal." Matt, a former student of mine, has been watching the owl for an hour. "Watch it," he says. "It's chasing the mice coming out from under the trailer. It nailed one, but then it got away." Other men join us, but the owl seems unconcerned. It's definitely interested in something on the ground beneath its feet. Twice, it changes vantage points, fluttering along the edge of the roof only ten feet away from us. After fifteen minutes, the owl suddenly jumps into the air, climbs high into the blackness where it hovers momentarily, a soft, white sphinx moth caught in a wash of light, and then darts away. To no one in particular, I mention the great horned owl that hunted for mice along my run at Santa Rita. "Beautiful animal," I say. "Restores my faith in things wild, supernatural."

At 3:00 AM I can't sleep because I'm thinking about Karen and how prison affects her more than me. Lately she won't hug me at the end of our visits. I'm having a recurring dream involving her. In it, I'm following her, chasing after her as she moves through some routine that doesn't include me. I never catch up with her. I know why Karen's affections toward me have cooled. A few weeks ago at visitation, we held each other a little longer than normal, Karen nuzzling my chin in a rare display of intimacy. When I looked up over the top of her head, an officer was wagging her finger at us.

There's an irony in the different way prison affects us both. It's not uncommon—one reason marriages on average don't last two years in this context. I won't let this place get into my mind, control my thinking and emotions and behavior. I won't give anyone more than my body. I will avert my thoughts to wildness. But Karen, I fear, responds to this environment with anxiety, attitude, and anger, precisely what the prison system wants. It's a kind—the worst kind—of control, and I find this peculiar, coming from a woman who prides herself on control. Tomorrow, Melissa will be twelve years old. Twelve years ago I held onto Karen's hand while Melissa slipped wet and pink into our lives. Twelve years ago I made a decision to stay with my family and prepare for prison. If we hadn't won my Rule 32 in 1994, and then lost it, I would be going home in two months. Instead, it will be twenty-one months. I wish Karen would hold me despite this place, despite that it reminds her of what I did to her twelve years ago. I wish Karen could see pelicans and burrowing owls.

THE HOUSE OF REPRESENTATIVES impeached President Bill Clinton today for lying about his sexual relationship with a twenty-one-year-old intern. I'm certain the Senate won't convict him; he understands how the justice system works, which has nothing to do with the truth.

The word adultery has fallen into disfavor these days. I guess it sounds too much like a criminal act—in Arizona, adultery is still a crime. Representative Henry Hyde, Republican of Illinois, calls it a "youthful indiscretion" even though he was forty-one when he began his sexual affair with twenty-nine-year-old Cherie Snodgrass, a mother of three small children, and carried it on for five years, destroying Snodgrass's marriage in the process. Another Republican, Representative Robert Livingston of Louisiana, who was briefly Speaker-designate of the House, says he "strayed" from his marriage. Bill Clinton won't even call what he did "sex." He's careful. To tell the truth only leads to greater legal problems.

Karen can hardly discuss these recent events with me. She won't watch the news. She thinks Monica Lewinski should be charged with treason. "She knowingly undermined the presidency of this country," Karen says, "saving evidence and making spreadsheets of their relationship. She knew exactly what she was doing. When Clinton didn't keep his promise to her about their future together, she turned on him. He was stupid, but she is evil." Karen sees too many parallels in her own life, and her sympathies focus on Hillary and Chelsea. "I can't understand how he could do this to them," she told me in visitation yesterday. "And I don't understand how you could either."

I had no answer for her, at least one that might make sense, ease her pain. *How could I place my hand on your swollen belly while you slept that night before I left with another woman?* I thought. *How could I say good-bye to my sleeping children early the next morning, believing that, by my own choice, in a few minutes I would never see them again?*

Now I wonder how I could so easily lose the battle within myself. The day I drove away from my family with someone else in the seat next to me, only my foot, numb against the gas pedal, kept the truck adding miles between us. My mind was reeling, backtracking, searching for a way to end the affair, to erase the shadows the following days would bring to everyone who loved me. But fate, I believed, held my foot to the pedal. What I needed was a deus ex machina of Greek theater, for a god to come from the machine and miraculously resolve my impotence.

Later, after the two of us had stopped at my home in Mesa, I collapsed on the couch and stared out the window. I was watching for someone, anyone, to pull into the driveway and take my next decision from me. It wasn't too late. Our discovery now might allay the damage of our discovery to come. She perceived my hesitation, my confusion, and settled it with seven perfect words. Putting her arms around me, she said, "I know we can make it together."

COLD, WINDY LAPS on this morning of the winter solstice, but this obsession of mine with walking keeps me on the perimeter. The birds are smarter. Mourning doves gather into lint balls at the edges of buildings. Blackbirds and cowbirds stick to the dead grass as if magnetized by the wind. Only the ravens seem unaffected, the gusts chafing their feathers as they shift in the wind like stringless kites.

On Christmas Eve, the sky is perfectly clear and melodramatic in its sullenness, the curve of darkness seeping along the rim of the world. A quietness slumps against me. Later, moonlight stretches over the prison like fresh mesentery. Three coyotes yelp in feral harmony, soft palates quivering. It's an ephemeral song and only half-remembered.

For dinner I ate beef and bean burritos, rehydrating one package of Cactus Annie's dehydrated refried beans and combining it with one can of Hormel roast beef. I then wrapped the mixture in flour tortillas, adding jalapeños, squeeze cheese, and salsa. I would heat my burritos in a microwave, but the machines are in continual use this time of year. Plastic bedpans used as cooking pots and filled with food make for long lines, so I eat my dinner cold.

On Christmas morning I walk around a deserted prison yard. No one is out. Holidays are for sleeping in: sleep helps one get over those days normally devoted to family. I pass along B run of Housing Unit Two on a narrow path above the tents, and a window opens. Someone calls my name, so I backtrack to the window. Two of my students, Manny and Greg, their eyes wide and glassy, stare at me with pale faces in the dimness of the room. "Merry Christmas," Manny says. "What are you guys doing?" I ask, thinking they both look peculiar, shell-shocked. "Nothing," Manny says. "It's our first Christmas in prison. We don't know what to do." They believe I have an answer for them; they know I've seen enough of these days locked up. "Treat it like any other day," I suggest. "Easy time—it's what most do. Or face it; celebrate it. Put up some Christmas cards on your shelves, listen to holiday music, and call home. Today's also my daughter's birthday, so I spent some time this morning on the phone with her." The two look at me blankly. I'm not sure they want to hear the latter, what I call doing hard time. Better to put Christmas out of your mind, family too. Greg, however, suddenly remembers he needs to call his mother.

THE NEXT DAY is shirtsleeve weather, and Karen and I sit together in visitation at the farthest picnic table. She seems subdued, and I wonder if she's off her medication. Since my return to prison, Karen has been taking Valium to help her sleep and Prozac to help her deal with being awake. This morning, her face turned away from me and hidden in loose hair, she twists the gold band on her finger. I tell her—and later regret it—about my former coworker who was released two weeks ago and immediately transported to Cholla Unit at the state hospital. Keith apparently had failed the predator evaluation after the department raised his custody level and transferred him last October. The men in my writing workshop at Santa Rita, however, say that Keith didn't know this, that he'd been told his release was approved. In a letter from Keith, circulated among workshop members, he described how his escort led him in handcuffs to a van destined, the officer assured him, for his Phoenix halfway house. He had lied.

"Keith is so lame," I tell Karen. "Most of what he talked about in that letter was how good the food is at the state hospital, how he has to use the treadmill machine to work off all the ice cream he's eating." It's my attempt to lessen the gravity of Keith's situation and its possible link to my own future. But it's weak, and Karen doesn't want to hear any of it. I decide not to tell her that another friend of mine, Dennis, who also recently left for the evaluation, is at the state hospital with Keith, and that three men at Santa Rita attacked and beat Colin because of his crime as soon as he arrived there for his evaluation. Instead, we sit in silence, until Karen suddenly pulls off her ring and complains that it hurts her finger. I replace it, saying, "Your marriage is getting too tight for you, isn't it?"

TONIGHT, the sky is a bloody skullcap, but I have no reason to stay up and usher in the New Year. At midnight, another second will be added to my sentence, the additional time needed to synchronize our atomic clocks with Earth's rotation, which is slowing down. One more second. I hope the planet doesn't slow any further.

IN PERFECT JANUARY WEATHER, with dry, balmy, La Niña days, the cottonwoods still hold onto a few yellowed leaves and the irises have begun to flower. Ravens simmer in thermal kettles, and somewhere among the shrubs three cactus wrens use their voices for ratchets. I pause at a bare shrub decorated with birds: a male house finch airbrushed with crimson, two white-crowned sparrows, and a delicate Brewer's sparrow. The birds eye me, heads tilted like lizards.

On the day of our eighteenth wedding anniversary, Karen visits. We sit at the farthest table outside in the visitation area (always her choice), where dozens of blackbirds feast on popcorn someone has scattered for them. The birds entertain us, *check-checking* excitedly and scrabbling among themselves for fat kernels. Karen points out a peculiar behavior: Each bird takes a piece of popcorn and retreats to the fence line to eat in peace among the coils of razor wire. All along the perimeter fence, blackbirds station themselves within the security of sharpened steel, preventing others from snatching away their food. I'm shocked. "They're yardbirds," I say. "Prison has institutionalized them."

This place changes everyone, its residents, and its visitors. Today, Karen isn't wearing her wedding ring. "It's cutting into my finger," she says through thin lips, flicking her fingers again and again as if a vileness were still clinging to them. The pale absence on her hand shouldn't bother me. A marriage is more than rings; ours has been. The ring Karen gave me eighteen years ago is long gone, dropped into a river at Silverton, Colorado, by the hand of a girl ill fit to wear it, its gold returned to its source. (I'm still not certain if she lost the ring intentionally or not; I remember feeling pangs of regret at seeing it slip beneath the swirling water, while considering the event a profound sign, an act of fate.) I have no right to care so much about her missing band, but lately Karen has been talking again about changing her name, another one of her painful constrictions.

Gene Roddenberry's Klingons believe that marriage is a declaration of war. Albert Einstein said marriage is an attempt to make something permanent out of an incident. I like to tell people that marriage is what results when nature uses love to fool us into doing something irrational. "Love is the triumph of imagination over intelligence," says newspaperman and political commentator H. L. Mencken. But regardless of how anyone defines it, there are lasting effects of the union that reach beyond our human institutions and contracts and promises, effects that linger even long after separation. The apostle Paul writes that to be joined physically is to become one body, reiterating what the author of Genesis says about two becoming "one flesh." Nothing illustrates this "marriage" better than its usual result—a child, literally one body from the joining of two. And nothing illustrates better the devastation divorce causes: no one would think of tearing apart a child. It's this mingling of the flesh of individuals that's truly permanent.

No matter where I am, Karen is with me. She isn't just constantly in my thoughts raising powerful feelings. She has more of a presence inside me than one of neural pathways blazed among my brain cells by the repetitions of chemical transmitters—the essence of "love." She shares a deeper intimacy—one that touches my lymph nodes and double helixes. According to immunologist Gerald N. Callahan, my immune system holds the viruses my wife has passed to me, those causing flu and fever blisters. (I never had a cold sore until after I met my wife.) And our intimacy doesn't end here. Today, Karen's own lipids and proteins, her own personal nucleic acids, DNA and RNA, carried in "envelope" viruses from her body to mine, live within me, in my lymphatic system and in my chromosomes, in the same way dead copies of smallpox live within me. Karen has infected me, and I feel her fever in my cells most acutely whenever my defenses slip, which is often in this place.

winter 1999

The Balm of Crime Economies

Today is my laundry day, if I can find a free machine. On this run, we have two washers and three dryers for forty men, and they're in perpetual use. One of the perks of minimum custody is getting to do your own laundry; you can actually separate your whites from your blues if you're so inclined. At other units, you stuff everything—socks, boxers, shirts, jeans, blankets, and sheets—into fishnet bags, tie them closed, and drop them into a pile for delivery to Complex Laundry where huge machines soak the bags in gray water and tumble them semidry. Dirt is removed (relocated?) and wrinkles are added.

While waiting for my turn at a washer, I sip caffe mocha (one Milky Way candy bar melted into hot Folgers instant) and read the paper. *USA Today* reports that 1998 was the warmest year since measurements began 119 years ago. Scientists blame El Niño, one of the strongest this century, and an increase in greenhouse gases. Blame isn't the right word—praise is better. I love the heat: 110 degrees in the shade.

On this warm January day, I'm treated to a rare sight: high in a naked desert willow a male northern cardinal flashes red, like a bright holiday bow left over from Christmas. On my last circuit, I see that one of the cactus wrens now chatters from a loop of razor wire next to East Gate. The cactus wren is our state bird, and I can't help but think how appropriate. The scene should be on Arizona's state seal. *Ditat Deus Incarceratamus*: God enriches, we incarcerate. Currently, the "Great Seal of the State of Arizona" features mountains and sunset, valley farmland, a miner with a shovel, a cow—all symbols relating to once-important economic activities like mining, ranching, and agriculture. The three C's: copper, cattle, and cotton. Since the decline of these industries in the seventies and eighties, and the curious subsequent boom in crime legislation (not crime itself, necessarily, but its definition), prisons have become the ore and livestock and crops to stimulate the economies of dustbowl towns like Douglas and Globe (mining), Florence, Yuma, Safford, Perryville, Buckeye, and Picacho (farming). Altogether, more than fifty prison units in ten major complexes crisscross Arizona, creating ten thousand jobs and making the Arizona Department of Corrections one of the largest state employers. In 1998, the ADC's operating budget was 479 million dollars. In fiscal 2000, it will be more than half a billion. Arizona should revise its state seal of 1912. It's outdated. Today the three C's really mean "crime, convicts, and corrections."

All this concerns me. Arizona has developed an economy based on disadvantaged people as raw material. Poor and minority people. If resources run thin, if we need to boost the economy of another depressed town, simply write a new law. Pass another statute making it illegal to be poor, homeless, or mentally ill. Make it a crime to transport people in the bed of a pickup truck, to rummage ("trespass") in trash dumpsters for food, to panhandle on city street corners, to be addicted to crack cocaine (but not the powdered form). Stop funding the social programs, the rehab centers, the state hospitals, and hire more law enforcement. We might even start prosecuting children as adults. Prisons are good for Arizona. Don't we have bars on our state flag? Isn't there a convict with a shovel on our state seal?

Flags, state seals, cactus wrens, and razor wire. This is all wrong. I shouldn't allow the way things are to form a patina over my view of the world or I'll find it impossible to reenter the world and see the wonder of the simplest things, like a gift-wrapped cardinal in a winter-bared tree.

But reality has a way of erasing the wonderful, particularly if reality has Orwellian overtones. Kasondra, who's in eighth grade this year, told me she had a bad day at school last week after a Tucson police officer from the DARE program visited her class. (DARE: Drug Abuse Resistance Education or some such nonsense. The police officer at the school where I once taught educated my students about drugs by selling them to the kids.) Kasondra came home from school crying after the officer, whom she described as a "big, fat cop," told her class that he wouldn't hesitate to shoot any one of them in the ass. *My God!* I thought. Karen wrote a letter to the principal informing him of the incident: "I wasn't aware Tucson police were in the habit of shooting children who were running away from them." I told Kasondra, who said, "It must be because the cops are too fat to catch us."

Kasondra *should* run from role models like this one, and I hope she does, this perfect example of abusive authority. As if this aggressive posturing really impressed kids. Kasondra's school is on the west side of Tucson, and the student body is largely minority, Hispanic. (I'm betting you won't find DARE officers like this one in the more affluent north- and east-side schools.) Kasondra's peers are already well acquainted with belligerent law enforcement, and the exposure has only made them more callous to *all* authority. Interestingly, the tough students the officer had hoped to reach got a message he didn't intend: they thought he was "cool." They understood that if you have the power, you also have the right to wield it. But most kids react to threatening, ass-shooting cops with worse attitudes and greater disrespect. My girls, all straight-A students and class leaders, don't trust the police and wouldn't call them in an emergency, which is something I find unbelievable as I write this now. I blame, first, the sadistic, uniformed officers they've encountered in prison, but I also blame cops like the DARE officer who visited Kasondra's class. Intimidation has never and will never keep kids off drugs, and I'm surprised at the ignorance of those agencies that continue to use it. I'm now teaching eighteen- and nineteen-year-olds so hardened to intimidation from authority figures that prison has become a rite of passage. They are a new kind of convict—young, violent teens with no respect for life, with no conscience, willing to do anything—even kill—to earn their prison badge of honor. A lifetime of threats and intimidation from authority figures has taught them nothing but how to threaten and intimidate. For these kids, this kind of role model is all they know.

In our prisons, security consumes all other programs and more than half of inmates return to custody shortly upon release. What should we expect when security comes before learning in our schools? When *controlling* students becomes more important than *graduating* students?

Maybe it doesn't matter. Society seems to be throwing in the towel concerning its youth, gating up its communities in response to the problem and passing new juvenile legislation (why do politicians call it the "juvenile crime bill" and not the "*children's* crime bill"?), while making the transition to institutionalization smoother at the same time. Schools have lockouts and lockdowns, dress codes, armed security officers, on-site probation officers, drug-sniffing dogs, video surveillance, controlled access with high fences and padlocked gates, and a lack of landscape vegetation. Older schools have barred and painted-over windows, and newer schools have no windows at all. They are as secure as our cold war technology can make them. Gateway drugs? We have gateway prisons.

ON MY MORNING EXERCISE CIRCUITS, I keep my eyes open for a loggerhead shrike. The men have been telling me stories about a gray bird with black eye-stripes killing other birds, pinning them down and pulling them apart in the midst of the wild complaints of spectator birds. One friend asked me why shrikes kill their own kind. "They don't do it for fun," I told him.

Anthropomorphism, assigning human traits to animals, has never really bothered me. I do it often enough in my writing, justifying it some-what because I'm convinced some animals experience a degree of human-like emotion, feelings we call sadness, joy, fear, compassion. Only recently has science begun to study and document such behaviors, once thought to belong only to humankind. How anthropocentric of us. Still, I don't believe predators like shrikes kill for fun, something many men here find easy to accept, as if an act of senseless violence in the animal kingdom can help us feel better about our own brutal natures. "Only man kills for plea-sure," we say with self-incrimination. "We are lower than the beasts."

It's true. We are fallen creatures, capable of the worst atrocities. When we assign human characteristics to animals, we bring them down to our level, not the other way around. I've never known a bird to act despicably, to imprison its own kind.

This week, Karen got a call from the DARE officer who visited Kason-dra's physical education class. The school's principal had forwarded Karen's letter of complaint to the officer, and he felt the need to call her and defend himself. "He called me at work," she told me, "and he let me know that he knew all these things about me: where I live and work, who my parents are, by name. I thought he might even mention you." Whatever his purpose in this was, Karen felt intimidated. He then began making excuses, saying that it was a windy day and that our daughter must have misheard him. He would never tell children he wouldn't hesitate to shoot them in the ass. Typical, I thought. No admission of guilt. No apology. In so many words, Kasondra is the liar.

IT'S OFFICIAL: There's a memo stating that over the next two years the department will change our clothing from blue to orange, what we call "carrot suits." Our jackets, hats, T-shirts, even our socks will be orange. The ADC will exchange our personal blue sweatshirts, sweatpants, and athletic shorts for the new color, which makes as much sense as painting over the fake wood paneling in our rooms. The department must have extra money to spend. Can't have a surplus; it will be harder to ask for that half a billion next year.

Prisons are elastic entities, morphing through time and space with unexpected and often monstrous twists of character. That Aspen grove in Colorado isn't the largest living organism on the planet. In Arizona we have an undifferentiated mass, erupting with huge spores and sprawling over the landscape where cities place their landfills. I'm reading an editorial in the *Tucson Citizen* by Mark Kimble, captioned, "Sign of the Times for Arizona Prisons: 'No Vacancy.'" By June 30, 1999, he writes, the Arizona Department of Corrections will employ more people than any other state department, including the Department of Economic Security. "In other words, there soon will be more state employees working in prison than investigating child abuse and providing social services to children, to food stamp recipients and to people on welfare."

The editorial says that presently Arizona spends ten cents of every tax dollar to run the prisons, but that this is not the end. "Every month, Arizona has to find room for 132 more inmates." (As of January there were 25,633 men and women in prison.) In September, Florence will get 1,400 new beds; then in January 2000, 350 more. By June 2000, private prisons will add 400 beds, and over the next year, 1,000 more. But inmates will fill these on the day they become available. Just recently, the legislature approved the budget for another "prison city," a 4,300-bed complex that should finish construction in 2002. (Rumors say it will be "Tucson South," right down the road from here.) It also will offer no vacancy upon completion.

Mark Kimble blames mandatory sentencing for this new "Arizona Field of Dreams." He believes that laws passed since 1978, when "tough on crime" attitudes began removing sentencing discretion from judges, have inflated incarceration rates, from 3,622 inmates to over 25,000 in twenty years. (Isn't 1978 about the time our mining economy began failing?) He adds that 60 percent of these inmates are convicted of nonviolent offenses, 20 percent for drug offenses, and that taxpayers spend $50 per inmate per day, or $18,250 a year, to house each of them, twice what it costs to educate people at our universities.

We're losing the war on crime, and I'm wondering what else we'll lose for a false sense of security, some insignificant peace of mind. Society is mistaken concerning crime and punishment, duped by agenda-driven politicians and media. Prison will never be a solution, particularly the current warehousing without rehabilitation; prison is not even a deterrent to crime. Prison is a black hole, sucking up both resources and human lives.

This is nothing new. Consider this statement from a recent *USA Today* article about a study by the American Bar Association's Criminal Justice Section: "Increased drug arrests and longer prison sentences have not slowed illegal drug use." The study found that 1.2 million people were arrested on drug charges in 1997 alone, "a 73 percent increase over the number of people arrested in 1992." Myrna Raeder, chairwoman of the section, says the statistics suggest the policy of arrest and incarceration doesn't work.

The article then underscores the continuing ignorance of law enforcement by quoting Jim Pasco, executive director of the Fraternal Order of Police: "The study shows the need to stop drugs before they get into the country and onto the streets." This was the same mistake during Prohibition. Sixty years and we haven't learned a thing. Finger in the dike. The problem is not with the trafficking; it's with the demand, with the addict and recreational user, with individual people like star athletes and the children of politicians. Even in prison, with all its security—strip searches, urine testing, K-9 units, fluoroscopes, and fences—drugs flow like water. If we can't keep drugs out of our prisons, how will we ever keep them out of our country?

Imagine the results if we poured our money and resources into treatment rather than "justice." If we stopped fighting a war and sought peace rather than peace of mind. There could be salvaged lives, and it could begin with people who care enough to touch them. Not an easy thing to do from a gated community.

WE CELEBRATE Valentine's Day in visitation with homemade food. My wife and daughters bring chicken cordon bleu, fruit salad, and blueberry cheesecake. Later, my mom arrives with fresh strawberries and blueberries and a heart-shaped box of chocolates. I ask about the candy, since I've recently learned that chocolate contains substances chemically similar to marijuana. Did the drug dogs at the gate alert to it? I joke.

This particular Valentine's Day is significant: today I begin serving time to make up for my temporary release. Before Judge Minker sent me home in 1994, February 14, 1999, was my release date, the completion date of my twelve-year sentence. But, although the state would keep me closely supervised with home arrest and probation during my nineteen months of freedom, the time would not count if my release were overturned. This was our agreement with the prosecutor, and we never asked for the time credit when I returned to prison. Essentially, what's happened is we've added nineteen months of supervision to my sentence, our punishment for bothering Pinal County by asking for a postconviction relief. The fact continues to anger Karen. The Rule 32 was her work, years of research and study and expenses—all for nothing, a mistake, she insists, although I'm still thankful for the vacation from this place. She gave me some time with my girls when they were young enough to enjoy having me around.

Now, Karen tells me that Alan Minker, my judge, has left the bench and won't return. "More fallout from your case," she says, speaking the words like a curse. I'm reminded of my original prosecutor, who killed herself on a deserted country road near Casa Grande, rolling her truck in the early morning darkness. Reports said she was intoxicated and wearing only a thin negligee. I suspect that Judge Minker knew when he ordered me home

to my family that the appellate judges would overturn his decision. I wonder what the decision ultimately cost him.

WE'VE HAD EXQUISITE EVENINGS with dustless skies ripening from
peach to plum. Venus and Jupiter, bright in the southwest, do-si-do after
sunset. It's only the second time in twenty years that the two planets, really
400 million miles apart, seem to kiss each other.

A single Mexican goldpoppy renegade blooms with the white irises outside the education building. It's a rarity, not only for this dry year, but for
this place—only once before have I found them here. I point out this one
to everyone nearby: students, friends, my supervisor, the complex chaplain.
It's special, a visitation. With a twinge of regret, I pick the single flower to
preserve in my notebook.

Peter, one of my Hispanic students to whom I teach math, works on
one of the ADOT road crews and sees wildflowers all the time. But this
evening he tells me about the drive-by women who favor the men on his
crew by flashing them a little skin. Other highway workers don't get this
kind of attention, he says, only the men who wear orange pants lettered
ADC INMATE. Some women, usually in convertibles, beep horns and
wave; others simply slow down and wait for an audience of eyes. Then they
slip out of a blouse or peel up a body sock, as if the act made perfect sense.
This is not maliciousness. It's not some cruel tease toward womenless men.
It is a sign of compassion. A random act of kindness. These same women
would hand loose bills to the homeless on street corners or buy transients
a beer on a hot day. When he gets out, Peter wants to buy himself a pair of
orange pants and walk the highways. "I'm going to find myself a beautiful
jaina," he says, "and treat her real fine."

ON THE LAST DAY OF FEBRUARY, with the help of two friends, Larry and
my neighbor Darrel, I haul property boxes, books, clothing, my bedding,

mattress, and metal bunk out to the basketball court and my designated tent slot. It's moving day. The whole run is a termite nest of activity as forty men strip their rooms of bunks and file cabinets, dresser drawers and window blinds, even mirrors and bulletin boards—anything left behind will be cannibalized by men on other runs looking to replace something missing. Nine other men (and all their furnishings) live in my tent, an army-style construct of khaki canvas over a steel frame. It's a Boy Scout jamboree, and the air inside our tent is heavy with the oily smell of canvas and unwashed bodies. From the back door I have a view across Cottonwood Park where, presently, a man crumbles bread crust for the blackbirds and sparrows. To the west, beyond the sweat lodge and the perimeter fence, dozens of ravens chase a lone coyote across open ground. He's an agitated, tail-flared, rear-looking canid, and the huge black birds make sport of him, dropping on him in relay as he pads away.

My tent is crowded, but it isn't so bad. We even have our own toilet, a four-foot-high, topless, port-a-potty on wheels, which just arrived for the evening lockdown. I can pee while looking at the stars, riding in my own chariot privy.

The next morning I'm cold. I slept in my thermals and sweats, but it wasn't enough; the cold sank deep into the ball sockets of my hips. Portable space heaters or no, I'm going to need another blanket. Most of the men in my tent have already left for work, their wake-up being 4:30 AM. Now, there are three of us; two sleep while I write. I intend to keep my schedule: up by six thirty, write until nine thirty, exercise, and then open the classroom before the noon lockdown and count. My job fills the afternoons and evenings until 8:00 PM. I'll shower as usual on Tuesdays, Thursdays, and Sundays, attempting to avoid the crowds in the two housing-unit bathrooms. It's a routine that works for me, one that keeps me occupied and busy. Routine is essential for doing time.

By the noon lockdown and count, sunlight has raised the internal temperature of my canvas envelope, thawing out my hip joints and suffusing my skin and clothing with the pungent odor of petroleum, warm and heady, like newly laid blacktop on a summer morning. My tent has become a mustard poultice, a remedy for winter doldrums. I close my eyes and I'm napping at Horton Springs in the heat of the day, my tent fly open to the sounds of birds, to the smell of pines and mountain duff.

OUTSIDE THE TENT a stiff wind combs through the pine tree, making mountain sounds. It's been windy all day, keeping temperatures down. Above me, the canvas snaps viciously, rhythmically, as the tent inflates to capacity. Darrel, my neighbor, wears suntan oil, coconut scented, that instantly brings in summer because my vasonasal organ is a time machine. The smell is nearly as powerful and moving as the blue scarves of mesquite smoke that curl up from the sweat lodge on weekends. My neighbor on the left, a Native American the men call "Chief," often smells of burning mesquite or sage, wearing the smoke like cologne.

Jim, another one of my tent mates that everyone calls "Wild Kingdom," has found a friend for company: a large horned lizard. He keeps it in a drawer next to his bunk, taking it out occasionally as if it were a charm, and presently he's holding it for a group of men and discussing "horny toad" attributes such as blood-squirting eyes and thorny defenses against being swallowed by snakes. The men listen to him, asking questions of their friend, the expert herpetologist, and getting impressed with his answers. Some of them have never before seen a flat toad with cactus spines.

THE COTTONWOODS have begun to flesh themselves out while the bird of paradise shrubs unfurl maroon fronds. Great-tailed grackles warm up their vocal striations as the courting season approaches. Every day on my exercise circuits I pass by the window of my room to check on the progress of the workers. More than a week ago, the men removed my shelves and desk, closet and drawers. The next day Darrel painted the walls as a favor to me, volunteering the work to speed up the whole process. By Tuesday carpenters had the plywood floor in place, and then the tiles went in. I peered through my window into a bare, white cubicle—no longer a room but a cell. At least the project is moving along. Rumors say we may return on Friday or Saturday.

On Saturday, I sit outside my tent and sip hot tea with real lemon. *Real* lemon—the actual fruit . . . from a tree, no less. I found it in the trash in the education building, intact except for a small slit where someone, my supervisor possibly, had squeezed out most—but not all—of its contents. I tore through the thick peel, inhaling the volatile oils and letting its juice run over my fingers. My nose still tingles.

It's a beautiful evening. I'm enchanted with spring's gloaming; even the prison can't resist it. Chain link and razor wire remain stoic, unmoved, but unable to shirk the sun's last garnish from their hard, metal shoulders. And now, another threat: a Cooper's hawk, red-barred breasted and lanky, perches on one of the fence's uprights. She's familiar and gorgeous, silhouetted against burnished pomegranate skies.

Prison raptors and urban raptors: This week I received my copy of *Tucson Lifestyle* with the article I wrote before my return to prison three years ago. It's about Tucson's raptor invasion: great horned owls, Harris's hawks, and others, especially Cooper's hawks. The idea for the article came to me after I began noticing a pair of Cooper's hawks nesting annually at my daughters' elementary school and hearing about a rising incidence of hawk sightings within the city. It was some kind of phenomenon, wildlife experts were saying. I called Clint Boal, who was studying the birds while finishing his doctorate at the University of Arizona, and learned that Tucson is attracting raptors from the surrounding desert because, Clint believes, the city offers three things the birds need: food, water, and security.

We also have food and water: doves and sparrows and rabbits, birdbaths and cement basins. We have large eucalyptus, palm, and peppertrees, all things raptors like our resident Cooper's hawk find enticing. Prison has become her sanctuary. And why not? Don't the blooming ocotillo, bird of paradise, and desert willow benefit the long-tongued nectar sippers like hawkmoths and hummingbirds? Aren't we a highway rest area for migrating warblers and orioles? We harbor bats in our buildings, toads under our shrubbery. Even the ravens find sustenance in our dumpster oases.

I'M SITTING on the edge of the basketball court outside my tent, magazine and notebook in hand. We've had two weeks of tent life so far. Except for some details like touch-up painting, the remodeling of our run is finished. No official word, however, on when we will return to our cells.

Between a pine tree and greening cottonwood, where the slender whips of ocotillo stand upright like disembodied animal spines and slip on leafy skirts to hide winter's thorn, I see the familiar dimple of Sentinel Peak, "A" Mountain, and its corrugated neighbors. The fence line between us hardly divides us, hardly separates me from my wife and girls, who live so close on my horizon. I look up from my notebook in time to glimpse a pair of coyotes trotting across the open ground beyond the perimeter. One follows the other, seemingly halfway between me and my family. I hear their voices almost nightly now, these perfect vagrants that thread the seams of my life back together.

Sparrows search for leftover cracker crumbs in the gravel where, earlier, Cecil sat in his chair feeding them, the birds like children at story time around his feet. Cecil is a large black Muslim at the far end of his fifties who never shuts up; he's an endless ribbon of language, verbal froth, circular stories about family history and past adventures with prison, banal conversations for anyone with ears. Every thought spills from his tongue; he's a mind open to the wind. But the birds don't care that Cecil is lonely and that he talks too much, as long as his words come with a few crumbs.

Cecil wants me to bring my wife and children to his place in Tennessee after we get out. "We'll have a barbecue, and I'll fix you up some ribs and cornbread," he says. I accept his offer, an easy promise to make on this side of the fences.

THE WORD ON when we move back into our cells is "indefinite." It seems the deputy warden has found a few nail holes in the walls and a cracked window. Also, the wax on the new floors isn't drying fast enough.

There are now more than 1.8 million adults imprisoned in the United States, according to a recent *USA Today*. The number "has more than doubled in twelve years, reaching its highest level last year," the Justice Department reports. At this rate, the article explains, we could be the world's leading jailer in a year or two, surpassing even Russia. This speaks poorly for the greatest country in the free world, and reflects precisely what's happening in Arizona, whose incarceration rate exceeded the national rate by 18 percent in 1997. When I came to prison in March 1987, exactly twelve years ago, when mandatory sentencing was a new rage (judges were supposedly too soft on crime), I received an inmate number in the sixty-one thousands. Today, the Department of Corrections is handing out numbers in the one hundred forty-four thousands. These are not repeat offenders, but new offenders.

I wonder if prisons aren't becoming a new kind of slavery, if saying so doesn't diminish the horror of this country's historical treatment of African Americans. America locks up a disproportionate number of minorities, as if poor minorities have no economic value until they're imprisoned. Louisiana's Angola prison, for example, is 80 percent black; the warden is white. Angola was once a cotton plantation where black slaves were forced into hard labor. Today, Angola still produces cotton, but there's a difference. The *inmates* are happy to work the fields because they get out of their cells.

Our society is finding it more and more acceptable to lock up its citizens, and keep them locked up, particularly if they are minorities and their crimes are of a "despicable" nature. Monday's *Tucson Citizen* has an article about a sex offender being touted as the first test of the predator law. Willie Boggess Jr., an African American, completed his sentence in 1990 and, after his release, moved to Tucson where he registered as a sex offender. He was arrested again in 1997, not because he committed another crime, but because he failed to reregister with the county sheriff after moving to Nevada (where he registered) and then returning to Tucson. While Boggess served another year for parole violation, the result of his registration lapse—a prison "psychiatrist," his own therapist "Doctor" Steve Gray, testified he'd likely reoffend. In 1998, when his release date came up, the Department of Corrections transferred him to the state hospital. "Under the 1997 law," Patty Machelor writes, "the state can continue to confine a violent sexual offender for treatment even after his prison term, if he is found not to have been rehabilitated in prison."

Rehabilitated in prison? Even former prison director Sam Lewis admitted that the department doesn't rehabilitate anyone. Why do people continue to think that prison makes you better? Now we also pass laws based on this misconception. The article mentions that the offender "underwent six months of mental health treatment, as required by DOC, while he was serving his prison sentence." I know about the Sex Offender Treatment Program (SOTP), and, first of all, it's not required; it's "voluntary" in the sense that if you choose not to participate you risk transfer to a prison unit where other inmates routinely attack and beat sex offenders. You also risk, since the legislature passed the predator law, a poor evaluation and commitment to the state hospital.

In January of last year, after an initial interview for the program and subsequent conference with my attorneys, I decided against participation. At my first session in "the trailer," before signing permissions for polygraph and plethysmograph tests, I told a therapist that, on legal advice, I would not return. Fortunately, within a few months the program folded and the department has yet to contract with another provider. It's probably the reason I'm still at Echo.

A friend who's completed the two-year program, and who is now nearing the end of his sentence, recently received a letter from the state hospital. From it, and much to his distress, he learned that the hospital had gotten copies of his "confidential" records, records now open for the purpose of the state's evaluation for predator status. "I never would have done it, Ken," Jon told me, "if I'd known. We were promised no one would see our files." What Jon was concerned about was something called a "full disclosure" letter—details about his offense, known and unknown, that the program requires before completion. "I made things up because my crime wasn't good enough for them."

It was the six months of mental health treatment that Boggess received after his return to prison, I suspect, that was his undoing. This is how the supposed "psychiatrist," working on behalf of the state like a prosecutor, determined to commit him. For seven years after his original release in 1990, Boggess had gone on with his life without further criminal behavior.

Still, the courts have decided, Arizona's predator law doesn't violate a person's protection from double jeopardy; nor does it violate issues of confidentiality, even if the law seems to blend what's criminal with what's civil. "A low percentage of sexual offenders is found to have clinically recognized mental disorders," says Deputy County Attorney Kathleen Mayer in the article. "We are not sending these people back to prison." What she *is* doing is asking the courts to lock up people—who have served their time—for treatment that is both indefinite and uncertain. According to professionals at the state hospital, they have no way of determining whether or not anyone will reoffend. So how will they know to let anyone go? Boggess's attorney criticizes the whole civil nature of the law: "The court is attempting to claim this is a civil proceeding," he says, "but they are bringing in these people in handcuffs. They are civil proceedings in name only."

We are fooling ourselves if we think civil predator laws will help mentally ill people, something Mayer wants us to believe. We send all kinds of mentally ill people to prison; more than 280,000, according to the Justice Department, are currently behind bars. The laws make certain they stay there.

Prison will never be a solution, although for some offenders it may be a necessity. It certainly shouldn't be a landfill for people with emotional/mental disorders. (South of Tucson, one road takes you to the prison, another to the dump.) But I see these men every day, men with the "Thorazine shuffle," the "watch-swallows" who line up at the medical unit for their next fix (courtesy of the state) like homeless people at a soup kitchen. Prison is not a hospital. Nor is it a place of rehabilitation, despite the "Corrections" designation in ADC. Some compare prison to a warehouse, as if inmates are dusty stock resting on shelves, unchanged until their release. That's drive-by mentality—quick, unreasonable, destructive. At the very least prisons function as factories, a place where raw material is turned into some kind of product. This is my concern: 95 percent of this product eventually ends up back on the streets.

WE ARE FINALLY back in our cells on the vernal equinox and after three weeks of tent life. My white, sterile lozenge of space. Tuesday, the wax wasn't dry. Wednesday, the hallway needed repainting. Thursday, there was paint on the floor, so it had to be stripped and waxed again. Friday, the captain wanted all the shelves in place, so he could order us to dispose of our file cabinets, chests of drawers, and footlockers. The shelves are inadequate for all my books and clothing; I'm living out of legal boxes again.

The sycamore's winter-pruned branches relax with the blooming temperatures and don a tentative canopy. Ash, chinaberry, and cottonwood have also begun to warm to spring, a noticeable boldness that worries me. Deputy Warden Steve Heliotes, the man who cut down most of the trees at the Santa Rita Unit while I watched, has come to Echo, replacing Scott Yates. I hope the trees at Echo are safe.

"JAILING 1.8 MILLION men and women, most of them non-violent, is not something we should be proud of as Americans," says Representative Charles Rangel, responding to a report by a private organization opposed to mandatory minimum sentences. The Justice Policy Institute found that this country's nonviolent prisoners number more than one million. Recently, the Arizona Department of Corrections conducted its own study and determined, not surprisingly, that Arizona's trend of locking up more people is responsible for the present decline in crime. What ADC didn't take credit for was fixing the statistics by ignoring property crimes, such as burglary, and drug offenses, both of which account for most of the nonviolent inmates in prison. The balm of incarceration, the department would have us believe. We *should* be ashamed of ourselves. We are hypocrites. For more than a decade, our nation has been carrying out a kind of "ethnic cleansing," disguised with tough-on-crime rhetoric. We imprison nonviolent minorities and poor in the hundreds of thousands. We jail children tried as juveniles and, more and more, tried as adults. We lock up the mentally ill and seventy-year-old geriatrics with canes and walkers, more people per capita, in fact, than most other countries in the world. But it's war, we say, a war on "crime." Today, Yugoslav president Slobodan Milosevic says his war against Kosovo is just; he's fighting a rebellion whose militia, the Kosovo Liberation Army (KLA), has ties to Iran and Islamic fundamentalist groups.

So what's the difference? The rhetoric. We don't call our war on crime "ethnic cleansing." We call it justice.

As I write these shrill words in my notebook, I can smell Karen's perfume on my hands. It's not her usual, Lady Stetson, but something more subtle and unfamiliar. Karen came out to see me today by herself and stayed for several hours, a rare treat, although every visit never seems long enough. She wore my ring for a change, I noticed right away, which pleased me, but I couldn't help wondering if she hadn't just slipped it on before leaving the house. When I hugged her from behind, she turned her head and nuzzled my ear—her unexpected affection sends pleasant shudders through my body even now as I recall it. I held her hand the whole time, the only physical contact allowed that takes more than five seconds. I could hold her hand and listen to her voice for days. I hope that I'm her favorite mistake, as the song goes. It had been two weeks since I last saw her; she seemed different somehow: an unfamiliar perfume, a new haircut, even her figure got my attention. Is she gaining weight?

We discussed my release in eighteen months and the logistics of three growing girls, the limited space for them, whether or not another place would be wise, and where I fit into the picture. "You might be just as comfortable living in the bathroom," she joked, referring to an environment similar to the one I spent nine years in at Santa Rita. She would have to install an electronic locking mechanism to the door.

Before Karen left, a friend walked over to the perimeter fence near our table. Bruno had been visiting with his brother, who, after returning to the parking lot, now led to the fence a family member Bruno hadn't seen in many years, one not allowed to visit. "Hey, boy!" he called through the razor wire. "Good boy! That's a good boy! That's a good boy!" When the small dog, a shaggy brown Chihuahua terrier mix, recognized Bruno, it began barking and leaping into the air, turning tight excited circles, stretching and knotting its leash, scattering dust and paw prints across the sand trap. It was a beautiful scene, rare for this place, one of reunion and forgiveness.

spring 1999

Migrations and Abstractions

Kim Stafford says that walking is what the wind does, the sun. It has "nothing to do with destination. Not a plan, but a way of being." Often when I walk the exercise track I have one destination in mind—anywhere but here. I unwind my circular course into trails along coastlines and mountain ranges. I've hiked the Arizona Trail, the Pacific Rim, and the Continental Divide. My eyes see hundreds of miles of chain link and razor wire and gray, numbered buildings, but nothing registers. On a good day, these are hardly shadows, vague images without substance, at most an annoyance, like the eternal white noise of tinnitus. When it's right, when the sun is high and the sky holds light against my skin, I can smell the streamside sycamore, hear grassland sparrows. Ravens croak in old-growth forests; swallows dip over pastures. On these trails the sun burns my nose and lips; I get stones in my shoes and blisters on my heels; ratlines of spider web brush across my face. In this place I embody the words of poets and philosophers as a way of being. And I walk. It's more than obsession; it's penitence. Who said, "Illusions mistaken for truth are the pavement under our feet"?

Destination or no, walking as a way of being knows no boundary, no limit. This morning, snow layers my knuckled horizon—the Catalinas, Rincons, and Santa Ritas—after yesterday's storm. A male hooded oriole, colored like an overripe mango, ravishes the ash tree next to the library. The bird jerks and twitches, blurring the uppermost leaves of the tree, while I hold my breath, hold the moment by its frame. At last it leaps away in a puff of flame as if the act were perfectly ordinary.

I PHONE KAREN on Easter Sunday as flanks of brown clouds close in on me. I expect to get soaked, but the rain never comes. Instead, the wind rises, whipping up a dandruff that slants from the sky and sticks to my hair and sweatshirt, cutting visibility to less than a hundred yards. I curl up inside the telephone booth. "It's snowing at home, too," Karen says into the phone, and I feel another dimension of connection to her as the storm out of the west allows me to share her elements.

An hour later the wind has subsided and flake size has quadrupled. The ground is white outside my window, the trailer, the tents, and the fences coated with cotton duff. Men throw snowballs at each other (and the cops when they aren't looking) and shout greetings of Merry Christmas. Anatomically correct snow women appear. There's a festive mood. Snow in the desert at Easter seems as miraculous as that other desert event two thousand years ago.

THE OCOTILLO ARE BLOOMING—those plants that the landscapers haven't brutally emasculated by chopping off their upper stems. I pull off a few fiery buds and pop them in my mouth. I expect some sweetness, the flavor of hummingbird tongues, but the buds immediately blot the moisture from my mouth with the astringency of crab apples. I consider brewing some ocotillo-flower tea, sweetening it with 7-Up. Or maybe I'll pluck the flowers for a garnish, a bit of color and texture to add to the wilted brown lettuce the food service calls salad. This time of year I could forgo the nasty lettuce altogether and eat salads made from the tender new pads of prickly pear. I've noticed the pads don't survive long on the cactus. Every day more are missing. Some of my Mexican friends are collecting the nopales to cook with canned roast beef, green chilies, tomatoes, and cheese, eating the traditional food with tortilla chips.

Later, I clip pertinent articles from various local and national newspapers for posting on the classroom bulletin board. I prefer to choose pieces about science and nature (melting Antarctic ice shelves, new species of carnivorous dinosaurs), but the men read only those articles concerning prisons, of which there are reams to clip. This is a curiosity to me, this attraction prisoners have for stories of crime and punishment, though I admit my own interest. But I draw the line at newspapers. Unlike most of the men, I won't watch *America's Most Wanted* or *Justice Files* or *Cops* or even the local news. I see through to the blow-it-out-of-proportion, scare-tactics agenda, and I don't find it entertaining. It's how legislatures get bad laws passed.

This afternoon I read that the Charles Keating story is in its final episode. After serving less than half of his original sentence of fifty months before a federal court overturned his conviction on a technicality and ordered his release, the swindler has accepted a sweet deal. To escape a retrial and probable life sentence, Keating pled guilty to four counts of fraud for siphoning nearly a million dollars from American Continental Corp. before declaring bankruptcy. His sentence? Time served. Four years served in the federal penitentiary across the street for costing taxpayers $2.6 billion in the largest S & L failure in this country's history, four years for destroying the finances of countless people. Who wouldn't jump at that deal? Money talks even when you supposedly don't have any. Convicted felon Governor Fife Symington, who still hasn't seen a day in prison, should be encouraged.

AT THE OLD FIREHOUSE I pause from my laps at a particularly large senna erupting with flower clusters of cadmium novae. Bulbous carpenter bees, honeybees, digger and leafcutter bees—it's a hymenopteran orgy. The female leafcutters press themselves provocatively into petalled loins, rubbing pollen onto their bristled abdomens, seducing the blooms of pollen in order to knead their "bee bread" and provision their brood cells. I pluck a single flower with a leafcutter buried inside. This one's a male—I can tell by the white muffs on his front feet—and he has no intention of releasing his prize. Even when I knock him off, he circles once and thrusts himself back into the bloom.

Later, the yard closes as new sex offender movements begin. A memo from Warden Hallahan says that Santa Rita, Winchester, Rincon, and Cimarron Units will be on lockdown Tuesday and Wednesday while the department transfers more than two hundred men from Santa Rita. So why is Echo Unit closed? This is only the beginning. Over the next three weeks close to a thousand inmates at the Tucson complex will change places with the same number from the Eyman complex at Florence as ADC moves to consolidate all sex offenders at Meadows and Cook units.

I called Karen earlier after I read the memo and heard rumors of an imminent lockdown. More than a hundred sex offenders will be rolled up from Echo, too, some officers were claiming. "I don't know what to tell you," Karen said, after I expressed my anxiety about the news. "If they move you, at least you won't be alone." I had hoped she might phone the warden and relate her concern, but she didn't seem concerned. I had become a burden to her. I told her: "I guess it would be easier for you if I were transferred to another prison farther away. You wouldn't have to visit as much." She agreed, unexpectedly. "You're like a hobby I don't have time for," she said, "between my work and school and the kids." She was right and I knew it.

Now, back on my run, I learn from one of the men that my neighbor with Alzheimer's disease has died. Two weeks ago, the guards took him to the Rincon health unit, the facility for the terminally ill and critically hospitalized, for an infection, possibly pneumonia. For several days previously, I could hear him through the walls, wheezing and coughing—a strange and at first unrecognizable sound, like machinery with worn bearings running down.

Sometimes I think I live on a geriatric run in a geriatric prison. The hallways are too narrow for passing slow traffic, and it seems I'm always getting caught behind old men with canes, crutches, or walkers. During count time we're all supposed to stay in our rooms, but Mike never understood this, and I would often hear him making his slow, cane-thumping way to the bathroom. Mike was in his sixties and he needed full-time care, someone more vigilant than the men here who tried to make sure he stayed in place, that he made it to meals and picked up his medication. The cops had had enough of him and his constant interference with their duties. A few weeks ago, a guard yelled at him for locking himself out of his room for the third time in recent history. "You'll go back to the tents," the officer threatened, "where it won't matter if you misplace your key." I thought they'd probably assign him to an upper bunk.

I suppose the cops will be relieved. Mike will no longer wander the run during count. He won't be locking himself out of his cell.

AFTER TWO DAYS of lockdown, I wait with a stack of books and magazines at East Gate for transportation to the writing workshop at Santa Rita. Richard Shelton's revolving library, which he carts in to us each week in plastic milk crates, is a godsend, especially for writers with long periods of cell time. Suddenly, a Cooper's hawk slides across Sycamore Park and kills a blackbird. "Look at that," I shout at Ralph, John, and Ken, other workshop members and fellow writers. They turn to where I'm pointing. "See the hawk? It shot toward a flock of blackbirds and at the last second twisted into a short dive, slamming into one of the birds." The hawk stands on the grass, its wings mantling its prey, and then it flies off with the dead bird to a copse of mesquite trees beyond the perimeter. I marvel at this simple act of life and death. If things live in this place, then they must also die. If we are a reservoir for Cooper's hawks, then we are also a sink for blackbirds. If our planet is the only one in the universe that harbors life, then ours alone has death.

On my way back to my cell after the writing workshop, I detour to the umbrella plants adjacent to the old volleyball court. When I had spoken on the phone to Melissa and Kasondra this morning, they told me about finding three duck nests at the Reid Park Zoo where they spent the afternoon with their grandparents. My daughters' excitement with the discoveries reminded me to look for our resident mother mallard.

The umbrella plants reach only to my knees. I search among the thin, papery stalks for the length of the hedge and then turn to the other side. There's not much cover; the plants seem neglected, destitute. In places the hedge is broken into segments. Just as I begin to think that our mallard may have gone elsewhere this year, I see her, tucked into one of the thickest clumps. She's on her nest, the lines of chocolate brown against ecru on her feathers blending her outline, a perfect camouflage in the dry patch of vegetation. "There you are," I say, kneeling down. "How are you doing, Mamma?" She's motionless, watching me with one black eye, brooding life among the dead.

THIS MORNING, birdsong catches on the razor wire and pools among the gray-sided buildings; it threads through the chain link and trickles into the pea gravel. In a desert willow outside the education building a Wilson's warbler forages for insects. The black-capped male is the first I've noticed this year.

On my last pass along the southern leg of my circuit I see that the Rincon Unit is receiving new arrivals, dozens of them. Three buses disgorge a spume of orange jumpsuits, replacements for the more than four hundred sex offenders who left Rincon yesterday. Major movement, and there's more to come. I think about Don, a friend who left for the predator evaluation last week, nine months before his release date. Don went to Rincon; now he's at Florence. I met Don the first day I arrived at Echo almost two years ago. He was in a small group of Christian men who would gather in the evenings in Cottonwood Park to sing choruses while I played guitar. When we sang "Jehovah Jireh" or "Blow the Trumpet in Zion," clapping our hands and shouting the words, Don would get up to dance. He claimed to be a prophet; he once told me that God spoke to him directly, in an audible voice, and that he knew things about people. It was a burden he found difficult to carry, this personal knowledge about everyone. Don had few friends and many enemies. It's likely that the state will commit him to the mental hospital, but I hope not. Don and I had the same judge. We received the same sentence for the same crime.

BIRD MIGRATIONS CONTINUE. The barn swallows have returned to Santa Rita and the blackbirds have finally departed. The white-wing doves ask only one question, incessantly: *"Whose crook are you?"* It's a rhetorical question, annoying, derisive. The doves have flown a thousand miles or more from wintering grounds in southern Mexico and Central America, but I can't tell if they're here more for nesting or mocking.

Other migrations: the major sex offender roll-ups continue this week at Rincon and Cimarron Units, hundreds of men in orange jumpsuits on the road. Rumors abound, but I can't get a straight answer from the staff concerning movement from Echo.

THE MEXICAN BIRD OF PARADISE stain the heavy aspect of this place in gala colors. The mesquite trees have begun to drip with caterpillar catkins, while buds on the Mexican paloverde explode like popcorn. Desert willow flowers, like tiny pink ear candles, are also on the way.

Four warblers pick through the desert willow outside the education building. They're yellowrumps, I'm sure, the males having a distinctive black breast patch with delicate pollen smudges on their sides and rumps. I feel self-conscious standing under the tree with my head cocked skyward while men in line for chow watch me. But the birds excite me, this colorful new species that's suddenly appeared here, zipping from branch to branch *chip-chipping* to each other. Their images stay in my mind. I tell my students about the yellow-rumped warblers outside the classroom. I get only one response: one of the men says, "I think if someone called me a yellow-rumped warbler, I'd have to hurt him."

YESTERDAY, on her way through the gates to visit me, Karen bent back the ears of a K-9 officer who had the audacity to tell her that exposing herself to a drug-sniffing dog was "completely voluntary." "Sure," Karen said, knowing that if she opted out of the humiliation the officer would deny her entrance, "then why aren't you at the malls? Try 'voluntarily' violating people there and see where that leads. Try strip-searching them." The officer hardened. "We aren't mall cops, ma'am."

Prison is such an abstraction. I understand Karen's attitude; it's not a result so much of the necessary security but the deceptive language, the political propaganda and lies from people responsible for the security. Why not just say that crotch-sniffing is required upon entrance? These days people understand that personal rights of citizens are becoming more and more optional, elastic. But it goes way beyond the definition of words. Prison is an abstraction in the sense that nothing is real. The crimes that bring men and women to this place may or may not even be crimes, depending on time and space. The definition of crime spasms from year to year, border to border. Prison itself may be hell or home, a badge of honor, a rite of passage. It's only the grace of God that separates the convict and his keeper, that and the color of the clothes. I know officers and staff who are thieves and embezzlers, liars, drunks, and brawlers. Today, Officer Ochs patrols the outside perimeter as punishment for stuffing his socks down another officer's throat at a staff meeting. His victim had told him to "put a sock in it," which Ochs did. Then there are the drug dealers and sex offenders. More recently, two food service employees at Echo lost their jobs for giving up both the drugs and their bodies. I still hear stories about them defrosting the walk-in freezer with inmates. While I was at Santa Rita, the captain's secretary had an inmate lover, a homosexual teacher at Cimarron had several, and Officer Rhonda had anyone for five dollars (I don't know if she took payment in cash or commissary items). Years earlier, a sergeant at Santa Rita sexually assaulted one of his staff at a party. I knew the victim; she couldn't have been much older than twenty, a petite, soft-spoken girl who never came back to the yard afterward. The sergeant, who reminded me of Lee Van Cleef of spaghetti Western fame, lost his rank and ended up at another unit where he eventually worked his way to lieutenant. I still see him here, the last time at Main Point, gossiping with the young female officers. Another officer was once charged with emptying her gun into her housemate, reloading, and shooting him again. The men call her "Two-clip" Robinson. After her case was dismissed, she went back to work with the department; she's now a program supervisor. A Pima College teacher once asked me if I knew that her hobby is quick draw. He was serious.

As I said before, Tacitus's question remains timeless. I like to say that if you want to commit crimes, you should work for the Arizona Department of Corrections. At least if you get caught, you won't do time. No criminal, staff or inmate, will be permitted to mar the image of this institution. Last Friday, I read a letter from the director printed in the department's news-letter, *Directions*. In it Terry Stewart discussed the settlement of a lawsuit against ADC concerning the sexual harassment of women prisoners by male officers whereby the Department of Justice alleged that "defendants were deliberately indifferent to staff's sexual misconduct and invasions of privacy of ADC's female inmates." ("Deliberately indifferent" is putting it mildly. The department refused Justice officials' requests for access to the women who made the complaints.) Stewart's words in the letter are typical of a politician: "Nothing in the Agreement can be construed as admission that the Department of Corrections violated the constitutional rights of any female inmate. This resolution reaffirms the integrity and professionalism of the Department and those personally named as defendants."

Integrity and professionalism. Words from the same departmental dictionary that "voluntary" comes from, no doubt. This place *is* an abstraction. It doesn't even register in the mind.

AT 7:30 AM Echo went on lockdown. After three weeks of major movements at Santa Rita, Rincon, and Cimarron, this lockdown concerns me. Radios squeal on the run. I overhear that someone's delivering barbecue grills and wood to visitation, the sign of an all-day affair. (The Tactical Support Unit enjoys a picnic lunch.) In the last three weeks more than nine hundred sex offenders have transferred off this complex.

Yesterday, Karen told me she'd read an article in the *Arizona Capital Times* about a new mental hospital for sex offenders. State health administrators have asked the legislature for additional funds to improve mental health treatment, add programs, and, in general, raise the standard of existing facilities. The legislature rejected all requests, except the one to build a new hospital to house the sexual predators. "It's just another prison," I told Karen. "This one at the expense of Arizona's mentally ill, those who aren't in prison already."

At one thirty, I hide my toothbrush, my illegal but luxurious seven-inch red toothbrush. It's a shakedown; no roll-ups. My appetite returns. Momentarily, two officers, a man and a woman, paw through my property, tossing out paper sacks, cardboard boxes, and my drawing board. They do not find my toothbrush!

Later, a friend and neighbor taps on my door. He offers me something warm and chocolaty from a plastic tub. "Would you like a brownie?" he asks. Brownie? I thought I was imagining the aroma. I'm curious about how he made them and take notes as he relates the recipe:

Gary Hayes's Perfect Prison Brownies
Finely crush one 24 oz. package of chocolate-chip cookies in a plastic
    bedpan.
Add one 1 oz. packet of hot cocoa mix.
Stir in hot water to form a thick batter.
Add three scoops of crunchy peanut butter and three crumbled Her-
    shey chocolate bars.
Microwave about six minutes (stirring batter first two minutes) until
    firm to touch. Cool.

The next morning the yard opens and I head for the track. I can finally
smell the sycamore: the heavy, wet odor of algae-rimed pools in desert grot-
toes that fingers my mind, stirring memories. For those who are intimate
with the tree, this must be a common phenomenon. Annie Dillard reacted
this way: "The past inserts a finger into a slit in the skin of the present, and
pulls." Yes! My riparian tonic of hot summer days soothes my mind.

No cicadas sing from the desert fringe as yet, but foothill paloverde and
white-thorn acacia are attempting to gild their desiccated branches with
meager flowers. Yellow is a foresummer color, whether it's the sallow hue of
the drought stricken or the aureate glow of an El Niño bloom.

Later, I stop by the old volleyball court to check on our brooding mallard. She's gone. Her nest is a dry, empty bowl of grass and umbrella plant
leaves, lined with downy black feathers. I place my hand inside and recheck
the location with my eyes. Is this a mistake? I caught her sleeping here just
this morning. I can't believe I missed the hatching and departure again this
year.

When I find James, the unit's plumber and a friend, he tells me that
mamma and her eight ducklings got a special escort to the wastewater
pond. I express my disappointment about not witnessing it both this time
and last. He says he's known about her nesting here for four years running.

"But in ninety-six Officer Reeves took a rake and smashed her eggs. He said they were a security risk." A security risk? Each spring the mallard and her eggs avoid being turned into a casserole for a month as she incubates her clutch. In fact, during this period the men care for her, feeding her slices of wheat bread and cups of water. The only trouble she has had was with a cop.

"COURT UPHOLDS STATE SEXUAL PREDATOR LAW," reads the headline of an Associated Press article in Friday's paper. Arizona's appellate court has ruled to allow the state to hold sex offenders beyond their sentence expiration dates. The one dissenting opinion, written by Judge Thomas C. Kleinschmidt, expresses a lack of trust that Arizona can provide treatment: "The state record in caring for and treating the mentally ill is not a good one." Kleinschmidt also argued that the law is unfair to former prisoners who originally accepted plea bargains of guilt without knowing about the new condition of possible confinement for life. Judge Rebecca White Berch countered this in her majority opinion, saying that "confinement under the law is not punishment and does not have to be disclosed in plea negotiations." The two-member majority also rejected the arguments that civil commitment after prison constitutes double jeopardy and that the evaluation process (using information gained from "treatment" programs in prison) violates confidentiality issues. This latter ruling is the most frightening, since the court determined that the patient-physician privilege is created by the legislature and that the legislature is free to limit it. I know men who continue to believe in the value of "the program." I tell them differently. I tell them to think of their therapists as prosecutors.

WE REACHED one hundred degrees Fahrenheit at 1:58 PM today, which is right about on schedule for the end of May. Now, real heat begins, the dry, lip-splitting, nose-blistering, ear-ringing heat of foresummer. As sunlight talcums the landscape, shadows are reduced to thin anemic lines on the ground. They become territorial, slipping beneath their stones at noon and emerging late in the day to venture out tentatively across the sand. Shadows never go too far or stay away too long.

As if to celebrate the benchmark, the cicadas have begun to sing. Theirs is the quintessential sound of desert summers, of the energy held in the coming monsoons with their windstain of wet creosote, concentrated into a squat gray insect and unloaded when the desert is empty of everything except faith.

With the heat comes both an absence and presence of birds. I have just learned to see warblers and now they are gone. But the season's first turkey vultures have returned, and I'm expecting nighthawks, members of the weak-footed, dirt-sitting clan called goatsuckers, which should be returning from Mexico to nest on our abundant bare ground outside the perimeter, feeding after dark on insects drawn to the security lights.

Since I'm off work this evening, I decide to go looking for nighthawks. The sun touches the horizon, casting its longer, redder wavelengths into a reef of clouds. Mourning doves turn my head as they cross the sky on their way to find overnight roosts. It's still too early. On my third circuit of the yard I think I see boomerang wings and the languid maneuvering of a nighthawk, but the bird is too far away. On my next lap I'm certain one drifts by Housing Unit Two, sculling through bug-rich cones of light. I need to get closer. Before I'm ready to quit, another one glides past directly in front of me. Three nighthawks in less than an hour, but the birds still seem ephemeral, theoretical.

On my way back to my cell, I notice a low-flying nighthawk circling the area between Dorm Four and Housing Unit Two. The bird continues dipping between the buildings as I approach and cross into its airspace. It's feeding on winged insects, protean clouds of them vibrating in the air. I sit on some steps to watch and discover a termite hatch. As if gravity were unwinding, the alate reproductives spray out of the ground beneath a privet shrub directly to my left. I'm participating in something intimate, silent yet potent: termite nuptials and nighthawk gluttony; the ecstasy of consummation and consumption. The nighthawk is insatiable, and for fifteen minutes I enjoy trailing the owl-like bird with my eyes as it sifts silken chutes from the air with its wide-mouthed, whiskered beak.

ONE OF MY NATIVE AMERICAN FRIENDS, stripped of most of his clothes while preparing for the weekly "circle gathering," yells to me as I walk past the sweat lodge. "Aren't you getting out soon?" he asks. "Another year," I reply. Mesquite smoke from his fire pit stains the air, but as the wind rises I smell wet creosote bush, strong and pungent. Clouds have been bunching up in the southeast all afternoon, complete with the jellyfish tentacles of virga. Fool's rain. Virga makes promises and then mocks you, sending its moisture back to the clouds before it touches parched earth. My skin prickles with a few imagined drops of rain, and I realize this is only a monsoon tease. A pattern hasn't developed. The humidity is a sweat-sucking 17 percent, the dew point barely forty degrees. The numbers are too low. Still, the creosote smells of what's coming. A pendulum slows in its arc beneath my ribs, slows toward the height of its path, slows toward its opposite swing.

Two mornings later, the humidity is 35 percent and the dew point fifty-five degrees Fahrenheit. I find a single speckled quail egg on the exercise track, and the incongruence stops me; it's as if I'm seeing an Easter egg in November. Gambel's quail are rare inside the perimeter fence, and I've never known them to nest here, although I'm sure they do in the surrounding desert. So how did this fragile-shelled bit of grace get here? I lift it carefully between two fingers; it's too light. Something has broken into the egg and robbed it of its contents, the opening showing an eyeless socket of coagulated yellow humor. My nose recognizes the sweet, dark smell of peeled birds from my hunting and taxidermy years that I still associate with death. Perhaps a raven carried the egg here, stabbed it open and neatly gulped down its liquid, then discarded the shell as if it were a used Styrofoam drinking cup. I'll hang it up on a pushpin on my bulletin board.

In the evening, the monsoon tease continues, but the season isn't official yet. Herds of clouds graze along the southeastern sky in late afternoon bringing spotty activity: wind and dust, thunder and rain. Rising dew points encourage me. I feel the pendulum pausing in my chest.

IT'S THE DETAILS that make prison life interesting . . . and aggravating. My lap-walking has worn the soles of my Reeboks through to their spherical air cells, rupturing one in my heel so that it collects pea gravel, which rattles around inside the chamber. I walk with a single maraca strapped to my left foot. Karen sent me new running shoes last week, but they've become contraband. An officer at complex Mail and Property says the shoes are white and gray, and gray is not allowed. Because a few men use colors to indicate their gang affiliations, all tennis shoes must be absolutely white (what about "white pride"?), their soles, eyelets, even the stitching. Karen's upset about the pettiness of the department's policy, not so much because of the expense of albino shoes but because of the difficulty in finding them. The department, I tell her, would rather we wear only the cheap, ill-fitting, state-supplied boots.

Today, as Earth lists toward its solstice (14 hours and 15 minutes of sunlight today), my shoe beats a rataplan with my pace and the Rincon Mountains fume. White smoke billows from ridges and slopes, mushrooming into the troposphere like a wannabe Peruvian volcano. The forest service has decided to let the fires burn, and presently five or six separate plumes smudge the sky over east Tucson, rising and condensing into high cumulus clouds as the fires seed their own weather system, their own potential extinguishing. So far, three thousand acres have burned. Last night, topaz flames circled Tanque Verde Ridge like opposing warrior encampments on the eve of battle.

It looks like our former governor's battle for justice is about over. "It's a good day," Fife Symington said when he learned that the Ninth Circuit Court had overturned his seven convictions for fraud. The federal appeals court has agreed with the defense's argument concerning Mary Jane Cotey's illegal removal as a juror, the only juror of the twelve who believed in his innocence (when she was awake). Prosecutors have several options, including a retrial, but Symington, of course, feels vindicated and says he's not bitter about his treatment. Treatment? Does he mean doing time in Honduras? Right now he says he has six more weeks of culinary school to be concerned with, and he's "taking one day at a time." I wonder if he would show the same humility if, like anyone else with those convictions, he'd actually spent the last year in prison. Karen always said he'd never do time.

A SCARP OF CLOUDS poses in the south. Distant groans. There's a consolation of wind after a day when the air has that slack, draping weight of wet papier-mâché. The National Weather Service has issued a severe storm warning for Pima County. Monsoons? The pendulum slips toward a new arc.

The monsoon season is official. We've had three consecutive days with dew points averaging fifty-four degrees or higher. The season began on Saturday, June 26, the third earliest date on record. The annual winds, my ambassador of places made foreign to me by the nature of fences.

monsoon summer 1999

Exiles of Nature

"There is no such thing as nature," says Charles Siebert in *Outside* magazine. "We are no less natural than the next creature, except that thinking makes it seem so, makes us invent a place called nature from which we can think of ourselves as having been exiled, and into which we can constantly seek re-admittance, whether it be through encounters with a collapsing cabin, a vanishing African nomad, or the airy portal of a noiseless dawn."

I am an exile of society certainly, and perhaps one of the reasons I write is because I'm seeking readmittance into society, even forgiveness, as undeserved as it is (and as pitiful as it sounds). I've said before that nothing is as unforgiving as nature. I could be wrong, probably am. Nature, as I define it, has never rejected me. It's never judged me and found me lacking. It's never imprisoned me against my will. And, it's never been offended by my faithlessness. "Life is where change and redemption are possible," says Wendell Berry. It's no wonder that in this place I embrace nature, and even if I were prevented from walking the yard and encountering cottonwoods and constellations, if all I had was my eight-by-eight cell, I would tune myself to the wind and rain on the walls, to the singing cicadas outside them and the stridulating crickets within them. I would visit with the recalcitrant spider crouching at the hub of her spinning wheel. I would glory in the furtive cockroach.

Rick Bass says that a writer must learn to fit his or her skin "and, inseparably, the cycles and characteristics of the place around the writer. And then, once you do fit it—your skin, and your place—I can't stress how important I think it is to step out of it. To seek the perimeter, if you are on the interior; or search for the interior, if you have been camped too long on the perimeter."

Today on my perimeter a pair of Scott's orioles weave a wheat-colored nest among the highest branches of the tallest cottonwood. The male is quite striking in his black hood and cloak and deep yellow vestments. He's by far the most formally dressed visitor in the prison.

Noel is the inmate landscaper responsible for the upkeep of Cotton-wood Park. He earns a top wage of thirty-five cents an hour for mow-ing grass, raking leaves, pruning shrubs, and watering, but he would do this for nothing. He doesn't need the salary; the job is worth more to him for its intrinsic benefits, those that grow out of having the earth and sky rub against your skin. Noel is past retirement age, and I imagine that if he weren't in prison he'd be caring for another green corner somewhere, admiring his work from another stone wall under another cottonwood. He shouts, "Mornin' to ya," as I walk by, his Southern drawl baritone and nasal. I stop to talk, asking him about the Scott's orioles. "Them yellow birds? They've been hanging around for a few days." Noel then points to a hedge at the far end of his yard. "I seen a roadrunner yesterday, sneaking along those bushes. It was stalking the sparrows and eating them. I knew they eat snakes, but the Mexicans are beating them to it, hunting all the rattlesnakes. I can't plant anything them Mexicans don't eat, prickly pear, aloe—I got tired of cleaning up all the aloe leaves, so I dug up the plants."

I know that people slather aloe on burns and rub the sticky sap into brown age spots; I don't know why the men eat it like celery. I've seen them harvest nopales, the young prickly pear pads. I've helped friends locate patches of *hierbabuena* (mint) and pull down leaves from eucalyp-tus, both for medicinal concoctions. Then there's rattlesnake weed, a com-mon euphorbia, and jimsonweed to round out our natural pharmacy. Who needs the health unit? I tell Noel that I'm encouraging the Mexicans to eat more rabbits because an overpopulation of the bread-fattened, furball locusts is destroying the shrubbery.

There's no rabbit on today's lunch menu, just the usual hotdogs, potato salad, vegetable soup, and orange Jello-O. I carry my tray to a table where Marra sits alone at the opposite end. "Hey," I say when he looks up. He slides over and asks, "What? You don't want to be seen with a queen?" He sounds like he has a cold. "I lived with you for a month at Santa Rita," I say, "and that never bothered me . . . much." Marra says he has something confidential to tell me. He rises with his tray and says, "I'm going to whisper in your ear," which I think is silly since with all the noise in the chow hall he has to shout to be heard. "Okay," I say, and he moves closer to me: "My voice is changing." I look at him, noticing some other subtle changes, too.

Later, I stop Marra by the phones and we gossip about Michelle, the newest queen to arrive at Echo. I tell him that my work supervisor, Al Benz, saw Michelle sitting in front of the disciplinary office and asked me why a woman was dressed in blue on this yard. I said, "Just because someone in prison has hips and breasts and beautiful, long blond hair tied into a ponytail, doesn't mean he's a woman." Marra laughs when I tell him that Benz thought I was joking, that he continued to insist Michelle is a woman. "Everyone is talking about her," he says. "Especially since she went to the health unit to order a bra." I'd heard a rumor that Michelle had had a sex change, that the department had originally placed her at the women's unit but the women promptly ran her off. Marra says this isn't true. "She's taking hormones, but she hasn't had the operation." I say: "So, are you girls having a good time, getting together to share makeup secrets and do each other's hair?" There's humor in my voice. I'm sure Michelle is supplying Marra with estrogen, and that this is the reason he seems more feminine lately, but when I ask about it he says another friend has smuggled the hormones for him. "I've been taking them for a month," he explains. "At first I was really depressed, but now I couldn't feel happier. I should have done this a long time ago. My breasts are growing, even my hair is growing back!" I mention to him that I've noticed. Then I remember the question my daughters wanted me to ask him. They're curious about the way Marra looks at his fingernails. Girls, they say, look at the back of their hand, fingers extended. Boys look from the palm side, fingers curled toward it. So I ask Marra—and he fails the test. He's a man, through and through, from chromosomes to fingertips. Later, I give the same test to my coworkers. All three of them also fail. "I can't believe it," I tell them. "The queen is more of a man than any one of you!"

I MAKE DARK LAPS around the prison yard this quiet, humid evening. The moon turns away from the horizon as if snubbed, and I walk my course with air, thick as glycerin, moisturizing my skin, thinking that this place scours you down to essences—shelter, food, and hope. Here, the moon and stars are excesses, sprays of termites and nighthawks and even an abandoned feather that holds a slip of sky against its vane are extravagances. There's something to be said about the ability to recognize this. There are those here who never see, who've been camped too long inside themselves. Prison has the power of a lapidary with his rock tumbler. It can produce polished gems or worthless sand, depending on the time, depending on the rock.

Tonight's extravagance: fireworks bloom above Sentinel Peak. On the northwest bend of my circuit I see the rumpled silhouette of the mountain where this year's Independence Day festivities are just getting under way. Men gather on the basketball court and above the sweat lodge to glimpse the distant display before lockdown. Patriotic inmates celebrating the Fourth. Right now, my wife and daughters and in-laws have dragged lawn chairs up to the end of the driveway and are barbecuing hamburgers in an old rusting wheelbarrow in the lee of the mountain. I miss being with them, but, momentarily, I'll be returning to my cell when the yard closes. I can do without the fire alarm this year: sleep means I do less time, feel less time.

At nine fifteen a cop walks the run, ordering us all to leave the housing unit: our Echo Fourth of July tradition. I head for the far corner of the basketball court where friends Ralph, a bearded, Harley-loving desert poet, and Ken join me. We sit and watch dandelion-eruptions of color, some the size of half-dollars, with their time-delayed detonations and talk about family—what they are doing now, what we've done on previous holidays at home with them. The poignancy sticks to us like the humidity.

THE TENTS ARE sailing ships on a brown sea, an armada of Spanish galleons with their sails hanging limp in this region of the doldrums. The monsoon season is flexing its muscle with afternoon thunderstorms and their requisite gully washers and puddle makers. Real male rain.

Today, a long noon shower saturated the hardpan, making sponges of even the rocks. In the last two days we've had more than twice as much rain as we've had all year. Sabino Canyon is closed due to flooding; Mount Lemmon has lost whole sections of road. After work I follow the smell of creosote bush down to the steps (the "porch") at the west end of my housing unit where I know Ralph and Tom will be waiting for, and cheering at, the revelations of tonight's lightning-blanched landscape. Together, we watch sudden, deep incisions of light ignite clouds banked like coals against the Baboquivari Mountains, and we listen to thunder a hundred miles away. Opiates of cloud and plasma mesmerize us; we wear the same awe on our faces. The colors seem hypothetical: lurid saffron, liver, and amethyst. The sky is too instantaneous to be real, but the fiction is a page-turner and we can't put it down. The "dark head of weather," as Cormac McCarthy says, entertains me until I see that the rain has brought out the first hawkmoths of the summer. The insects fall into several bird of paradise, swooping and blurring among the blooms, sipping nectar but giving *me* the sugar high. The moths are luminescent sprites of the monsoons, resurrected from buried, overwintering pupae as the seasonal winds flush moisture into the desert, and now they dance in the half-light, exuberant in their second chance at life, in their reprieve from a prison sentence under ground.

Annie Dillard, my mentor of late, says insects "lack the grace to go about as we do, softside-out to the wind and thorns." Hard, chitinous exoskeletons, jointed appendages, segmented body parts don't generally make for elegant and lithe creatures. Even medieval knights couldn't do much more than sit horseback and deflect arrows. Yesterday I found a dead giant mesquite bug on the exercise track. It lay on its elytra, four black- and red-banded legs—two were missing—bent back on themselves and lifted skyward, its knobbed antennae splayed like tiny divining rods. The thumb-sized bug still displayed its mouthparts, a muscular siphon through which it recently sucked the sap of only one kind of tree, the mesquite. Even fussy bugs can be ugly. Watching hawkmoths from the "back porch" on this monsoon evening, I can't believe that they have the same ancient pedigree as mesquite bugs. "Nature will try anything once," Dillard writes. "This is what the sign of the insects says. No form is too gruesome, no behavior too grotesque." The sign of humans must say the same thing.

OUR RECENT PRECIPITATION and rise in humidity has been a boon for the hallucinogenic plants. I walk past the sweat lodge where one jimsonweed has quadrupled in size to washtub proportions. It has more than a hundred leaves and a dozen pearl white blossoms, which trumpet above the murky green foliage. At night, these flowers seem to glow from some internal light, like Mexican luminarias, scenting the area with the delicate fragrance of petunia. Some of the men have learned to harvest the flowers, dry them, and then crumble them into their Bugler tobacco for a more relaxing and satisfying smoke. A better life through chemicals. Where the cops pulled up the jimsonweed last summer outside Dorm Three, there's now a score of new sprouts, some with four or six oval leaves, others with only a pair of elongated cotyledons, all of them spread out over the whole flower bed. I'm also finding morning glory, another hallucinogenic crop, that's just starting to push tendrils and heart-shaped leaves across the ground. If I used drugs I'd never have to rely on the cops for my supply, or pay their inflated prices, which can be three to five times the street value, depending on what you want. (Heroin is always cheap at Echo, but presently a quarter ounce of marijuana sells for a hundred dollars, a fivefold mark up. Dealing drugs in prison is both lucrative and safe, reasons some officers succumb to the temptation.) Instead, I could get high on the weeds outside my cell, or the toads.

On my second lap I pass two friends, Dan and Bill, who immediately notice my new Nikes. As one of the few articles of personal property still available to us, athletic shoes have become symbols of status relatively equivalent to Rolex wristwatches or sports cars. Inmates' eyes always rove to footwear. "I'm flashing my gang colors," I tell them, indicating the gray stripes along both heels. "Not *white* pride but *gray* pride." "Property let those in here?" Dan asks, and I explain that the warden approved them only after my wife called him to complain. Bill says, "I talked to her once and I remember thinking: *Ken, you've got your hands full there.*"

"INCARCERATION is now considered the American version of mental hospitals," claims a recent article in the *Arizona Daily Star*. According to a Justice Department report, 16 percent of the country's prison population is mentally ill, and the number is growing. The article cites causes including the trend since the 1950s of closing mental hospitals, the lack of outpatient care, and the unwillingness of profit-making hospitals to cover the costs of often long-term treatment. "In the meantime," the article continues, "this country embarked on a national incarceration craze. Instead of addressing social shortcomings through prevention and education, this country chose to build more prisons to house more people. Nearly 2 million people now live in our prisons." In fact, we lock up more men and women per capita than any other nation in the world. America: home of the Brave, the Free.

I know about the mentally ill. They sit in my class, live on my run, and shuffle across the yard, "sniping" stale cigarette butts from the ground for the tobacco. They are the "watch-swallows" whose high point each day is morning meds: Thorazine, Elavil, Zoloft, lithium carbonate, valproic acid. I knew Tim for eight years before the department shipped him to a higher-custody level to protect him. He had a third-grade education when he came to prison for a sex crime. He was eighteen years old, and his face showed the features of a Mongoloid child, naive and friendly, a face I'd seen every summer while directing a camp for mentally disabled people. Tim survived prison by allowing men to sexually abuse him. He had accepted this as a way of life, and it was no more a burden to him than washing their laundry or giving up his commissary purchases to avoid more serious trouble and to stay on the prison yard. He should be safe now, in protective segregation, alone in a cell where he will serve the remainder of his long sentence.

When I remember Tim, I wonder about the wisdom of a system that will eventually turn him, and so many others like him, back out to the streets. The emotionally disturbed, the impulsive exhibitionists we now call predators. Without treatment, without a modicum of rehabilitation, perhaps lethal injection would better serve all concerned, society and the inmate. Maybe for all prisoners we should draw the line at, say, five years. Five years of warehousing might fall within a margin of acceptable damage. Anything longer, in our present system, is a kind of death sentence anyway, one much more cruel. Lethal injection would show us to be humane, civilized, and it would save the taxpayers some money at the same time.

The brutal treatment of prisoners, whether they're mentally ill or sociopaths or just sick, is in vogue. And it all comes down to money and politics. Today, on CNN, Arizona's Maricopa County Sheriff Joe Arpaio is defending his claim as "the toughest sheriff in the West." He says he's doing the taxpayers a favor with his jail policies: zebra-striped clothes and pink underwear for inmates, green bologna sandwiches, no cigarettes, no coffee. "Took away their coffee," he brags on national television. "That saved a hundred and fifty thousand a year." He says he also saved half a million a year by serving bologna sandwiches. The sheriff, his gut bulging from his uniform as he walks his tent-city jail with reporters, brushes off charges of brutality. "That's garbage," he yells. "Look at my officers!" I'm not sure what he means by this. Do his officers eat his bologna? I'm also not so certain he's as brutal as he wants people to believe. He didn't take away coffee and offer only sandwiches just because he has a sadistic streak. He can't afford it. According to one CNN estimate, he must pay his lawyers to battle more than eight hundred lawsuits by inmates, including one for mismanagement of funds. (He pays the salaries of some of his staff with money from inmate family-supplied funds.) Lawyers are pricey. Anyone with Sheriff Joe's legal expenses would be eating bologna, too.

I've never had the pleasure of visiting Arpaio's jail, but I've met many men who have. No one speaks favorably of the conditions. (When I came back to prison in the summer of 1996, his officers killed a man by restraining him and "cattle-prodding" him to death with electric stun guns.) Sheriff Arpaio uses the standard cliché when confronted with prisoners' complaints: "You should have thought about that before you did the crime." Even my wife uses this line; but I hate it. It's one of those clichés that perpetuates the fallacy that punishment is a deterrent to crime. I've said it before. Tough jails and tough prisons, even tough-talking imbecile sheriffs, will never prevent criminal behavior. Francis Fukuyama, Hirst Professor of Public Policy at George Mason University, said it this way in the *Atlantic Monthly*: "Most people do not make day-to-day choices about whether or not to commit crimes based on the balance of rewards and risks, as the rational-choice school sometimes suggests. The vast majority of people obey the law, particularly with regard to serious offenses, out of habit that was learned relatively early in life. Most crimes are committed by repeat offenders who have failed to learn this basic self-control. In many cases they are acting not rationally but on impulse. Failing to anticipate consequences, they are undeterred by the expectation of punishment."

I like to equate Sheriff Arpaio's style of "rehabilitation" with kicking a chained dog. People respond the same way, either with cringing submission or vicious attack. Tonight, after writing all day, I walk the perimeter in the wet and dark to clear my mind. But it's no use. Prison saturates my thoughts. As I pass near the band room, inmate musicians are practicing an old Eric Clapton tune, singing with relish: "I shot the sheriff."

WE'VE BEEN LOCKED DOWN ALL DAY while the tent dwellers drag their property, mattresses, and bedding to their new homes on the softball field. The old tent city outside my window is coming down; my skyline is changing. When I peer through the venetian blinds I think I'm in a different cell. The living conditions in the new tents are much improved. All twenty tents have concrete floors and steel frames, and they are no longer double-bunked. And, not only will each man have his personal floor space, but he will have his own power outlet for his appliances: a television, lamp, fan, or radio. Headphones are mandatory.

In the evening, I prowl the yard after the lockdown for pinacate beetles, those shiny black insects that go by many names: *Eleodes*, darkling beetles, stink bugs. The men call them "punk bugs" because they crawl across the ground with their rear ends in the air. Pinacate beetles appear here after the monsoon rains, busying themselves with some obscure search pattern familiar only to insect nerve ganglia. Near the inmate commissary, I reach for one navigating the seam in a sidewalk. The beetle immediately stands on its head and mists my fingers with a tobacco-colored stain. The smell is faintly sweet, like almonds and skunk.

Other mindless insects on missions have been drilling tunnels under the largest palm outside the education building, where last year's seeds now slip narrow green ribbons through the hardpan. The solitary wasps resemble delicate damselflies, with thin black bodies drawn out rearward half an inch beyond the wings to a bulbous abdomen dipped in orange pigment. But they are unmistakably wasplike in the air, their dark bodies and legs dangling beneath hovering wings. I've watched one insect dig her pencil-width hole and disappear down the shaft to jackhammer into the dirt with a vibrating whine. When she exited, she flew off one or two feet, tossed away her burden with the quiet tick of falling rock, and then returned to her work. She was obsessive in her task, a committed escapist, and she ignored me although I was practically kneeling over her. Later, I watched another wasp stretch out a smooth green caterpillar next to her tunnel. She appeared to be using her body as a ruler, laying it alongside the caterpillar to measure the proper depth of the hole, which she continued to excavate. When she was satisfied with the proportions of her larder, she emerged and dragged the caterpillar inside to attach her single egg. The caterpillar, imprisoned underground and unable to move, will slowly wither as the wasp grub feeds from lesser to more and more vital organs.

About a hundred years ago, the French entomologist Jean-Henri Fabre conducted a simple experiment with a digger wasp of the genus *Sphex* that illustrates how profoundly fixed instinctive behaviors can be. Normally, the digger wasp drags her paralyzed prey to the threshold of her tunnel and leaves it there to inspect the condition of the tunnel before pulling the prey inside. Fabre, typical of a naturalist, wasn't content to just watch the insect. He *had* to get involved. So, while the wasp was inspecting her nest, Fabre moved the prey—in this case a cricket—a few inches away. When the wasp reemerged, she dragged the cricket back to the burrow, left it there again, and disappeared inside for a second inspection. Whereupon Fabre moved the cricket a second time. And a third. The wasp repeated this "drag and inspect" subroutine forty times before Fabre finally gave her a break—she never could make the leap and pull the cricket straight into her nest.

Scientists have since labeled this kind of chronic behavior "sphexishness" in honor of the digger wasp. It is the inability to adapt to new circumstances, to adjust to change. It is a revolving door with no exit, a one-dimensional Möbius strip. A kind of mindless feedback loop that uses up resources without any beneficial result, precisely like the function of corrections. Could anything be more sphexish than our prison system?

THE NATIONAL WEATHER SERVICE has issued a flash-flood warning for Tucson, and I walk the track in the rain with Ralph, my poet-friend and desert compadre who's both a professional wrestling and John Wayne freak. I found him alone on the back porch, his regular cadre of sunset watchers opting for dry skin and clothes. Tonight, our shoes crunch in the wet gravel and the sky is aged sheet metal. Sluggish lightning strobes clouds and mountains and our faces—we could die at the speed of light. Ralph talks about poetry and freedom, what it would be like to actually visit the places he writes about. I'm thinking freedom is a wilderness he's been away from a long time. It will need getting used to. He's been in prison for seven years, and he recently made home arrest. In the next month or so Ralph will be going home, back to the desert north of Tucson that he loves, to a son who's grown, to friends who never gave up on him. He plans to continue his writing, perhaps joining a writers' workshop at the University of Arizona, and work on publishing another poetry chapbook. His latest poem is about a man with no shoes who feeds the rabbits outside Ralph's cell window. Ralph feeds them, too. He says he won't eat any food the rabbits won't eat.

After dark we're soaked, but the rain has stopped. A great blue heron toes the edge of a large pool in the tent area—only it isn't the tent area any longer, just a broad, flooded ditch. The heron stands, footed to its own featherless shadow in the security haze for several minutes, but when nothing edible presents itself the bird wings away. Hawkmoths flutter in urgency over the bird of paradise, and a small Sonoran Desert toad, the first of its kind I've seen this summer, squats alongside the housing unit, praying for fat insects to blunder within tongue reach.

"MUST EVERYTHING WHOLE BE NIBBLED?" asks Annie Dillard, after observing a mosquito fill its belly by piercing the neck of a copperhead snake. She continues: "Here is a new light on the intricate texture of things in the world, the actual plot of the present moment in time after the fall: the way we the living are nibbled and nibbling—not held aloft on a cloud in the air but bumbling pitted and scarred and broken through a frayed and beautiful land." This week is kissing bug week. The men I teach complain about itching welts on arms and buttocks, fattened lips, eyes swollen shut, so I choose the conenose as the bug of the week. I've been doing this all summer. Last week was pinacate beetle (stink bug) week; before that we had mosquito, cicada, hawkmoth, harvester ant. The themes are part of my "almanacs," which I post on the chalkboard daily, and include drawings with interesting facts. The students now expect something new on the board every Monday. Some are insistent. They want to know what sucks or stings or stinks, what eats them. Kissing bugs are the latest nuisance, particularly to men in the tents. The insects normally feed on the blood of packrats, and in late spring the adults go searching for the mammals' nests after dark. Unfortunately for tent dwellers, light draws the bugs, and the security lights, those outside on poles and those inside the tents, glow all night, calling them to feast on exposed lips and eyelids. Foreign proteins in the bugs' saliva raise welts like oversized mosquito bites. With me, one nibble ignites every hair follicle with insane itching. My heart pounds and my ears ring. Kissing bugs are my personal thorn in the flesh. God's grace may be sufficient, but I still tear apart my bedding whenever the assassins appear. I tell the men to sleep in their tents with one eye open.

In the back of the classroom on a large sheet of white paper I've started gluing down insects. And not only insects but spiders, centipedes, egg-shells, hawkmoth wings, and a mummified bat. It began with the bat, a fleshless Mexican freetail one of the men found outside the education building. Then the eggshell, a mourning dove's capless hatchling discard, pale and thin as a cuticle. And the moth wings, brittle flakes of zebra, stolen from the jaws of ants. Each I've labeled and fastened into place with Elmer's white. As the men caught on, we added bumble bees, fetal-curled in death; black, bulbous carpenter bees; metallic, blue- and green-bodied wasps; rhinoceros beetles (a female and horned male); an eight-inch giant centipede; a pressed and dried tarantula; a tarantula wasp; paloverde and pinacate beetles; and a Halloween-colored horse lubber, among others that pinch, sting, or spit. The collage is our objets trouvé, envoys of this "frayed and beautiful" place, and it continues to burgeon as the men add wild garnish.

Prisoners have the propensity for collecting things. These aren't necessarily natural objects; I know a man who still has the spring he cannibalized from a ballpoint pen six years ago. Another always wears his jacket, even in the summer, so he has pockets for all the paper he scavenges on the yard. You never know when you might need a piece of string or a rubber band, paper clips, sandpaper, razor blades, screws, a length of wire, an old toothbrush, used tea bags, or a broken watchband. This place turns people into packrats. I keep a plastic tumbler filled with my own salvage: colorful paper clips, a button, two small combs, Moldex earplugs, half a tube of Carmex, a glue stick, Liquid Paper, and four used typewriter ribbons.

THERE IS NO hyssop of purgation. On this date thirteen years ago, August 19, 1986, I was arrested in Aspen, Colorado, while holding hands and window-shopping with the girl I loved who was not my wife. Some sins you may atone for, but they will never be forgiven or forgotten, not by legislatures that continue to pass retroactive laws, not by family and friends who remember. Prison, my garment of sackcloth, loads my past onto one day. All events pile up to yesterday, the only past allowed. Yesterday, I committed a heinous crime. It's as if I haven't changed in thirteen years and can't change, forever being defined by this one act. Just recently I overheard an inmate talk about sex offenders. "You know what really gets me?" he asked a friend next to him. "When I see them with their families in visitation. I don't know who's worse, the sex offender or the person bringing in the children. It just allows them to do it all over again." I've seen this inmate in visitation when Karen and my daughters come out. I'm sure he knows why I'm in prison; I'm certain he meant his words for my ears. But his mock concern for children doesn't extend to those in visitation who regularly see him with his hands under his girlfriend's clothes.

AFTER LAST EVENING'S TERRIFIC STORM, sunlight rolls out on the wet ground and insects speak to one another in hyperbole. Clicking dragonflies in fluorescent hues orbit pools, competing for air waves with cicadas, beetles, and the weapons range clacking of grasshoppers. Alongside the housing unit, butterflies—pipevine swallowtails, painted ladies, monarchs, and yellow sulphurs like flakes of sunlight—garland the blooming privet and lilac. With my thumb and forefinger I snap onto the wings of a swallowtail and carry it to the classroom to glue to our objets trouvé, but the men won't have it and make me release it. I comply.

If last year was toad summer, then this summer belongs to the bugs. In the evening, hawkmoths replace butterflies at the privet and lilac. Rhinoceros beetles shuttle and scull over the dirt. Orb-weaving spiders, whose web hammocks seem to be everywhere now, wrap tiny moths into triangular tents. As they feed, the yellow and black arachnids first recycle their own silk, reprocessing its protein within twenty minutes.

When I join Noel, Ralph, Ken, and Tom at the back porch, Tom says he's watched sunsets here for the last six and a half years. Sunsets on the porch seem to be the constancy that Tom draws strength from. Overhead, nighthawks and hawkmoths knit the sky, and with my arrival comes a pair of great blue herons, their dark outlines sounding off with a hoarse *frahnk, frahnk* as the two drift into the vacant but puddled tent area. As daylight wanes and imaginations take shape, the stilt-legged birds begin fishing at the water's margin.

Later, a scarp of purple nightfall rims the horizon beneath pure, dustless, indigo skies. The constellations haven't been so bright all summer. Ursa Major in the north bends its tail toward Arcturus in the west, and farther along the same arc Mars is Scorpio's red eye. The desert amplifies the stars. You can lie on your back and listen to them.

I look to the stars for confirmation that I'm not stuck in one place. From one hour to the next I can tell by marking the counterclockwise motion of Ursa Major that the earth moves beneath my feet. I'm spinning with it at 700 miles an hour. From season to season I can feel the earth coursing against a backdrop of constellations, summer's Scorpio and winter's Orion. I'm circling the sun at 66,000 miles an hour, a million and a half miles a day. I am not in prison; I am a traveler. I am a galactic tourist, visiting the sun and moon and gas giants. I watch the universe pass by from the window of this fenced plot of ground. I should have motion sickness.

IN THE FIRST WEEK OF SEPTEMBER, the sun begins dilating in its course; its light has an attenuated cast, less demanding. Summer leans toward the equator, and already turkey vultures turn circles toward Mexico.

September's peregrinations are under way. Migrating hummingbirds refuel among the aloe at the library. I've rarely witnessed such activity. The tiny vibrating dabs of green chase each other, rest on branches, tongue flowers on the wing. Later, the evening is aflutter with bats, which zip and spin and loop in pursuit of radar-sensitive insects, moths with "fuzz-busters" that warn them to fold their wings and fall from the sky once scanned.

It looks like I won't be migrating anywhere soon. At my six-month classification review (my pass said, "You must attend your work assignment; however, you must also make time to attend your hearing") I waited outside the Service Center under a butchered peppertree until an inmate called my name. Once I was seated in his office, my counselor John Payne asked if I wanted to participate in the Sex Offender Treatment Program. Before I answered, another counselor, Therese Schroeder, added: "You'll have to transfer to Meadows." I don't think so. Schroeder recommended my continued placement at Echo: no change in status.

AT THE AUTUMNAL EQUINOX, melancholy phoebes sigh with twin notes, a peculiar, depressing way of announcing their return to prison. This morning, there is an absence of white-winged doves as the "cactus pigeons" return to Mexico.

The monsoon season presses toward record length, as thunder resonates against the housing units. I walk in the rain, checking first to see if the sun will set without Ralph at his post on the back porch. Ralph went home today, and I'm already missing him, his relaxed presence at sunset or jogging on the exercise track, the poetry he shares with me. I've known him since the early years of my incarceration when I traveled to Cimarron for the creative writing workshop. When Ralph came to Santa Rita we connected there, and again after my return to prison when I finally arrived at Echo Unit. Ralph and I grew up in the same desert, Pima Canyon and Pusch Ridge. We were disciples of the same cactus and sand and stones.

I circle along my northern perimeter and its frayed hem of razor wire.

My narrow path is scored with shadow and the wind-pruned branches and leaves of cottonwood. Poststorm debris. In prison, this place where trouble is always walking toward you, I am the marginal, excerpted one, and because of this I'm always looking for ways to knit myself to something significant, something greater than I am—to feel what Charles Siebert calls "the wide accident, the inherent anonymity of existence." Perhaps he is right. Maybe there is no difference between man and nature, that the "otherness" of nature is purely a human invention. Maybe he would say that prison is simply a "natural" extension of the human presence on the planet, like a bird and its nest. Like a brood cell with its paralyzed tarantula is the natural extension of the tarantula wasp. Even so, for me this place erects barriers, physical as well as metaphorical. Prison attempts to delineate and separate—if only feebly, thank God—what is wild and what is tamed, controlled. And so I walk and write, embracing this wilderness of fences and razor wire, trying to believe that I am not an exile.

aftersummer 1999

The Symington Effect

Birds don't measure time, Thomas Merton observed in his *Conjectures of a Guilty Bystander*: "For the birds there is not a time that they tell, but the *point vierge* between darkness and light, between nonbeing and being." Today, September 25, 1999, I begin my twelfth and my last year in prison, and I sense the closing of time as a ship-bound rat senses the coast is near. Four thousand days locked up in this overcrowded cargo hold. Just as the mass of an object increases with its velocity, it must also be a physical law that as time increases it also gains weight. Einstein's relativity modeled in the ways of birds and prisoners. "Eternity is always present in the animal mind," says Wendell Berry; "only men deal in beginnings and ends."

I find myself measuring the remainder of my time in strange ways: How many more haircuts will I need? How many bottles of vitamin E, 100 count? How many more times do I have to wash laundry, if I stretch it to once every other week? How many more visiting days will Karen have to endure? Then there's the wear on my Nikes. Will they last another year? Will my sweatpants, already hand-stitched in places, hold together? Should I walk fewer exercise circuits on the yard and save threads and treads? I'm even counting the remaining number of flycatcher exchanges and blackbird migrations. For forty-four seasons in prison I've gauged my life by the birds: barn swallows, kingbirds, and phoebes among others. Their world is cyclic: they live within the land's pulse. Ebb and flow, rise and fall, I feel their rhythm and mark it as a passage of time. And now, as I discard the pages of my last calendar—in this place where calendars are meaning-less—I count the birds. The birds don't measure time, but I must.

Charles Simic is right; he must have done time: counting *is* an activity of a lonely soul. I count, and I write down what I count. It is my first obsession. A way to save myself. Counting allows me a kind of communion. When I record weather, woodpeckers, and planets, I'm more than a mere observer. My words and sketches grant me an intimacy with wildness. The lines on the page, whether literal or pictorial—descriptions of color and scent of sycamore leaves or the penciled texture of a rhinoceros beetle—etch images deep inside me, images that impose themselves on the auster-ity of this place. Images that have significance beyond fences and razor wire. I write about nature because I'm doing time in prison. I have to. Scott Russell Sanders says: "I write about hope because I wrestle with despair. ... To write about the natural order that sustains us is not to ignore the human condition, but to insist on our most fundamental needs—for light and earth and water and air, for companions, for beauty, meaning, grace." For me, marking the days, the seasons of migrations of birds and bugs, reminds me that I need more than what prison offers: food, shelter, and institutionalization. It reminds me that I need to find my sense of place, even with this sentence of place.

I'M ENJOYING classic aftersummer weather: days relax, cool and dry out, night skies clear. After the sun falls sideways to the horizon, Arcturus, the star dipping far into the west, emerges through a thinning sheet of day-light.

Flights of mourning doves sound off with the rusty hinge squeals of their wings. A single barn swallow seines the air for insects beyond the west perimeter; it's time for the swallow migration, and I feel a pang of emotion upon seeing the lonely bird.

There's also an absence in Cottonwood Park. Noel, the landscaper I've come to know on my exercise circuits, sits in one of the East Gate holding cages, waiting transfer to another unit—his turn for the predator evaluation. Dan, another friend, has joined him. Seeing Dan concerns me. His release date is very close to mine. I could be sitting next to him.

The public salivates over sex offenders, and the media feeds this appetite with news broadcasts, talk shows, and programs with titles such as "The Sex Offender Next Door." I don't know what Dan and Noel did, and I don't care. I do know both understand the magnitude of their crimes. They would agree with me when I say some people belong in prison. What I wish people understood, however, is that not all sex offenders are predators. Some of these "predators" are children themselves. Arizona will soon indict seventeen-year-old Jessica Jeffries from Phoenix on eight felony counts for her sexual conduct with two twelve-year-old boys. She may spend the rest of her life in prison as a sexual predator. Others are exhibitionists. I remember meeting one man who had a sex score on his record for "streaking" twenty years ago. I can't help but think our justice system is overreacting to a public hysteria about sexual behavior, deviant behavior that incarceration will never prevent or correct, particularly because incarceration focuses on punishment rather that treatment.

Six billion people now inhabit the planet, a population that has doubled in my lifetime. About one person in every three thousand is in prison in the United States: the greatest incarcerator in the world.

LAST NIGHT AFTER DARK I collected a fistful of jimsonweed seeds from one of the two plants in Cottonwood Park, pricking my fingers on the dry, thorny pods. Each pod held scores of hard, black, heart-shaped specks, which I slipped into a small manila envelope. In a few days I plan to scatter the seeds across the prison yard, doing a Johnny Jimsonweed seeding around the sweat lodge, the education building, and along the margin of my walking path. The plants in the park are thick with leaves and still flower conspicuously, but no one bothers them. I think of the jimsonweed as part of Noel's legacy. This morning, I stop by one plant and pick a dried and split seedpod to draw.

The hallucinogenic plants may be safe, but tree cutting is under way at Echo courtesy of new Deputy Warden Heliotes. I wondered how long it would take after his arrival before the trees would begin to suffer. Santa Rita saw the removal of most of its vegetation under his reign. And just like at Santa Rita, Echo is also losing part of the visitation area with its playground equipment. Heliotes is too predictable. What does he have against trees and children? Today, a landscape crew lops off branches from the pair of giant eucalyptus at the southwest perimeter near Kingbird Park.

I watch in disgust as the men chainsaw the eucalyptus. The lieutenant says they're blocking the security camera's view of the tents. (So why not move the security camera?) For me, the trees block the view of the fences and razor wire, the stark, gray buildings. There will be two fewer places for orioles and flycatchers, two fewer places to rest my eyes. When I turn away to leave, I see our resident Cooper's hawk, a regular visitor to these trees, has also been watching the butchery. She flies off, and I read disgust in the beating of her wings.

IN SUNDAY's *Arizona Daily Star* I read that Charleen Lease, a twenty-eight-year-old inmate at the women's unit, died on July 10 of primary pulmonary hypertension after the department delayed her medical care. Doctors at St. Mary's Hospital didn't diagnose her condition until two days before her death, "because prison medical staff—who learned in May that she had an enlarged heart—waited nearly two months to take her to a hospital to find out why."

I've learned that, where the department is concerned, ignorance is the best health care. ADC practices a kind of "Don't ask, don't tell" health care.

Recently, a friend and coworker in education discovered he had hepatitis C. He didn't, however, learn about his condition from the health unit. He learned about it after first requesting to review his own medical records and then combing through the paperwork in the allotted half hour. He had no idea he had the contagious disease; he wasn't looking for it. But there it was in his blood work. Hepatitis C. Later, he asked the nurse practitioner, "How come no one counseled me on this matter?" She didn't know.

I wish someone had told me. I've eaten food from his meal tray. I do know what the department advises the staff: treat everyone as if he has AIDS. Several years ago we had an active case of tuberculosis at Santa Rita. Everyone received skin tests. What mostly concerns me are those like my friend who may be carrying communicable diseases unknowingly and who are going untreated. Prisons could be festering sores of resistant organisms waiting outbreak. My friend will be on his way home soon, one of more than several hundred men released statewide each month. And what's the first thing these men will want upon release? It won't be a blood test.

Charleen's story, based on the newspaper's investigation, only gets worse. The headline caption is telling: "Corrections Finds No Fault in Death: Prison Nurses Ignored Ill Inmate's Pleas, Records Show." On the day of her death, Charleen Lease was vomiting blood and complaining that her legs were going numb, but the unit nurse, Beth Thompson, was busy with other "emergencies" (the article reports these as a flesh wound and a dental problem). I've met this nurse. She occasionally works weekends at Echo, passing out medications and addressing minor complaints. Her attitude is caustic toward the men. One encounter I had with her last June inspired me to write these words in my journal: "Another angry nurse at the health unit. Squinty eyes behind thick glasses, thin hair tied back because it's unwashed or has begun to fade to gray. I imagine the woman treats the men as she treats herself . . . her bedside manner isn't appreciated anywhere but in a prison system." That day at Manzanita she finally called 911 after Charleen had turned blue. Shortly after 8:00 PM St. Mary's Hospital admitted her; a note on her emergency room chart says she was being treated a few days prior but the department of corrections "wouldn't let her stay." (ADC denies this.) At 8:45 Charleen's heart arrested; a half hour later doctors pronounced her dead.

Camilla Strongin, a spokeswoman for corrections, reported to the *Star* that the medical staff's lack of knowledge about Charleen Lease's previous test results "wouldn't have made any difference" one way or the other. "The bottom line is that this inmate would have died anyway."

Attitudes like Strongin's and Thompson's are prevalent in this place. Prison seems to attract people with a disregard for life, people who the system then encourages with promotions. While I'm writing this, Lieutenant Trudeau stops by my cell to make certain my blue jeans aren't hanging where only towels are allowed and to see that I don't have any unauthorized pictures, like those torn from magazines, pinned to my bulletin board. He asks me, "What's that smell?" and I notice that his head is the same narrow diameter as his neck. I tell him that I don't know and then explain that the whole run smells like urine, that it has even after the remodeling. On his way out my door he says, "Have you been wetting your bed?" *The pencilneck idiot*, I think, recalling that it's the lieutenant's habit of disrespecting everyone, including his own staff (who does the same to him behind his back). "I wouldn't do that," I answer, shutting my mouth before I ask, "Do you wet yours?"

Trudeau incites people as a kind of job security. What good is a "trained" security officer if there are no problems with security? If your job entails little more than baby-sitting inmates as well as staff? In this system it's tough to gain a promotion or recognition without some incident to demonstrate your ability. Trudeau justifies his existence by inventing ways to unzipper his puny authority.

When Trudeau treats his staff with similar contempt, it has the same effect—insubordination. Disgruntled officers are more willing to disregard security policies, break protocols, and violate direct orders from superiors. Presently at Echo the brown shirts are skirmishing: officers versus administration. You can hear it in their radio conversations, the way the cops step on each other's calls, ignore or refuse requests, voice derogatory (and often humorous) comments. I haven't seen Officer Ochs since he stuffed his socks into a coworker's mouth earlier this year. Most of the staff I've talked to seems to have the same opinion of Sergeant Abt, who is a clone of Lieutenant Trudeau. The staff hates him, believing Abt will do anything to anyone to advance his own career. During the last shakedown, I explained this to Officer Macy, who is Abt's current target. "What do you know about it?" he asked me. "Just what I hear," I said. "That Abt is out to get you. That he's accusing you based on the word of an inmate, that you're selling state computer parts on the Internet." Macy wanted me to write a letter to the deputy warden on his behalf. "Heliotes, Trudeau, they all believe Abt. I could lose my job." Fear and intimidation—the administration uses it to control its own staff as the cops use it to control us. The result, however, is a lack of control. Macy is now more of a security problem. He isn't selling state property, but he is smuggling personal property to inmates and selling inmate-authored computer programs.

Inmates appreciate disgruntled corrections employees. These officers and other support personnel are the most willing to look the other way. I know one who claims to have never written up an inmate, something he brags about. Grudge-bearing, resentful employees are the ones who treat us to contraband like coffee and doughnuts, pizza and movie videos, alcohol, drugs, weapons, or sex, depending on your pleasure. We should be more grateful for belittling Napoleon-types like Abt and Trudeau. We have to put up with their pettiness, but in the end they make doing time a little easier.

AFTERSUMMER CONTINUES with cool nights and days. I walk laps on my fortieth birthday in my sweatshirt while Gila woodpeckers call from the desert's edge with hesitant, arrhythmic pings. Ravens post themselves on power poles as negative beacons against a blue, kiln-glazed sky.

The blooming desert broom at the west perimeter quivers with pollen-saddled honeybees, bee-mimicking flies (bubble-eyed copies of honeybees), and stopover monarch butterflies. Every honeybee has her panniers packed with gold. A dozen or more queens and monarchs droop from the tiny flowers, and I imagine I can hear the monarchs panting as they refuel before the next leg of their fall migration. I easily capture a queen butterfly to draw.

When I return to my cell, Steve, one of my coworkers and a neighbor from A run, asks me about an animal that resembles a cat with a long black-and-white tail. I think he's referring to something he saw on *The Discovery Channel*, but he says he watched it last night crawl out from under Dorm Four, cross the sidewalk, and slip under our housing unit. "I was sittin' outside, smokin' a cigarette before count," he says. "It stopped when it saw me, and then disappeared under the building." I'm amazed by his story. Occasionally, we have feral cats here, but what Steve is describing, I believe, is a ringtail, a small reclusive carnivore whose most conspicuous feature is its long, bushy tail with alternating black and white rings. Ringtails do venture into the lower Sonoran Desert and love enclosed spaces such as outbuildings and attics. While I was teaching in public school, I trapped a ringtail in my mother's attic and kept it in a display case in my classroom for a semester, feeding it rats and mice. My students named it "Max." If there's a ringtail inhabiting the prison, I'm guessing it spends the days curled up in some dark recess under the trailer and prowls around the yard after lockdown. I desperately want to see it.

Later I take my mammal guides to Steve and show him a lineup of suspects: a raccoon, a coati, and a ringtail. Other men, claiming to have seen the animal, are calling it a coati, another relative of the raccoon. I want to get a positive ID; Steve immediately points out the ringtail.

THIS MORNING as I write in my journal, I hear the chainsaws punishing our unruly trees. Deputy Warden Heliotes, Captain Patterson, and Lieutenant Trudeau are on a mission. The cottonwoods and desert willow, the pines and juniper and chinaberry, are out of compliance. They have too many branches, more than the allotted three, and some of them have grown within reach of the buildings, a certain security problem. An inmate might climb to a rooftop and escape upward if not outward. I suppose someone could tear branches from the trees and use them for ladders or pole vaults, but this seems unnecessary when you can twist rope from toilet paper. (I hope the department doesn't take *that* away from us, too.) I just learned the rope-making yesterday and it gave me an idea. Since millions of people are in prison and millions more undoubtedly will be going there, I propose the need for a prison survival manual. The book wouldn't have to be entirely seditious in nature; it could offer other helpful advice for adjusting to cellular life, including recipes, like 101 ways to cook with potato chips.

"ARIZONA CRIMINAL JUSTICE is making national news again," I add to my journal. According to yesterday's USA Today, Arizona has condemned Claude Maturana, a mentally ill murderer, to die by lethal injection. "'Healthy' would be a fatal diagnosis for prisoner," the article says. The problem is that a psychologist at the state hospital has refused to treat him. "I'm upholding the ethics of my profession," says Jerry Dennis. "It's not right to give a patient treatment just so he can be executed." Arizona, however, will not be denied. Officials have conducted both a statewide and then a national search and found a psychologist in Georgia who will declare Maturana fit to kill.

I'm obviously biased, but aren't the executions of mental patients a shortsighted solution to crime? Aren't prisons, for that matter? (The Department of Corrections now prefers the politically correct—and ridiculous—term for prison: "secure care facility." I still prefer "gated community.") Fear is the motivator. Texas columnist Molly Ivins says, "Fear is the most dangerous emotion in politics. People do terrible things to one another out of fear." Fear replaces common sense. It has elected presidents and started wars. Fear is what builds prisons and fills them to overcapacity—at the same time diminishing our constitutional rights. We have a U.S. Supreme Court justice who would gladly give up his right to dally on a street corner to keep his neighborhood safe. There's security in martial law, too.

Here's how fear works. In the "Comment" section of a recent *Arizona Daily Star* (November 7, 1999), our director of prisons, Terry L. Stewart, published an editorial entitled "Imprisonment Prevents Crime." In it, Stewart responds to FBI reports that serious crimes have declined for the seventh year running by taking credit for the trend in Arizona. "I firmly believe one of the reasons why crime levels are down is imprisonment," he writes. "Not only does the thought of spending years behind bars act as a deterrent to crime, but prison also provides something else—incapacitation." He then goes on to explain why "keeping violent and dangerous individuals away from society" prevents crime with the example of ADC being "forced" by old early release laws to free an inmate after serving "*only*" sixteen years on a twenty-one-year sentence. The inmate was back in prison with a life sentence in six months after committing a long list of crimes, including aggravated assault and murder. "Clearly," Stewart argues, "had this individual been in prison during those six months, he would have been unable to commit murder or threaten public safety." At least not until his mandatory release in another five years, I think. But this is how Stewart uses fear. The message: Keep locking them up and keep them locked up. Or else. It's an extreme example used by design, and he could have used others. Why not mention James Hamm? (Admittedly, another extreme example.)

After serving seventeen years, the courts "forced" ADC to free him from a life sentence for murder, whereupon Hamm completed a Juris Doctor at Arizona State University and is now a law professor. (Jim received his undergraduate degree in prison at a time when that was still possible.) But Hamm's example doesn't send the right message.

Fear, once you establish it, is a powerful persuader. Fear sells—one reason the media feeds it to us. Fear is subtle. It has no taboos. It reaches across gender and age and culture lines. Consider those Brinks security systems commercials showing hooded figures watching your sleeping children. It's the same as the salespeople who, after Karen and I bought our first home, attempted to sell us fire protection systems by showing us photographs of horribly burned kids. Fear makes anything believable: the exaggerations, even outright deceptions and lies.

Terry Stewart would never use an example like James Hamm because it wouldn't sell his mythology: that prison is a deterrent to crime. Even so, his example seems to be a contradiction. Sixteen years of imprisonment certainly couldn't deter the inmate from committing an even worse crime after his release. In fact, the example speaks of what's wrong with our system. I want to ask Stewart: "You had the man for sixteen years. Did you really need another five to correct his behavior before returning him to society?" It's obvious from his editorial that Stewart knows little about rehabilitation and cares even less. He says he supports rehabilitation but that spending taxpayer money on it won't make a difference. He writes, "When an offender identifies to us that he or she is serious about making a change, we are ready to help the inmate meet that need," and he lists available programs including education, vocational classes, and those to curb substance abuse and manage anger problems. It sounds good on paper, but I know these "programs" and have seen the disposal of many others over the past twelve years. For those below the eighth-grade literacy standard (excluding Mexican nationals, which the department forbids educating), education is mandatory, and therefore another punishment; the state rejects offering incentives for participation. Treating substance abuse and managing anger are self-guided "packet programs" often with answers for sale by inmate clerks. Alcoholics Anonymous, directed entirely by volunteers, has much more merit. Just at Santa Rita, we lost horticulture, building technology, maintenance, and culinary school. The inmate machine shop is now a "Service Center" of offices off-limits to inmates. Pima College no longer offers associates degrees, only certificates in subjects like automotive repair, wastewater management, and computer applications, classes that are only partly filled because they're not available to everyone owing to travel/security restrictions. The department prohibits these programs to all the men at the Rincon and Cimarron Units and all others who can't meet the security criteria.

But Stewart isn't selling the benefits of rehabilitation to the public, only that punishment is a deterrent to crime. I like to say that no one in his right mind would want to go to prison—and that's the problem. Most criminals aren't in their right minds. In my own case, I discussed with the girl I ran away with the possibility of my imprisonment, even asking her if she would visit me in prison. I didn't really believe it would happen, but if it did, I didn't care. I was out of control emotionally, overwhelmed beyond reason. I wanted one thing: the object of my obsession. After my arrest, I actually told my wife that the love affair was worth going to prison for! I've since reconsidered. Now, I have a fuller understanding of how addiction, whether it's drugs, alcohol, sex, or love, erases the threat of consequences, how to many offenders prison may not even enter the mind.

Stewart, however, is convinced punishment is the key to society's criminal justice woes. Since replacing Director Sam Lewis in 1996, he's adopted the "get tough" policy of our former governor-convict Fife Symington. Stewart has removed all weight-lifting equipment from the exercise yards, confiscated personal property and hobby-craft supplies, and locked down once-open units (a necessity for securing men who now have few activities to occupy themselves). He's put an end to Christmas food packages from home, and he's limited phone calls and visitation with family. He's decided inmates are unworthy of clubs and organizations. Currently, what little property is allowed must be purchased—at ADC-set prices—through the inmate commissary, and soon we will all be clothed in Day-Glo orange. Stewart should be pleased with himself. The increase in protests, strikes, and revolts—"riots" the department consistently claims to be "racially motivated"—has given him a way to justify the need for more security and even tougher policies.

Earlier in his editorial, Stewart also wants us to believe that incapacitation, "keeping violent and dangerous individuals away from society," reduces crime. This is curious to me, how Stewart compares *serious crime* rates to incarceration when there is no relationship. We aren't locking up *serious* felons; most felons are drug addicts with mandatory sentences. Last March, the Justice Policy Institute reported that, of the 1.8 million men and women in prison, more than one million of them are nonviolent. "Do Drugs. Do Time" our state vehicle license plates boast. Stewart's editorial is simple propaganda. He misinterprets statistics (crime rates could be down merely because the economy is so healthy) and employs fear tactics to sell his position: prisons will keep you safe—we must continue to build them and to fill them.

I suppose prison, and the deterrent to crime it creates, will keep us safe from criminals like Charles Keating and Fife Symington. And how about Morgan Gramm? CNN reports that police stopped the twenty-one-year-old son of Minnesota Senator Rod Gramm for suspicion of driving under the influence. Officers found beer and more than two ounces of marijuana in his vehicle. The police did not arrest Gramm, however, but drove him home. Instead, they arrested and charged several "juveniles" (children) who were with him.

Prison sensitizes you to injustice as frostbitten fingers forever curse the cold. I don't wish prison on anyone, but stories like this one anger me, stories of blatant favoritism. The Symington effect: laws are written and prisons are built to control the poor and irrelevant. I hear "Morgan Gramm" cases all the time. Recently, a counselor at Echo and onetime parole officer told me about a former prison director whom sheriff's officers would drive home after pulling him over for driving while drunk. Police escort. The privilege of position. Gramm, at the very least, was contributing to the delinquency of minors, but apparently only the minors broke the law. I guess none of the kids had influential parents.

WHAT ANIMAL wears black and white and lives in prison? Answer: Arizona's state mammal, the ringtail. Sheriff Joe Arpaio, who dresses his inmates the same, would be proud. Fifteen minutes before the evening lockdown and count, Steve sticks his face in my cell door window and says I should come outside. I pull on my shoes and follow him onto the front steps of the housing unit. "See it?" he says. "It's poking its head out of that second grill." I look where Steve points, but it's dark and I'm not sure I can see anything. I move down the steps and along the sidewalk toward the grating. A few other men stand in a group, smoking, and unaware of the animal. I stop when I see its head and quickly sit down on the stone wall; it's twenty feet away and staring directly at me. Neither of us moves. I wait. The animal could be a cat, only it looks weasel-like, with a long neck and pointed face, round ears and large, liquid obsidian eyes. When the animal finally slips from under the housing unit through a hole in the grating, I'm surprised at how delicate it looks, and how gracefully it moves, carefully placing its short legs and kitten feet on the gravel. Then I see its tail. It's as long as the ringtail's body and held level with the ground, fluffed like a feather duster and banded with black and white. "Ringtail cat," I say to the men who have joined me. Others walk past without noticing the animal, which silently ducks inside every time someone gets too close. It's nervous, but definitely wants to venture out. More men stop to watch; a crowd gathers. When a friend approaches from the opposite direction, I point to the ringtail and he pauses to toss it pieces of a Snicker's bar. The ringtail reaches out, deftly snatches a bit of chocolate, and then disappears under the trailer.

Later, I lie on my bunk and stare into the swimming darkness overhead, trying to convince myself that what I just saw is real. Ringtails carry emotional weight for me. They are ghosts out of my past. Unwanted images come: vague, black-and-white shadows slipping along the edge of firelight of a winter desert campout; Max, a ringtail I kept in my classroom thirteen years ago; a sleek Siamese cat I gave to my daughter that disappeared within days of my return to prison. My wife says Kasondra and her sisters held hands on the front lawn and prayed to God for Mittens to come home. She didn't, and the girls no longer pray like that, for their pets or for me. Why is this memory coming to me now? Mittens and Max. Max the ringtail was only one of the many wild creatures of my classroom menagerie. Students I'd never had on my roll would visit my classroom before and after school to help me feed and care for the animals. Others simply came to look. The men I teach today do the same, coming to see the shoe-box tarantulas, the tadpoles swirling clockwise in their bucket of muddy water, the forty-some dead, dried, and pasted animals of my objets trouvé. It's ironic, this work I do with the men in prison, the math and science, the show-and-tell with toads and "field trips" for rattlesnakes. Karen says she could never handle me being a teacher again. I understand her distrust. But I've never *stopped* teaching. Only now, I reach out to a few lost convicts, sharing with them my encounters with wildlife, with ringtails.

DONNA LEONE HAMM, a retired judge and wife of former convict James Hamm, and the director of the prison advocacy group called Middle Ground, rebuts Terry Stewart's editorial in the *Arizona Daily Star*. Her words are severe, denigrating. She accuses the prison director of distorting the facts "to fit the interpretation that best serves his own interest, which is building more prisons." She concludes that the Department of Corrections must accept some responsibility "for the kind of people who exit the prisons after serving time," and she suggests that the department facilitate more public involvement, particularly the use of volunteers.

Volunteers: this is what I want to hear. I immediately think of Richard Shelton, who has volunteered in prisons since 1974, and who has made a difference in the lives of hundreds of inmates, including some very successful writers and poets like Jimmy Santiago Baca and William Aberg. Dick's workshops, which cost the department nothing except a space on weekends, have accomplished more toward the rehabilitation of prisoners than all the department's "programs" combined. I wish ADC placed more emphasis on attracting volunteers rather than discouraging their participation. Church groups, lay ministers, Alcoholics Anonymous, Narcotics Anonymous, Prison Fellowship—these volunteer organizations are wonderful, but more from the community is needed. Today, I'm thinking we need counseling help from the mental health community.

Benny, a very large black man and student of mine who talks seriously about running for president of the United States, is in trouble, again. Currently, he's locked inside one of the East Gate cages awaiting transportation to Central Detention Unit. He's railing—his booming voice carrying halfway across the yard. I won't repeat his words—what he wants to do to Lieutenant Trudeau, and to his wife, to his brother, to his dog. Benny just got back to the yard last week after spending sixty days in lockdown for what he says was "a disagreement with the nurse over my meds." He takes powerful psychoactive drugs to control his behavior. I'm guessing, as it often happens here, that the unit pharmacy messed up his prescription, his dosage, or simply failed to order his medication. It's also possible Benny asked the nurse to take him off of his meds because he didn't like being a zombie, a form of control the department keeps within arm's reach. Lieutenant Trudeau, apparently, has an even better approach. He prefers the control of a lockdown cell.

There are men who find ways to hang onto their sanity, with or without drugs. I'm not the only one who watches wildlife. Others work out, walk laps, or play chess. Some play jokes. There's an unknown student in our classroom who is quietly chewing off all the erasers from our pencils. This is the kind of behavior I like to see: subtle, subversive, and comical.

Pat has been focusing his subversive attention on the health unit. He visits there daily for medications to treat his diabetes, high blood pressure, and depression. Pat also has limited use of his legs and depends on crutches for mobility. He's the most intelligent man I've met in prison. A Vietnam veteran, after being wounded during his tour of duty (and losing his closest friend, a friend Pat convinced to join up with him on the "buddy system"), Pat finished college and went to work for IBM as a computer programmer and consultant. He's doing ten years for living with an underage girl.

Today, Pat stopped by my cell on his way to dinner and told me he had a new complaint for the nurse. I was already smiling. Last week he had told the same nurse that his medication had made his wristwatch stop. She stared at him from her window. "Yeah," he said. "I think my meds are causing my joints to swell. Now my watch won't work." He held it to his ear while the nurse examined his prescription. Finally, she said seriously, "I don't know what could be causing it." This time, Pat complained to her about another problem: "These meds aren't helping me with my addiction." "What addiction do you have?" the nurse asked him. Stone-faced, he said, "I'm hooked on phonics." In response, the nurse checked Pat's medical file and then explained, "You have to give your medication a little more time."

PREPARATIONS HAVE BEGUN for the new 4,300-bed prison complex adjacent to Tucson complex. Friends and former students work on a crew with several biologists to tag pineapple cacti, a rare succulent that grows in the desert enclosing the prison. Environmental regulations require that the department transplant any of the cacti located on the new site before construction may begin. The men, walking in a search grid, are finding dozens of the plants, and other rarities like the night-blooming cereus. Today, Joe returns to the yard with three shards of Hohokam pottery the color of rust. I hold in my hand the largest fragment, an irregular hexagon the thickness of skull bone. I wet it with my tongue and pray that the Hohokam will rise up against the new prison. It tastes warm like stone and smells like history.

We don't need any new prisons; we need to change the way we're "helping" people raise their children. The state makes a lousy parent—Arizona consistently rates among the worst places to raise kids. Children can't vote, so what should we expect from a population that's largely retirement age and sequestered in gated communities? It's not hard to understand why building more prisons is the popular solution to Arizona's inadequate child welfare system and poorly funded schools. We rate dead last in the nation for funding education. The greatest proportion of the state budget goes to prisons, not economic security, not health care, not education.

We tag endangered pineapple cacti to save them from the destruction wrought by building prisons that destroy people. Chewing on the irony is like biting down on aluminum foil. Author William Kittredge believes that society has lost its direction, its "privileged long-faced citizens trying to figure out what to do about our global troubles without forgoing their privileges." One result is that we raise fences around ourselves, whether it's voluntary or mandatory. This is the new segregation, and unless we find ways to put an end to it we will never feel safe *without* fences. Kittredge's answer is simple, and profound: "It would help if we could lower our defenses, stop trying to conquer aspects of wildness that frighten us, and admit and follow our passion to care, for nature and for each other."

fall 1999

A Degree in Minor Frustrations

Aftersummer closes with the first Pacific cold front of the season, a rainless tease with wind and clouds and cooler temperatures. This morning, sunlight powders my walking path and the air smells like contentment, something sweet and forbidden. The cottonwoods, bright and robust in their leaves, find all that they need right where they stand. The winter sparrows and blackbirds flit and cheet with all the exuberance of bodies with wings. Sometimes there are days when I sense only my landscape, reading it as I move through it as if the birds and stones were unscrolling letters on printout pages. In prison, where the most privacy you find is under a blanket, solitude, and the peace of mind that comes with it, is an act of willpower.

On my last lap I pass Lieutenant Trudeau, who seems concerned about a breach in the perimeter fence where workers have recently dug a trench for power lines. A voice from the lieutenant's radio wants to know if it's okay to allow a certain inmate back on the yard. The name rings in my ears. "Legend," people call him, is the man who couldn't keep his mouth shut about sex offenders, who couldn't keep his hands off his girlfriend in visitation. A week after I overheard his comments, the prison administration rolled him up and sent him to Central Detention Unit following another incident in visitation, this one inciting some Mexican inmates. They said Legend was disrespecting them by continuing his public display in front of their children. Echo's white leadership, Legend's own "friends," said he was on his own, that they would not get involved in a race war over his behavior. Legend asked to go to PC, protective custody. Now, with the permission of Lieutenant Trudeau, he's coming back to the yard, something almost unheard of, and I'm wondering what the fallout will be.

At lunch, people chew their food and stare when Legend walks in. The chow hall is quieter than normal. I hear the word "snitch" several times. This is all wrong. No one should come back to the same yard after going to PC. If I believed in conspiracies, I'd say Lieutenant Trudeau planned this: a nice prison crisis to justify his existence.

After work, walking back to my cell, I can feel the tension. Groups of men, all Mexicans, stand around. Their faces, hard as the steel concealed beneath their denim jackets, are turned in the same direction. I keep moving to my housing unit, my back to the object of their interest. I don't look until I reach the door, and then I see Legend, standing in the center of a crowd of men.

Lockdown. The yard had just opened after the mandatory count and then closed again before half of us had eaten. No dinner tonight.

Lockdown continues the next morning. Controlled movement to meals: we file out to the dining hall one housing unit at a time, brown shirts stationed at junctures along the way in a show of force. There are turnouts for ADOT workers, and for Solar Industries and the Motor Vehicle Division (telephone answering services), the contracted jobs. But there won't be any school; I'll be in my cell all day and possibly longer.

When the shakedown comes, a short, thick female cop stands outside my door and asks if I've been stripped yet. "No," I tell her, and she leaves to get a male officer. After the visual-exam-of-the-orifices routine, he fingers my books, clothing, and every ball of tissue in my trash can. He takes nothing, not even my contraband toothbrush, plastic containers, or extra socks. He's searching for weapons.

On the second day of lockdown and controlled movement, officers escort us to lunch: cold grilled cheese sandwiches, tomato slices, cucumber salad, pasta, and red Jell-O. The more I learn about Monday's incident, the angrier I get. A sergeant attempted to prevent Legend's return to the yard, knowing he would be in danger. Trudeau also knew this, but overruled the sergeant anyway. This is all too close to the bone for me; my once-fractured ribs ache in sympathy for a man who doesn't deserve any sympathy. A sadistic lieutenant just like Trudeau was responsible for the attack on me at Meadows Unit more than three years ago. Then an officer told me that Meadows Unit is what you get when the department allows incompetent officers to run things. Now, I see the same is true at Echo. People get hurt. In Legend's case, a dozen Mexicans beat him senseless. Trudeau will probably cover up his own involvement, while inflating the seriousness of the incident and his "professional" handling of it. He will explain it as "racially motivated."

IN WARM LIGHT and a stir of breeze, I walk laps along my perimeter—finally, after three days of lockdown. On my first circuit, I see water geysering from four broken sprinkler heads in Kingbird Park. The reclaimed water smells like a neglected fish tank, wet and green, liquid recycled through the bodies of single-celled organisms . . . and the kidneys of men. Blackbirds have discovered the foaming wetland. At least a hundred of them cavort in the rising pools, splashing and fluttering their wings like black flies rejoicing over an oozing wound. It's an indiscriminate gluttony, promiscuous, riotous.

At noon, I skip lunch, opting instead for a peanut butter sandwich, triple-decker, and a cup of coffee. I hear that the cops found fifteen shanks in the area surrounding the tents after scanning the pea gravel with metal detectors. One of the homemade weapons, described as "machete-like," could have severed someone's head from his shoulders. And I thought the department took all the predators off this yard.

Two more sex offenders went to Santa Rita for the evaluation. The unit is no longer a nice place. The men who attacked me several years ago could be at Santa Rita now. I hope they don't join our writers' workshop. I can't understand why the department continues to send sex offenders to Santa Rita for the evaluation, unless someone wants them hurt. A week ago it was Frank and Bill. Friday it was Brent and James. All of them I've known for years: Frank, a dark and broody librarian; Bill, a pleasant clerk and computer expert for the Work Incentive Pay Program; Brent, a former member of the white leadership; and James, a former preacher and the unit plumber who sings with me on Saturday nights at church. Brent and James warned officers that their lives would be in danger at Santa Rita, explaining that their counselors had said these roll-ups wouldn't be neces- sary any longer, that the evaluation didn't require a higher-custody status. Lieutenant Trudeau wouldn't hear it. He has other plans. He wants *all* sex offenders off the yard.

When I call Karen and tell her about the latest moves, she tells me she regrets the decision she made to stay married to me, that if she'd known the outcome of these last twelve years she would have left me. "I don't like what I've become," she explains, her voice shrill, "what prison has done to me." What she means is what being married to a prisoner—to a sex offender— has done to her. I have no argument for her; I can't deny her feelings. But I tell her that whatever she's become, she's been helpful to others, that her growth from naive housewife to cynical professional has changed other people's lives for the better. "I'm sure Cindy wouldn't agree with you," I say, "after all you've done for her." Karen's friend, a mother of two young chil- dren, had been trapped in an abusive marriage. Karen settled her divorce, child support payments, and got her on the state's health care system. She then helped her enroll in college and continues to assist her today with her studies. And then there's the legal work Karen performs without pay for those in need and without resources, the wills she writes, the probate she accomplished for the widow who lived down the street. I could go on.

Some of her work is far-reaching and touches many lives. Several years ago Karen won a lawsuit against Arizona's welfare system that established the present vehicle allotment criteria in accordance with federal guidelines. In 1990, she filed the lawsuit after the Department of Economic Security (DES) canceled her Aid to Families with Dependent Children (AFDC) because her 1986 Toyota Camry, a gift from her aunt, was worth just over the allowed nine thousand dollars. The checks immediately stopped. At the time, Karen was working through college herself, raising our three daughters while living at her parents' home. She needed the money. Selling the car wouldn't have solved the problem. Not only did she need the transportation, but she still would have been ineligible due to her new bank account balance. It was catch-22. This was the ultimate frustration with a system that already penalized her for attending school (grants and loans for tuition and books always slashed her benefits) and humiliated her for remaining married to me (social workers often counseled her to divorce me and find someone else as the only way of deleting herself from the welfare roles). In response, Karen did what she does best: she studied the law. Her research soon uncovered that, not surprisingly, Arizona didn't meet the standards set by the federal government concerning vehicle allotments for AFDC recipients, standards that would have still qualified her for the program had Arizona adopted them. Since most of the budget for AFDC comes from the feds, Karen knew she had a strong argument. First, she exhausted her appeals with DES. Then, with the assistance of Southern Arizona Legal Aid, who had been waiting for just this kind of test case (Karen had "good facts": married to an incapacitated man, three children, college student), she prepared a class action civil lawsuit and filed it in superior court. She won. The state responded by appealing the case (*Lamberton v. the State of Arizona*, rather than the other way around!) to the federal district appellate court. She won again. Her lawsuit became more complicated because now cases from the western region, including

Hawaii, were involved, but again the state appealed and again Karen (et al.) received a judgment in her favor. In the end, after more than six years, the state's appeals ran out. The decision held.

While Karen was arguing her case, she could have requested to continue receiving AFDC payment, but she feared that if she lost in court she would then have to repay the money, and Arizona is relentless at collecting on debts owed. Instead, she relied on the support of her parents and additional college loans (which she still repays today) and the generosity of her church and friends. People she never met but who knew her from the media exposure would mail her checks. Karen would rather owe her family and friends than owe DES. After the civil action settled, did the state send her a single back payment? No. Karen estimates the amount at ten thousand dollars. Also, neither Karen nor Southern Arizona Legal Aid has recouped one cent in legal expenses. The latter probably can't, since a separate ruling now prevents the state-subsidized organization from assisting people in filing actions against Arizona. To this day, DES has never even acknowledged that Karen won the lawsuit. I'm sure it would be different if she had lost.

I say all this because I disagree with Karen's assessment of herself. It's impossible to deny her feelings; however, how many inmate wives can say they've been responsible for setting a legal precedent that affects every welfare recipient in the western United States? What I find most ironic about Karen is that the one thing she truly can control—her attitude about herself (and God)—she lets slide. She finds it difficult to be proud of herself in humiliating circumstances.

IN EARLY DECEMBER, a Pacific frontal storm, only the second of the season, approaches southern Arizona with the possibility of snow in the mountains. Today, frost sheathes the still-flowering bird of paradise. I miss the eighty degree temperatures of November, but this morning a bird I've never seen before in prison calls me out to the exercise track. From my housing unit, I notice a raven-sized shadow slip over the sweat lodge and disappear behind a cottonwood. It's not a raven, I'm sure. I swing around northward, walking slowly along the track with the wind in my face. At first I don't see anything in the cottonwoods, and then suddenly there's a wild thrashing among the upper branches of one of them. The bird whirls and dips, its primaries clawing the air for purchase, feathers the color of a winter marsh, patterned with rotten tules. The American bittern *should* be in some backwater, hidden among the reeds and cattails of the lower Colorado River, where it belongs.

I like to think that these birds, lost or not, come to me because I cannot go to them, that there's some need within me that mysteriously draws them, occasionally, across the path of my eyes. Gary Nabhan says that what we have inside us is always of the larger, wilder world. "Nature is not just 'out there,' beyond the individual." For me, moored to this fenced desert section, every so often nature grants a sprig of wild garnish to what little I have on the inside—in this case, the smell of marshwater held among feathers.

After I return to my cell, my friend Pat says he's harassing the nurse again. This time he told her that one of his ears is colder than the other. She wanted to know if he's taking circulatory medicine. "No," he said. "And it's not always the same ear. Sometimes it's the right, other times it's the left." The nurse had no explanation. "Yeah," he said, gripping his crutches and gritting his teeth to keep from laughing, "I notice it when I wake up in the morning. The ear that's against my pillow is always warmer than my other one." The nurse just stared at Pat and then said finally, "You need to tell the doctor about this."

I love a modicum of payback, trading harassments for harassments. Prison lacks the power to transform, but it can be a provocative teacher for those willing to learn. Among its many curricula, prison offers a degree in minor frustrations. There are innumerable lessons—rules of inconsequence like those concerning smoking in designated, red-lined areas only. There are the policy memos posted on a whim that govern everything from grooming compliance to cell sanitation. And there are the unwritten dictates of each new lieutenant, captain, and deputy warden. (As I write this, an officer wakes my neighbor and orders him to make his bed. It's past nine o'clock. "You can sleep," he says. "You just have to sleep on top of your covers.") I feel ridiculous and petty trying to explain these things to people unfamiliar with prison—like I'm whining—but I can't deny that it affects me. It's as if my feelings about these harassments are inversely proportional to their true gravity. Even molecules have weight and energy. Even dust motes make my eyes scream. Prison turns trivial pricks into an art form. For example, today there's a memo stapled to the bulletin board near the exit of my housing unit. Among other things, it says that the department has lifted the color ban on athletic shoes purchased at the commissary. The inmate "store" is the only place we can buy them now, the only place we can buy anything, from a small approved list of overpriced televisions, radios, and athletic shoes. (No more typewriters or guitars!) And now the shoes no longer have to be solid white. For years, my wife searched the outlets and malls for footwear that satisfied the department's guidelines. When she found a pair, more often than not a property officer rejected the shoes or placed them in contraband. They might have a wedge of gray on their soles. The eyelets might be silver. The stitching might be black, or worse, red or blue, the forbidden colors of rival gangs. This was the department's reasoning for all-white, impossible-to-find athletic shoes, or so it claimed. Gang members advertise their affiliations by the colors on the sneakers. I never believed it from the beginning. The message I—and my wife— always understood from ADC went like this: "We provide cheap state boots. More expensive footwear is unnecessary, undeserved, and we will bury you under frivolous rules if you attempt to supply it." Today's memo only confirms the message. Now that the state will sell us athletic shoes at its own prices, colors, whether or not they announce certain gangs, no longer matter. Apparently, gangs flashing their colors never really concerned the department.

I *am* whining. I also sound trivial. Now I'm thinking that the memo itself is a cruel shot. The men who read it with me were disgusted, angry about it; they saw through it, too. Why tell us the color ban is lifted? Why not just sell the shoes? Inmates like to repeat that what comes around goes around. We're not all passive Buddhists. Payback isn't always as subtle or humorous as Pat's treatment of the nurse.

AT THE AFTERNOON SHIFT CHANGE, the yard closes because of insufficient staff. When this happened last Saturday afternoon the yard didn't open again until the next morning. Then, according to the transportation officer, three staff members failed to show up for work. Echo requires six officers. Officer Reynolds said the problem comes from Lieutenant Trudeau's treatment of his staff. Blue (brown?) flu. He said there's more to come.

Maybe the department shouldn't worry about staff shortages. According to Warden Parin, the average number of new inmates entering the prison system over those released is down from 143 to 110 per month. Since I've been locked up, an average of 567 new inmates each month have come to prison, which means well over 400 former convicts return to the streets statewide every month. It's a flood. But corrections officials *are* concerned; prison population growth is down 23 percent. Already, legislators are questioning the need for our neighboring 4,300-bed complex previously slated to begin construction early next year. Those inconvenient, rare pineapple cacti are no longer in the way of new building programs, but a loss of funding might be. I guess what's needed are some new laws, more mandatory sentences. I love the irony, how economic prosperity adversely affects the prison industry. Conservatives may want to consider cooling off the economy, taking steps to raise unemployment and poverty numbers. And plan better for the future by cutting education spending. This will help with not only imprisoning more people but with finding the right kind of employee to guard them. As it stands, the department is unable to hire enough staff to fully open the multimillion-dollar Sam Lewis complex at Buckeye, leaving a thousand beds empty. One officer in four quits to take another job; more than a thousand have resigned already this year.

I have the solution for the department, one that takes care of both problems—fewer numbers of corrections officers and inmates—at the same time. Yesterday, Pima County sheriff's deputy James Tracy Strickler, a twenty-two-year veteran, was arrested for his part in a drug ring involving other former Pima County deputies, Officer Richard Wayne Parker, the alleged ringleader (who already has a California conviction related to the theft of 650 pounds of cocaine from a police evidence locker) and his half brother, George Michael Ruelas. Officials accused Strickler of conspiracy to possess with intent to distribute cocaine, and also of being involved with several home invasions, wearing a raid uniform and bullet-resistant vest, to steal drugs, appliances, and cash. Also, two weeks ago, Tucson police charged two narcotics officers with driving under the influence. Both were driving department-owned vehicles. Sergeant Kevin Michael Tennyson collided with a tree and left the scene, attempting to flee from deputies investigating the accident. He refused field sobriety tests. Police also pulled over Officer Jaime Aviles for speeding and charged him with DUI. His breath analysis registered 0.112; Arizona's legal limit is 0.100. Then there's the case of Pima County Court Justice David Mark Anderson, whom officers arrested after he crashed into a street sign while driving home from a bar. Deputies discovered a warrant for his arrest for missing a court date concerning an August hit-and-run. "You don't know who you're messing with," Anderson shouted at the arresting officers. "I will pin your badges to your asses, every one of you!"

Now these are the kind of people corrections can use. I suggest that the courts sentence problem cops and judges to prison where, with their training and expertise in law enforcement and criminal justice, they could serve as inmate corrections officers, counselors, and even "trustee" deputy wardens. With top wages of fifty cents an hour, the department cuts its overhead, not only in salaries but also with the cost of training new officers. This could work. There are bad cops everywhere. Chicago, Philadelphia, New York. Los Angeles has a surplus of dirty cops, enough to loan to other states. Let them reform themselves while they reform the prisons.

THERE WILL BE NO creative writing workshop this morning owing to another staff shortage. No one is available to transport us to Santa Rita. No one is available to guard the inmates at Echo. More brown flu.

I do love to see the cracks developing. This is the fourth staff shortage in two weeks. Pettiness is at an all-time high at Echo. Yesterday, Captain Patterson and Lieutenant Trudeau went on a mission, searching the kitchen, kitchen workers, and their cells, cleaning out grease traps. It was the great Echo Unit spork hunt. Inmates won trips to the cages, write-ups, and lost jobs—all for stealing the plastic spoon-fork hybrids. The cops are experts at finding major significance in minor sins.

Recently, one of our mentally ill students was handcuffed, pepper-sprayed, and hauled off the yard because of an incident involving his headphones. Carlos loved his Walkman radio; I never saw him without it. Unfortunately, listening to loud Mexican music interfered with his school-work, more, even, than his medication. Al Benz warned Carlos several times to remove his headphones, and then he wrote an incident report. "Later, I had second thoughts," Benz told me. "I was going to tear it up, and I told Sergeant Acuna not to punish him because of his mental state."

This would have ended it, except that Sergeant Abt saw the paperwork. There's a reason his own staff call him a "kick-starter." Abt ordered Carlos to report to disciplinary where he confiscated his Walkman. Carlos immediately lost control of himself and attacked two officers, punching one in the face and kicking another in the groin. The cops threw him to the ground, cuffed his arms behind his back, and pepper-sprayed his face. Carlos continued to rage, screaming obscenities as more officers rushed him. With monofilament lines of mucus streaming from his mouth and nose, the cops jerked him to his feet, hoisting his arms high behind his back in a horrible contortion.

Carlos is in lockdown at the Cimarron Unit now. There, the health provider will adjust his medication, and no one will bother him about his listening to music.

AT LAST the earth begins to lean toward summer. Tonight, on the first evening of the winter solstice, I take a break from work with a few interested students to watch the moonrise. The moon is full and at perigee, the place in its orbit nearest the earth, an event that hasn't occurred for 130 years. The moon should appear both brighter and larger as it unsaddles itself from the Rincon Mountains. The cold air condenses my breath, which hazes my vision. Jupiter and Saturn dominate my zenith. Five minutes after six. Crepuscular mountains release the moon's pupil-less eye.

ON CHRISTMAS EVE I dress in sweats and wear my radio and headphones to walk the perimeter in the darkness where I can be alone with the wind and evening lawn bunnies and allow a selection of Christmas music to blur my eyes. The music warms my ears, shuts out the weather's distractions, and others. I taste the ocean through clenched teeth.

Christmas for me amounts to a dozen or so cards, and I think about Melissa's, a card in the shape of her cat, RainCloud. In it, she shared a

"Christmasy" metaphor with me, writing, "My dreams are filled with color as hot cocoa fills a mug." My mom writes that Kasondra is "quite the young lady," wearing the concert dress she hemmed for her, the heels, the pearl necklace and earrings she bought for her fifteenth birthday tomorrow. Kasondra's teacher invited her to sing with her high school chorus, which had three public performances with the Tucson Symphony Orchestra last weekend. On Friday, Karen, her parents and sister, and my mom, were all part of the audience. I should have been there as well. Instead, I read about it in a letter, those coveted, bittersweet pages of ink and reality that only magnify how impotent and alone prison makes you feel.

I walk laps in the darkness for two hours, until my legs and my emotions are spent. Afterward, I burn homemade cinnamon incense and roll three bean and squeeze-cheese burritos for dinner, eating them in the glow of my television.

ON NEW YEAR'S EVE, the prison administration granted us a special visiting day, and Karen stayed through most of it, even though we argued over our usual painful topics. She looked good in her cowboy boots, black wrangler jeans, and beige pullover. At the end of our visit, she caught me by surprise by grabbing my collar, pushing me against a wall, and pressing her lips on mine. It's been too long since she kissed me like that.

Fourteen years ago I began arranging my life and calling it fate. Now, I understand that event will always be the lens through which I see myself, but that is all. Karen, however, carries the burden of 1986 as if that one year has defined all others, and has defined her. Her wounds still leak. Every day now is tied to every day then: anniversaries and birthdays, vacations and holidays, equinoxes and solstices. Karen doesn't send me Father's Day cards. She won't speak of our wedding anniversary or even respond to my letters and cards concerning it. I'm teaching myself not to care so much. This is part of my New Year's resolution, even though I don't make New

Year's resolutions. The time has come to give myself a break. No more begging for forgiveness. And I need to give Karen a break, too.

At 9:30 PM, after being on lockdown for three hours due to the Y2K computer-malfunction scare, I'm having a late dinner with my neighbor, Darrel. On television, the new year arrives at every major city circling the planet while we eat super nachos. This is Darrel's concoction, a mixture of roast beef, rehydrated beans, summer sausage, Spam, jalapeños, and squeeze cheese, heated inside a plastic bag dumped into a tub of hot water (the administration disposed of our microwave ovens a while ago), and poured atop a pile of tortilla chips. Not a bad way to start the so-called new millennium.

ON THE SECOND DAY OF JANUARY it rains, the first moisture since the monsoons ended one hundred days ago. I walk laps as the sun collapses on the horizon, throwing bloody filaments into the sky's underbelly, and coyotes rhapsodize beyond the perimeter.

Except for a few glitches, the year begins well. Jailed inmates in Italy had one hundred years added to their sentences. The Y2K bug has affected the Work Incentive Pay Program (WIPP) computers, fouling up the gate logs necessary for inmates to travel off-site to jobs and school, travel that involves three-quarters of the inmate population. Pat, my computer-guru friend, is very pleased with himself. He predicted the problem two years ago and was in the process of correcting it when Lieutenant Trudeau and Sergeant Abt accused him of "having too much power" and removed the computers from Labor Pool office. Pat wrote all the programs that facilitate Echo Unit's operations. "They're doing it all by hand now," he tells me, "and they wanted me to fix the problem. I said I wouldn't do it." I can't believe they'd even ask him, after all their accusations of complicity with Officer Macy's computer programming side business. The lieutenant thinks Pat is a security risk, and now he has a real security problem. Someone could escape.

winter 2000

Compassionate Conservatism and Cruelty

In his essay "The Common Life," Scott Russell Sanders writes, "In our common life we may find the strength not merely to carry on in the face of the world's bad news, but to resist cruelty and waste." Simply surviving what life brings our way is not enough. Resistance is necessary because the end never justifies the means. And still, there's more required. I could have chosen to deal with prison by reaction, adjusting my thinking and behavior as necessary, remodeling my character to fit this place. But I resisted. I resisted the racism, the ignorance and self-serving attitudes, the hatred and violence . . . in most cases. I don't pretend to always get it right. Sadistic cops take up way too much space in my head. Fortunately, many officers are decent people, men and women who understand how easily they could be wearing blue instead of brown. I resisted the nature of this place, the kind that seeks to degrade me as a person, to institutionalize me. And I continue to do so. I won't wait in lines. Not for meals. Not for commissary. Not for toilet paper. Waiting in line is bad enough when you're free, but to have this dead time in prison is intolerable. I resist the waste of life, my own and others. It's why I write, why I teach. And, it's in this that I see more is required. I could have chosen to deal with prison by reaction. Instead, I chose creation. I chose to carry on, to resist along the way, and to give something back.

Today, I'm enjoying some wonderful shirtsleeve January weather. Blackbirds congregate with cowbirds along the fence top; the cowbirds, those unwanted nest parasites, redeem themselves with song.

My one jimsonweed survives the occasional harvesters. Although it no longer flowers, the plant continues to push out heavy green leaves; most of its thorny pods have loosed their seeds, either naturally or by manipulation. Recently, when a friend asked me about the availability of jimsonweed for his back pain, I showed him this plant.

I feel differently about drug users now than when I first came to prison. Their revolving-door recidivism bothered me, mostly because I knew that if I had the same opportunity I would never come back. The department seems to parole those who are primed for return. Now, however, I realize that these people can't help themselves without treatment. Prison becomes part of the culture, an acceptable consequence. For some, prison is their dope house. I know men who visit it on a regular basis, four or five times even. Recently, even America's drug czar has begun to question the effectiveness of prison for drug addicts. "It costs too much, and it doesn't work," Barry McCaffrey says, explaining that it costs $26,000 a year to lock up someone, while the most expensive drug program costs $18,000 a year, with many programs ranging from $2,000 to $3,000. "If you examine the reason why people are incarcerated, you'll find that somewhere between 50 and 80 percent have a chronic drug abuse problem," McCaffrey says. What a waste. One-fourth of all the prisoners in the world are locked up in the United States. We find it so much easier to bury these people, whatever the cost, than to help them. I suppose the problem is too complicated. It weighs too much on our conscience, so we pretend to have a solution. For my friend, society finds it best to simply keep returning him to prison. I find it best to simply show him the jimsonweed.

When I return to the housing unit, two cops are searching Pat's cell and boxing up his property. The department's internal investigators (INI) have confiscated his typewriter and a box of files. Pat is in lockdown at another unit. Another officer has escorted Officer Macy off the yard. I'm thinking there's a relationship. The officer working our housing unit says

Pat had computer disks and pages of personal information—social security numbers, addresses, financial records—on private citizens. I'd already seen these computer printouts. Pat was using them to correct a glitch in a computer program, a program that an automobile dealership in Tucson uses to keep track of its customers. Officer Macy, whose wife works for the company, had asked for Pat's help. Now, I'm wondering if I'll ever see Pat again.

LIKE ANNIE DILLARD, I, too, live in "tranquillity and trembling." Tonight, I walk the perimeter in my T-shirt as the stars form constellations: Orion high in the east, Cassiopeia higher in the north. I'm thinking about the priority package that plugged my mailbox: my book *Wilderness and Razor Wire* has arrived. Kirsten, my editor, writes: "I must say, I believe this is the proudest author copy I have ever sent out." She has always been a believer in me. Two years ago Mercury House accepted the manuscript; three years ago I penciled the first essay, "Of Swallows and Doing Time," at Santa Rita after I returned to prison. The book is a culmination of ten years of writing in this place. I try to believe that finally holding my book in my hands makes it worth the experience. One thing is certain: *Wilderness* wouldn't exist had not the appellate court overturned my release and sent me back to prison. Those three justices deserve some credit.

The lights of Manzanita, the women's facility, also form constellations on the western horizon of my perimeter circuit. A voice on the unit's loudspeaker plows across the creosote, ordering the women to return to their dorms. The department has plans to move the women to the Perryville complex in a few months and refit Manzanita as a medium-custody prison for men. I occasionally read letters from the women in the op-ed pages of Tucson's newspapers, letters of complaint mostly. Health care is a prominent issue, along with the poor quality of food and living conditions. Sometimes there's mention of other abuses. Last month, a federal judge dismissed the Department of Justice's lawsuit that accused the Arizona Department of Corrections of violating the rights of female inmates. ADC agreed to provide a half-day of in-service training for the staff in dealing with female prisoners, so the DOJ dropped its lawsuit alleging that male corrections officers had repeatedly raped and sexually assaulted at least fourteen women, that male officers watched the women as they dressed, showered, and used the toilet, that male officers ordered women to dance nude.

PAT HAS RETURNED to Echo Unit after three weeks in lockdown. He's assigned to the tents and still wears the requisite orange jumpsuit. He tells me that the rumor is true: Officer Macy has resigned. "They had nothing on me," he says, "which has Sergeant Abt's panties in a twist. Instead, they wrote me up for corresponding with an ex-inmate and made it a major violation." I'm surprised that this is against the rules since many people here write former inmates, myself included. "They'll make the write-up stick so they can transfer me off the yard. I'm going to Buckeye."

Buckeye, or more precisely, the new Samuel E. Lewis complex, is one of the lonely, isolated places like Douglas and Winslow that corrections administrators use to relocate their "problems," both staff and inmates. Pat's situation bothers me. This is his first write-up in seven years, and I've seen many other inmates receive a string of violations resulting in raised institutional scores but no transfers. But Pat will go to Buckeye with a major rule violation on his record, one that may—because he's a sex offender—raise his public risk score to predator status and send him to the state hospital upon his "release."

In the afternoon, two more friends, James and Brent, return to Echo after their transfer to Santa Rita more than two months ago for the predator evaluation. Neither one of them fit the criteria—no violence, no weapons, no multiple offenses—but the department still found it necessary to endanger their lives. I talk to Brent on the exercise track where he has stripped down to his shorts to lay some sunlight against his tattooed skin. He wears a golden nipple ring. He says that they ate a lot of meals in their cell, and he advises me that when my turn comes I should refuse placement there and go to lockdown instead. "The place is full of lifers who would kill you as soon as look at you," he says.

Brent is at the end of his ten-year sentence, a survivor of the Cimarron Unit where he fell into an Aryan gang and eventually earned his way into the leadership, which is rare for a sex offender. His tattoos—two full sleeves, chest and back, of black designs including spider webs, flames, and a girlfriend's portrait—are permanent symbols of those years. Although Brent no longer involves himself in what he calls "that craziness," his former gang affiliation continues to gain him respect from inmates. I've seen him use this respect to keep people out of trouble, protecting them from extortion or retrieving their stolen property. Brent is the Robin Hood of sex offenders.

Brent and James's return to Echo means that they both passed the predator evaluation, both judged unlikely to commit another crime. "We refused to talk to the psychologist," Brent tells me. "He already had all the information he needed in our files, and we weren't about to give him anything to use against us."

In a few months, the Department of Corrections will release Brent and James to society, rather than release them to the predator ward of the state hospital. Others haven't been as fortunate. Recently, a jury in Tucson decided that Paul Frankovitch, a former offender with a long history of crimes, should be confined because of the likelihood that he would commit another crime. Prosecutors, relying on the new predator law, claimed Frankovitch "has a mental disorder . . . that predisposes him to commit sexual acts to such a degree to render him a danger to the health and safety of others." The jury agreed and a judge ordered him confined at the state hospital "to receive care, supervision and treatment until his mental disorder is so changed that he is no longer a threat to public safety." So this is where he waits, with about seventy other men—many of whom I've known over the years—who have already served their time in prison. Each year, men like Ray or Dennis or Bill all file petitions to the courts, asking to be released but being denied. Imprisonment not rehabilitation seems to be the intention of our legislature. The American Psychiatric Association thinks so, saying that its profession is being used to "preventively detain a class of people for whom confinement rather than treatment is the real goal."

It would be an understatement to say that few people sympathize with sex offenders. We don't have many advocates: defense lawyers (on principle), mothers, and a rare wife. My children are the most forgiving. I'm not complaining. Anyone who knows me understands that I insist on consequences for behavior, whatever these are and however lasting. I deserved to do time, even twelve years. Still, I understand that for many people no amount of regret is adequate or punishment severe enough. In his essay "*Lolita*, my Mother-in-Law, the Marquis de Sade, and Larry Flint" from *Commentary*, Norman Podhoretz says these "monsters" receive shorter sentences than they deserve. "If it were up to me," he writes parenthetically, "they would either be executed or put away for life without possibility of parole, instead of being released after a few years with nothing to stop them from preying again but a sadly ineffective Megan's Law." This is the prevailing attitude, and it's surprisingly clichéd, coming from such a provocative essayist. I hear it everywhere, all the time: from the news media and network talk shows, from crime dramas and documentaries, from television personalities, politicians, and ordinary people—some of them friends. They all rub my face in what I did. It's the same judgment of even the white supremacists in prisons across the country, including the men who beat me senseless at Meadows Unit several years ago. I later learned that those three men originally intended to kill me but relented because my crime was consensual—Podhoretz may not have been as kind. The truth is, in my emotional state at my arrest, I would have accepted an execution. When my public defender said he had no defense for me, that I should take the state's plea bargain of twelve years flat and start looking forward to watching my grandchildren grow up, I asked for the death penalty. "That's not available," he said, as if he had already considered it for me.

Nothing in life is simple, and Podhoretz admits this, although he leans toward advocating a broad net of law, even if it means catching and killing a few trash fish. I hope we might at least allow the final authority to rest on our judges, rather than on the perfunctory anachronisms our mandatory sentencing laws are making them.

MATT, my mentally ill friend and chess-playing former student, stops by my cell and tells me he has something to show me. "What?" I ask, cautiously. He's more nervous than usual; his face is white, the pupils of his eyes pinpricks. He unfastens his pants and begins to drop them and I shout, "Stop!" "No," he complains. "I want you to see these sores." Matt has crossed the line, and I've had enough of his hypochondria. Every day it's something new: rashes and hives, throat lesions, kidney, heart, brain disease, lung infections. Lately, his scalp is too tight. I tell him: "I will not look at the pimples on your butt."

Two summers ago, I taught fractions to Matt for several months before giving up and convincing him that he had learned them. Fortunately, he fell under the sixth-grade literacy requirement and not the eighth-grade, or he would still be in school today. For a while he worked on the trash crew, then as a bathroom porter, then in the kitchen, for ADOT, for landscape ... and finally as part of the general labor pool, cigarette-butt chaser when the WIPP coordinator ran out of suitable positions. His mouth always seems to get him in trouble because thinking first is impossible for him. Matt's doing two years for criminal damage and trespass for breaking into his former girlfriend's apartment to retrieve his clothes.

Next month, Matt will go home to his parents and to his young daughter whom his parents are raising. I'm wondering if he'll make it. He's grown more and more psychotic since, six months ago, he accidentally drank reclaimed water from a hose, or so he says. He insists that the treated sewage is the cause of his symptoms, and he's convinced the health unit to perform blood labs and to take throat cultures. The results are always inconclusive. Now, I watch him as he fingers his uvula in front of my mirror, scaring himself when the fleshy appendage sticks to the back of his throat. Matt thinks he's dying, that he won't survive the night. He phoned his mom earlier today and told her so, using up his two-call limit, and then spent the afternoon in one of the East Gate cages for threatening a counselor when she wouldn't allow him to use her phone to call home. Tonight, as he's done recently, Matt will probably sleep on the floor outside the door of the control room, waiting for the cop on graveyard to locate a nurse.

MY THIRTEEN-YEAR-OLD DAUGHTER MELISSA spent yesterday at the capitol having brunch with legislators, former governor Rose Mofford, and Governor Jane Hull. Melissa was among about a dozen students who won a statewide poetry contest focusing on an Arizona theme. She won first place in her junior high school division with her long poem "Arizona Deserts," which begins: "Creosote sings its scent to me / the desert stills under the warm touch of the sun / here the wind has no purpose / except to buffet and pound on the silent rocks / shaping their solid bodies."

Karen told me that during the event Rose Mofford mentioned to her that she has much to be proud of. *You have no idea*, Karen thought. We talked about the many ironies in our lives, how our youngest daughter writes a poem glorifying Arizona's wilderness, winning an award ceremony with Arizona's governor, while her father sits in an Arizona prison. No one has any idea. Many children of prisoners follow the example of their parents. I've taught literacy to a father and son together in the same class.

But here's what's really crazy: Poetry contests aside, recently our Republican governor Jane Hull spoke about Arizona's public schools, listing problem after problem. She was aware of them all, but, she said, she would not increase funding for education. Arizona would remain dead last in the country for school spending. The prisons bulged at the news.

"IF YOU WANT TO KNOW MORE ABOUT THE RAVEN," Barry Lopez writes in *Desert Notes*, "bury yourself in the desert so that you have a commanding view of the high basalt cliffs where he lives. Let only your eyes protrude." This is the kindest euphemism for doing time in prison I've ever heard. It's what I do: bury myself in this place with only my eyes exposed. I watch, and I record what I see: the wildlife, the people, and I write about the insanity.

I wait with John and Tom at East Gate for transportation to the writing workshop at Santa Rita. Last week, the men in the workshop told me that Sergeant Murguilla, the sadistic cop I wrote about in the "Killer Bees" chapter of *Wilderness* (I had changed his name to "Basura"), is no longer employed by the Department of Corrections. They said he walked off the job in his uniform and badge and hasn't returned, and that he's now working at a local nightclub as an exotic male dancer. No way! Yes, they insisted. He's going by the stage name of "Flash." He must have needed the uniform and badge for part of his act.

The morning is cold, even in my sweatshirt. My fingers are as pale as slugs. But I'm not as uncomfortable as the men in the East Gate holding cells. Matt, my psychotic friend, has been locked inside a cage since 5:00 AM, without a jacket or sweatshirt. Matt won't be at my door tonight. He won't be waking me up after midnight and spitting into his hand to show me his foaming saliva. Two weeks ago the cops rolled him up after he told them he intended to cut himself open to find out what was wrong with him. He then produced a razor blade to prove it. They shipped him to

Rincon Nine, the health unit for the terminally ill and medically unmanageable.

Matt has lost at least forty pounds. His psychosis has been growing every day as he adopts diseases from the most minor suggestion. Recently, he began telling people he had syphilis after he overheard me reading its symptoms to a few of my students. He'll cough up mucus, claiming it's bloody lung tissue, for anyone who'll indicate concern. Once, he gave himself a rectal exam and later asked me what would cause internal swelling.

Rincon Nine returned Matt to Echo after a day or two of observation. He won't be visiting me tonight because today is his release day, when he'll become someone else's problem. In one final hurrah for all the grief he's caused concerning his wild medical complaints, the cops have rolled him up before dawn, feeding him a cold breakfast on a tray. He's nervous and paces in small circles. His short-cropped blond hair is nearly as white as his face. He tucks his arms halfway into the front of his jeans. "Do you think they'll put a detainer on me?" he asks me after I tell him to take care of himself. Even now, he doesn't believe the department will let him go home.

After nearly three years of prison, Matt is leaving three months early on his TR, or "temporary release" date. The department, at the discretion of the director, allows this form of early release during times of prison overcrowding, which has been the case for the past decade. Not everyone gets one, however. TRs aren't automatic, even if the date appears on your time computation, as it does on mine. Repeat offenders don't get TRs, nor do those with discipline problems. Nor do sex offenders. The present trend is for sex offenders to serve all of their time, and maybe more.

Last week, two more sex offenders—they travel in pairs now—left Echo Unit for higher custody. The roll-ups continue. Sex offenders don't get TRs, but, once the department does release them, they do get their faces, names, and addresses posted on the Internet. Arizona's new Web site lists more than ten thousand registered sex offenders, a convenience the media encourages people to use to find out about their neighbors. Occasionally, local television stations send their news anchors out into the streets to knock on doors and check up on these men during live broadcasts. The voyeurism is very sensational. "You know why they created that Web site?" an inmate recently asked me, after telling me the home address of a friend released six months ago. Doug feels that my friend disrespected him, and he still has serious issues about it. "It's so people can find them and harass them," he answers. "You think they're going to call the cops? The cops don't care." My wife has a similar opinion. Karen says they made the Web site "so your girlfriend can find you."

Personally, I think law enforcement shouldn't discriminate, especially since sex offenders as a class have a lower recidivism rate than the general prison population—you won't see pictures of released murderers passed out in neighborhoods. According to a 1998 analysis by the Research Unit of the Arizona Department of Corrections, of the 2,444 sex offenders released in the previous ten years, 509 or about 21 percent returned to prison. (This is less than half of the recidivism rate for all prisoners.) Not all had committed new crimes, however. About 7 percent were parole violators. "While sex offenders returned to prison for a variety of new crimes," the report says, "78 or 3.2 percent returned for a new felony sex offense." Three percent. That's lower than the rate of released murderers who kill again.

I realize that it only takes one, one repeat offender, and then the whole world comes apart. I wouldn't want it to happen to my family. But I also realize that justice must be tempered with mercy. Zero tolerance is an Old Testament god, and we no longer live under that dispensation. Justice *and* mercy, understanding that having compassion also means being willing to suffer grievously when compassion allows further tragedy.

I think the state should create a Web site that posts the names and addresses, crimes and mug shots of everyone released from our prisons, all four hundred or so of us dumped out of these places every month. Then people would *really* know who their neighbors are, and possibly show more concern about what goes on in prison, what kind of person the place produces.

THIS MORNING on Ash Wednesday the yard finally opens; we've been locked down since Sunday night. I've said before that prisons exist on the margins, places of adaptation and change where something new might evolve out of the muck. Prisons are like islands. Species either evolve or they go extinct. In his book *Systematics and the Origin of Species*, Ernst Mayr describes what he calls "genetic revolutions" that drive evolution more rapidly and are more apt to occur in small isolated populations. Evolution here is a fact, and I think evolutionist Stephen Jay Gould would be pleased to know that prisons prove his theory of punctuated equilibrium: we endure long periods of boredom, punctuated by rare explosions of drama.

Like last weekend's drama. An inmate broke into the contraband storeroom and walked away with a number of televisions and radios, appliances he promptly sold to anyone who wanted them. Sunday evening the cops discovered that the inmate porter assigned to Building 68, which comprises the commissary, property room, accountability and disciplinary offices, had broken through the ceiling tiles in his porter closet and crawled into the other areas. Property was missing. The administration ordered a lockdown and called in the Tactical Support Unit, which enthusiastically began searching the housing units and tents for contraband, checking property numbers with paperwork and rolling up suspects. Before TSU arrived on my run, televisions began to appear in the laundry room trash, unclaimed.

Monday morning a petite brunette woman knocked on my door and asked me to stand outside. *What? No strip-search?* She took my ID and began comparing my ADC number with those numbers etched into my television, radio, lamp, electric razor. When she got to my guitar case, she lifted it and asked, "What's in here?" "It's a machine gun, Charise," another officer, who had just appeared at my door, replied. "You should have been a blond." I laughed, but not too hard.

She took nothing. My contraband Lakewood fan and Coleman ice chest, two items I had illegally bought from other inmates, sanded off their numbers, and scratched in my own, were safe. By Monday evening the shakedowns and investigative roll-ups were completed.

This morning, I learn of more punctuation to our boredom. Because of the break-in, I can't be trusted. The teacher's aides may no longer work mornings in the education building without supervision. No more grading papers and preparing lessons before school begins. Evolution doesn't happen without change.

I stand at the top of the stairs above the exercise track at the western limit of Echo yard. The sky is a flat matte blue, hard against my retinas, Annie Dillard's "hollow, hammering sky." The air holds a warm, roselike scent of male monarch wings, and in every direction, on every mountain range, the snowline rests exactly at eye level. Sunlight is a balm that seeps into my cold-stiffened joints and muscle.

Winter's ashen thumbprint of mortality has faded. A dove carefully selects nesting material, testing every twig for just the right strength and flexibility, before lifting it to the beak of his mate, who, in turn, threads each into her nest. She regards his meticulousness with a flare of feathers and cloaca. Ravens, too, feel the rising heat. Couplets ride the thermals in tandem, spiraling upward and then falling upon themselves as if clipped together at the pelvis. I believe that spring's bird promiscuity might embarrass even Nabokov.

spring 2000

Civilization and Sex

Vivian Gornick, a writer who taught me the value of nature as metaphor, hates the desert. This she made clear while teaching at the University of Arizona, where she endured one semester each year away from her home in New York City. Gornick writes for the *Village Voice* and the *New York Times* on subjects that include women and feminism, people and politics—subjects more worthy, I think she would say, of literature. She did tolerate my nature essays, but she liked to remind me that civilization only happens in the city.

Since what Gornick means by "city" translates to "New York City," I might suppose that what she defines as "civilization" is actually American society, that minority part of the planet whose citizens use up the majority of its resources. America is a grotesque, insatiable animal. Like the mound-building termite, a species related to cockroaches and locusts, it is a colonizer of landscapes, with its obese, pulsating queen that sucks up raw materials at one end and spews out more colonists at the other. These offspring, blind and mindless castes of workers and soldiers, exist to serve the expanding colony. Those who lose their usefulness, or worse, those genetically tweaked who don't conform, live as outcasts on the fringe of the society.

This is the underside of our civilization, a kind of subconscious eddy of people, with all their spooled emotions and thoughts, who go about their lives without our awareness—mostly. On occasion, elements of the subconscious leak into the conscious and, like a recurring dream, leave an impression, a glimpse of stark reality lurking within. Poets, philosophers, and artists know that often profound and useful ideas rise from the subconscious, but civilized society prefers to forget, to plug up the holes. We have a moment of fascination, of voyeuristic curiosity, when something new and horrific presents itself, and then we put it away. The subconscious is a convenient place to keep that which we wish to ignore, those parts of ourselves too shameful to deal with. The parts we feel guilty about. Or fear. As this country's rivers and oceans have become places to conceal and deny our environmental transgressions, society's subconscious—our prison system—is where we dump and forget our human transgressions. But prisons are not some backwater region of endless capacity. From our prisons issues a slow, continuous, copious release.

But as prisons seem convenient for society, they are even more convenient for prisoners. Being locked away from society, being dehumanized, we don't have to face the consequences of our crimes—the people we hurt. The sixteenth-century essayist Montaigne writes that there is "a great favor for a criminal, to be so execrable that justice deems it unjust to touch and see him: free and saved by virtue of the severity of his condemnation." Prison frees us from our guilt. There is no remorse. Instead of looking for fault within ourselves, we transfer the blame to all the external tangents to whom we've defaulted control of our lives: judges, lawyers, law enforcement, and the Department of Corrections. Rather than repentant offenders, we become bitter victims. And then the prison gates open.

Today's latest form of dehumanization arrives on a flatbed truck. The driver, a "grayshirt" support staff member, waves to me as I walk past on the track. "Hey, Lamberton!" he shouts. I recognize him as a former property officer from my early years at Santa Rita, Mr. Brooks, who now works at Complex Intake and Processing. I circle around the yard and find him behind the property room supervising the off-loading of dozens of crates: new clothing. The time has come for the exchange of wardrobe: prison blues for institutional orange. If there was any doubt about inmates being nameless, faceless ciphers, there won't be any longer. At least in blue jeans and chambray shirts we appeared presentable as a labor force—my father-in-law wears the same kind of clothes to work in. But I suppose that was the problem: we looked too much like real people. Now, dressed in the orange polyester elastic-waist-banded pants and pullover smocks, both stenciled with the black block letters "ADC," there's no question about it. We are the dregs of society, and we are as visible as neon signs. My wife and daughters have already warned me that they'd rather not see me like this, would rather not visit me. Karen is really upset about our new outfits, clothing styles once reserved only for discipline problems. She wants to know how the department expects me to function after my release.

"I hate to see you here," I tell Brooks, pointing to the crates, "with all this." "Hey," he says, and we shake hands. "Look at all the gray hair. I knew you when you were just a kid." Brooks could use a little of my gray hair, but he looks like I remember him: short, balding, with the standard midriff paunch that must be a requirement for graduation from the academy. He asks about my family and wants to know how I'm doing. I mention my book. "You didn't say anything bad about me?" "Not this time," I say. He tells me that giving up his badge was the best decision he ever made. "Should have done it long ago." I sympathize, but can't help thinking that his gain is our loss. Good officers like Brooks are rare, and we need them to balance the sadists and the idiots, the attitudes and the incompetents who always seem to rise in the ranks. We need them to attenuate the orange glow.

HYPOCRISY IS INHERENT with a society that hides its dark side "out of sight, out of mind" in prisons and pretends it doesn't exist. Sometimes I think people are completely oblivious to the double standards. This morning, I'm amazed by the suggestive chatter of Christine and Alex, two local radio personalities, who are talking about the Ted Nugent concert last night in Tucson. They're interested in contacting a woman who peeled off her top up close to the stage. "Double-Dee," Alex calls her. They have another woman on the phone. She suspects that Double-Dee is a coworker. They laugh. Christine wants to get her on the air. Alex wants her picture and asks his listeners to send photos of her if they have any; he will pay for them. The caller says Double-Dee was at the concert with her young son.

Last week the news was about Mardi Gras, radio and television reporting on the rampant spectacle of revelers, mostly women, flashing to the crowds on the streets of New Orleans. The news anchors were all smiles. Mentioning that the displays are illegal comes only as an aside, if at all. Computer-blurred pictures left little to the imagination. Beads? They wanted to know. How *do* you get those beads?

I'm no prude. Not even close. But I know people here who are doing time for indecent exposure, exhibitionists who can't control their behavior in public, men like Dave who would parade naked in front of his living room window as people passed by. Or Brian, who liked to invite an acquaintance to his house and then remove his clothes just before his guest arrived. Or Andy, who, high on drugs, stripped off all his clothes and ran down the middle of a street in rush-hour traffic. These men will have to register as sex offenders with the county sheriff wherever and whenever they move, for as long as they live. They will have to renew their driver's licenses every year. They will have their faces, crimes, and home addresses posted on the Internet. But the television reporters don't mention this. Instead, we laugh at what we see at Mardi Gras and rock concerts.

George Eliot, the nineteenth-century English novelist who was not a stranger to social ills herself, said that even the quickest of us walk about well padded with stupidity. My own padding is bulletproof. But even before my unutterably stupid choices that led to my crime, I was ignorant of society's secret gated communities. Driving through Florence, Arizona, with a vanload of students on a field trip, I often pointed to the prison and joked about it being my alma mater.

This kind of ignorance—my ignorance—serves the prison system. Ignorance of the abuses of funds, abuses of people. What the public doesn't know about prison won't hurt them. Who needs meddlers and oversight committees? Just keep the money coming. The Department of Corrections in Arizona, and I imagine in every state, prefers, even fosters, a well-padded public. And, there are ways to sew up the weakest seams: humiliate the wives, frighten the parents, children, and volunteers, and they will all go away. Who wants to associate with criminals anyway?

I prefer to be uncivilized. For the most part, Gornick's cities—the seat of our "civilized" society—have made America's prisons necessary. Laws come from cities. Hypocritical laws. For example, in Washington DC, the U.S. Congress—a group of 535 people with an extraordinary number of arrests and indictments for crimes ranging from spousal abuse (29), fraud (7), bad checks (19), assault (3), drugs (14), and drunk driving (84)—is presently cranking out hundreds of new laws designed to keep the rest of us in line, us being, apparently, the poor and uninfluential. The United States locks up more than two million men and women, the greatest incarceration rate per capita in the world. We shouldn't call our flag the Stars and Stripes: we should call it the Stars and *Bars*.

Being uncivilized doesn't mean being lawless but being without law. It means being self-governed by the Golden Rule, which has no vague moral codes and penal systems. It means living lightly on the earth, having perhaps a contradictory lifestyle but never hypocritical, keeping in mind that there but for the grace of God . . .

THIS MORNING, spring migrants of the feathered kind arrive: orange-crowned and yellow-rumped warblers. Despite the drought, one of the worst on record, spring's flux begins. But the monsoon season's autoclave weather is still months away. Straight ahead lies foresummer's attenuation, when the heat and drought draw life into a taut, thrumming ligament. Even the phlegmatic endurance of lizards will be tested.

I've just picked up my Day-Glo orange leisure suit, and I feel like the state has arrested and convicted me all over again. That we are less than human, and should be treated as such, is the department's continuing trend. A recent memo from the director that's circulating among the staff spells it out: "Subsection 1.2 states that employees will not: Give any food or beverage to an inmate." I read this as, "Please don't feed the animals." Another order states that employees will not "Address an inmate as 'Mister,' 'Ma'am' or any other inappropriate manner." My supervisors can no longer call me "Ken" or even "Mister Lamberton"; I am "Inmate Lamberton."

My orange clothes are stiff and uncomfortable, fresh from the chemical vat, no doubt. I can't get over the waste of money: more than two hundred dollars per inmate for the wardrobe (three pairs of pants, three smocks, six T-shirts, and a ball cap—all orange). ADC's motto shouldn't read: "Security is not convenient." It should read: "Security is not cheap."

So now we all look like biohazard signs. The public is safe. Our orange clothes overwhelm personal identity to such a degree that I'm finding it difficult to recognize from a distance people I've known for years. We aren't people anymore; we are anomalies, outcasts crying "unclean."

TWO DAYS AGO we broke ninety degrees for the first time this year as we begin to move into the hot, dry foresummer season. The barn swallows arrived this week, their seasonal migration now "as inevitable as one shoe after the other," as William Kittredge says. Ten years ago I couldn't have predicted that the birds would return after that first tentative nesting at Santa Rita. But they have. Every year. This spring will be the last time I anticipate their coming, I think, as a pair of dark, narrow wings cuts across Cottonwood Park. The swallow abandons itself to the most trivial currents, lifting, twisting, and dipping with imperceptible feather adjustments. If it's true that to the birds I must seem as a bottom-dweller, limited by gravity to two-dimensional scuttling beneath an ocean of air, then at least when the time comes for the swallows to again leave this place, I will be following them. Expanding my range. My eyes lifted upward.

This afternoon my counselor, John Payne, calls me to his office to fill out a release packet. "Six months to your SED," he says. Sentence ending date. I tell him that I have a temporary release date of June 25, and he says, "You won't get it." I give him my home address and phone number, and then he hands me a single sheet of paper. "Sex Offender Registration/ Notification Requirements," it reads at the top. I must initial each one of ten "I understand" items, which list descriptions of violations for failing to do such things as: (1) registering as a sex offender within ten days of moving into any county; (2) notifying within seventy-two hours the sheriff of the county from which I move; (3) renewing my driver's license or identification card every year. The paper also informs me that registering as a sex offender is a lifetime requirement in Arizona, that law enforcement may post my picture, address, and offense on television, in the newspaper, and/or in my neighborhood for as long as I live in Arizona. The release of no other kind of prisoner garners such attention, this kind of ex post facto prosecution. I know a man released last year after serving twenty years for killing a woman and her child in a violent, bloody rage. He now lives a quiet life in Phoenix without any restrictions. I doubt his neighbors know anything—not that they should. Of the two dozen sex offenders I personally know whom the department has recently released from prison, only one has been charged with another crime, and that was for exposing himself in public.

I leave Payne's office with my copy of the notification requirements, thinking that all this makes me want to move to Mexico, maybe the Baja peninsula or Costa Rica. This was not part of my original plea agreement.

I'm also worried about being rolled up for the evaluation, something I've noticed happening to men after completion of this paperwork. "When there comes to be a soothing light at the end of your tunnel," the song goes, "it's just a freight train coming your way."

I WALK LAPS with legs angry and red from sunburn. Inca doves sing: "no hope, no hope, no hope." Before I finish, a friend stops me on the exercise track. Harry has been watching out for our mallards since their arrival, and when I mention that the female is missing, he says, "Didn't I tell you? Bruce found her in the lilies next to Dorm Three." Bruce, a sandy-haired man with a gentle face and manner, is Harry's partner and the one who first showed me the mamma duck on her nest in April of 1998, her third season at Echo. "Look on the east side," Harry says, and so I do. Sure enough, there she is, embedded among the high, broad leaves. I'm determined not to miss the hatching this year. If she's already sitting on a clutch, then she should lead her brood off the yard around the thirteenth of May.

Near record high temperatures have driven off the blackbirds, the last of the winter migrants to depart Echo Unit. I may never see them again at this place, and their absence now is a kind of negative reminder for me that soon I will be going home.

I hope. There's a new directive from the department concerning sex offenders. The department will no longer house us at minimum-custody units because of the new predator laws. Since our sentences now are essentially indeterminate, that upon release the state may commit us, all sex offenders are an escape risk. Never mind that we are free of serious disciplinary violations, or even that we fall outside the criteria of a sexual predator. It makes no difference; the perceived risk is there. Two of my friends went to reclassification this week and were reassigned to South Unit, one of the old medium-custody prisons at Florence, Arizona. My next scheduled reclassification is in September, the month of my release.

FORESUMMER'S YELLOW FLUSH is under way. The Mexican paloverde have burst with heavy clusters, followed by foothill paloverde and tassel-flowered mesquite outside the perimeter—all this beneath the sun's egg-yolk blister, which will all too soon burn the sulfur yellow to ash gray. Foresummer is a season of taking. Hooded orioles rob nectar from the blooms of aloe and desert willow, while cowbirds take this opportunity to parasitize nests, furtively swapping the orioles' bluish, speckled eggs for their own. This time of year, cowbirds seem the most selfish, fostering off their broods to the care of others. They even recoup the energy expended in egg-laying when they devour their host's eggs.

Selfishness is a human construction, a moral judgment. Nature isn't so opinionated, or black and white. But nature does keep it simple: species either adapt and evolve or they go extinct. When prison gives you no way out, when there's no chance of something better, when even the bottom rung is impossible to reach, then you're left with nothing but selfishness for survival. It becomes an anesthetic, numbing the isolation, the insulation, the disenfranchisement.

I prefer adaptation and evolution, as selfish as that sounds. And today I head for a perfect example of adaptation outside Dorm Three. While waiting for school to begin yesterday afternoon, I spotted one brown- and yellow-streaked duckling, still half-damp from the shell. Mamma mallard stabbed at my hand as I reached into the lilies for a clear view. A movement next to her drew my attention. The duckling's oversized head lolled to one side, then the hatchling squirmed beneath its mother.

When I arrive, mamma duck is standing at the corner of the planter, eyeing the few men who have already gathered. She seems cautious; several bicolored tennis balls hug her legs, ten by my count. I take a seat on the steps to the chapel. Ten minutes later she begins to move, stepping and then stopping, and then starting out again, gradually veering in the direction of the wastewater ponds. Her babies scoot on tiny legs, tumbling and rolling onto their backs, legs kicking the air. When their mother moves, the ducklings follow closely, bouncing over obstacles, falling into tree wells. More men stop to watch. Mexican landscapers lean on their shovels. Other inmates find seats. The family slips down an embankment and files past a man writing letters at a picnic table. He looks up to see them pass only three feet away, surprise and disbelief on his face. Once on the grass, she makes for the chain link, stringing out her family behind her. My friend Dennis, who's been irrigating the area and who has just joined me, says, "We should give her a break. She's done her job." When he returns with a box from the kitchen, we circle the mallards and trap them against a hedge of umbrella plants. I scoop up five ducklings with one hand. Dennis says, "I'll get the rest. You grab the mother." She lunges for my face, but I get both hands around her and drop her into the box with her babies. At East Gate, an officer chauffeurs Dennis and his charges to the settling ponds while I watch from Cottonwood Park. When he returns he says, "They're all in the pond. Made a beeline for it, and then Dad flew in as they got to the water." Dennis hands me a few brindled breast feathers and adds, "She left a gift for you."

VIC HAS READ MY BOOK. He represents the white race at Echo, an "unofficial" position that serves the department well by maintaining peace among the various ethnic groups—most of the time. Vic looks like an Aryan brother: shaved head, heavily muscled frame, and tattoos. His upper body is covered with them. A seated wizard fills his back, above which a diaphanous black aura now stretches across his shoulder blades. Not long ago Vic had the words "Thank God I'm White" in its place. When I gave Vic my book to read, he said he knew about my case, that he had seen me on television. He's the kind of man who would have ordered my beating at Meadows Unit four summers ago.

Vic's been locked up for eighteen years, off and on since he was twelve for crimes mostly related to drugs. In prison, he continued trafficking in drugs, enlisting the aid of corrections officers in units like Cimarron, Rincon, and Santa Rita where security is more difficult. At these units you can't simply walk back to the yard from your work site with contraband in your pocket. You need a friendly cop to do it for you. Some guards are passive, looking the other way. Others are more active, making pickups and serving as "mules." Vic, having the right connections to place him at the center of the prison drug trade, quickly rose through the ranks of the white leadership. These days, however, he's a changed man. He's met and married a woman. And he's getting out soon. I gave a copy of my book to Vic in an attempt to befriend him. I knew I was taking a chance, and I told him that he may not like all I had to say. On my part, it was an act of self-preservation. If he could get past my crime—which it appeared he already had—he might be an ally if I ever came to trouble at Echo. I'm still too high profile. And the department keeps stirring up attention about sex offenders by regularly sending them to higher custody for the evaluation. There are only about thirty sex offenders remaining at Echo; we're steadily losing our numbers, and there's safety in numbers. At least taking a risk with Vic seems to have reached him. Today he says my book brought him to tears. "As long as I'm running this yard," he tells me, "you won't get hurt here."

TROPICAL STORM BUD might kick start our monsoon season. Dew points are up; humidity is up; nubile clouds daub mountains.

At two thirty I send Karen home from visitation, hoping she beats the storm. All afternoon we sat hip to hip, holding hands and watching bruised lenticular clouds plume like disturbed sediments. She left with the wind kicking up her hair, and I ran back to my cell to the percussion waves of thunder. More thunder. Now, marbles of hail pepper the trailer and skitter over the ground's skillet. When I move to close the window, one piece strikes me in the face. I eat it—crunchy and cold. Then the rain comes.

In the morning, my orange T-shirt sticks to my back in the mossy air. Dew points remain high. Humidity as thick as egg whites curls my hair tightly against my head—definitely monsoon weather. Along my path I notice a curious scent, something that seeps out of the soil and out of my past, yet it's new. I recall a shoal of minnows swimming clockwise in my Red Arrow wagon the summer when I was six. The smell is vast, an exhalation of wet granite and duff after a storm. It is the smell of toads, of promise.

Tucson weather forecasters report that the monsoon season is official, thanks to Tropical Storm Bud. The date, June 17, is the earliest monsoon start on record.

monsoon summer 2000

Executions of Popular Justice

"All things are meltable, and replaceable," Mary Oliver writes in her essay "Sister Turtle." "Not at this moment, but soon enough, we are lambs and we are leaves, and we are stars, and the shining mysterious pond water itself." This evening, convicted murderer Gary Graham is scheduled to die by lethal injection, after he's spent nearly two decades on death row in a Texas prison. The execution will be number 135 for George W. Bush, unless he grants a reprieve, which is doubtful since the governor says strapping seventeen-year-olds to the death gurney "is appropriate." Graham, who was seventeen years old when accused of shooting Bobby Lambert, says he is innocent, that Bernadine Skillern was mistaken in her identification of him. Two other witnesses concur; Graham was not involved, but they never testified at his trial. Graham's 1981 conviction is based on no physical evidence, only on the words of one woman. His jurors now say that hearing the other witnesses probably would have made a difference in their decision.

I'm against executing anyone for any reason, but this case really disturbs me. Graham may be innocent of this crime. Eyewitnesses do make mistakes. In last Sunday's *New York Times* there's a story by Jennifer Thompson, a North Carolina homemaker who, in 1984, when she was a twenty-two-year-old college student, was raped at knifepoint. During the attack, Jennifer bravely determined that, if she survived, the man would never harm another woman. "I studied every single detail on the rapist's face," she writes. "I looked at his hairline; I looked for scars, for tattoos, for anything that would help me identify him. . . . I was going to make sure that he was put in prison and he was going to rot." The same day Jennifer went to the police and made a composite sketch. A few days later she identified her attacker from police photos and subsequently picked him out of a lineup. In 1986, when the case went to trial, she took the witness stand. Her testimony sent Ronald Junior Cotton to prison for life. "I knew this was the man. I was completely confident. . . . If there was the possibility of a death sentence, I wanted him to die. I wanted to flip the switch."

A year later after an appellate court had overturned Cotton's conviction, Jennifer learned that another man in prison with Cotton had bragged about being her actual attacker. When officials brought Bobby Poole into the courtroom, Jennifer didn't recognize him. She testified: "I have never seen him in my life. I have no idea who he is." It wasn't until 1995, eleven years after Jennifer Thompson first accused Ronald Cotton of raping her, that DNA evidence finally exonerated him—and condemned Bobby Poole. He later pled guilty to the crime. "The man I was so sure I had never seen in my life was the man who was inches from my throat," Jennifer says. "And the man I had identified so emphatically on so many occasions was absolutely innocent."

Two weeks ago Jennifer Thompson traveled to Texas to beg Governor George W. Bush not to execute Gary Graham and to grant him a new trial. She came with eleven men and women who had once been convicted according to eyewitness accounts and were later found not guilty. I doubt Jennifer would consider herself an advocate for death row inmates, but she does have a compelling story to tell, one that underscores the limitations of our justice system. "I know that there is an eyewitness who is absolutely positive she saw Gary Graham commit murder. But she cannot possibly be any more positive than I was about Ronald Cotton. What if she is dead wrong?"

Just now, the U.S. Supreme Court refused to stop the killing of Gary

Graham by a five to four vote. I'm watching a debate about the execution on CNN's *Larry King Live*. Tonight, Larry King interviews Harvard Law School professor Alan Dershowitz, the Reverend Albert Mohler, president of the Southern Baptist Theological Seminary, and actors Mike Farrell and Susan Sarandon, among others. Dershowitz is animated, calling Texas "the poster child for improper imposition of the death penalty." Farrell and Sarandon agree, adding that the whole process is barbaric. At first I think that all of Larry's guests are against the death penalty—until the Christian, Reverend Mohler, speaks. He claims a biblical authority for capital punishment, citing the books of Genesis and Exodus. "The taking of a life requires a life," he says again and again. It's the "eye for an eye" argument so often espoused by death-penalty Christians. Dershowitz, live on a monitor screen, jumps in, saying that he can quote Old Testament scripture, too: "Whoever is worthy of death shall be put to death on the testimony of two or three witnesses, but he shall not be put to death on the testimony of one witness." Even Mike Farrell, a lifelong opponent of the death penalty, turns to the Bible, referring to Jesus's words about how we must love people. Farrell says there are appropriate sanctions, like life in prison without parole, that protect society and punish wrongdoers "without forcing us to stoop to the level of the least among us." Wasn't it Martin Luther King Jr. who said that practicing "eye for an eye" would lead to a world of morally sightless people?

My Christian mother-in-law says she could flip the switch, and she believes Jesus would do the same. The Reverend Mohler sides with my mother-in-law. He believes that without capital punishment criminals would kill even more innocent victims. He uses the Bible to justify his biases. But it seems to me that if deterrence worked, America, the execution capital of the world, should be murder free.

At 6:15 PM Governor Bush has made his final decision: The execution will proceed. The taking of a life requires a life.

I see the worst kind of people every day. I am one of them: liars, thieves, extortionists, gangsters, addicts, sex offenders—I lived in the same cell with a double murderer. What I now understand is that it's the emotional part of me that desires to see *anyone* punished. We don't simply kill to show that killing is wrong; we kill to satisfy an emotional need to even the score. I wish we could set aside the emotion. There should be consequences to crime. But the consequences don't have to be wrath. They could be life.

At 6:45 PM, 8:45 in Huntsville, Texas, Gary Graham is dead. The taking of a life requires a life, even if it goes kicking and screaming to the death chamber, which Gary did, calling for an end to the brutality, the injustice, demanding that we stop all executions, last words that, because of the hopelessness they stir in me, thicken these walls.

Before he announced the time of the execution, Larry King asked Reverend Mohler if Graham could be saved. The Reverend assured him that Gary could be. He was confident, and he rose up in his chair. This is his area of expertise. "Gary Graham can find salvation through Jesus Christ," he said, suggesting that all he has to do is ask for it. I didn't believe him, however. If Mohler really thought Jesus could save Gary Graham, or if Mohler really cared, why wasn't he in Huntsville outside the prison holding a prayer vigil for him? Rather than appearing on national television in support of his killing.

Gary Graham might have been saved one day—but not after tonight. "We are losing so many things," my favorite nature writer Rick Bass says, "not just wild nature, but economic, ethnic, and social justice; we are losing our voices, becoming more brittle and fragmented—if ever our country had a social weave, it is unraveling." And yet we keep trying to be heard, even as we're being killed. I don't have any answers for you, Gary, and my vote no longer counts. I could forget you, since for me you symbolize all that is brittle and fragmented, and I shouldn't allow the despair associated with the world's unraveling to find a purchase in me, not in this place. I could, but I won't. Instead, I'll promise you this: When the voyeurs, the experts, and the pundits fade away, I'll see that your message doesn't—at least within the circle of my voice. I'll speak your name, state your case. Your death is worth that much. Your life. And, I'll believe that yours is one grave closer to an end to such graves.

ON SAN JUAN'S DAY, the jimsonweed is sprouting everywhere: along the sweat lodge, around Cottonwood Park, outside the education building—all the places I've been scattering seeds. It's embarrassing. All the twin knife-blade cotyledons pushing up through the dirt, rising above the pea gravel.

After three weeks we still can't travel to the creative writing workshop. There's a rumor that the administration at Santa Rita has suspended the workshop indefinitely because of the recent riot there. I've seen this too many times before: the best programs, usually volunteer programs like our workshop, canceled as blanket punishment for the behavior of a few. The Department of Corrections touts its programs, but there's a wide chasm between what's on paper (or on the Web site) and what actually occurs. It's all about perception. Tomorrow is the date of my temporary release (TR), and if I was almost anyone other than a sex offender, I would be going home in the morning. The last thing the Arizona Department of Corrections wants is the news media calling the department soft on sex offenders. Tomorrow, I won't be going home to my family on an early release. I wish that was the worst that could happen. I'm afraid, however, that something else is coming, for sex offenders, and for me.

TONIGHT, Phil begins working with us as a teacher's aide. He's the youngest among us at twenty-eight, but Laura Garrison, my new supervisor in education, was pleased with his test scores. "I had a good teacher," he told her three weeks ago when he applied for the job. Phil was referring to me.

Phil has been in prison for a few years for crimes related to drugs and credit card fraud. When he first arrived at Echo, I noticed him right away—not because he's a former student from my eighth-grade science class, but because he's a queen. His hair advertises his place, its strands pulled back into a ponytail at the feminine position. Before long, people started talking, and word got back to me that Phil was talking about being in my class my last semester of teaching. He was a member of our science club; he joined us on weekend field trips. He knew everyone, everything.

Phil still calls me "Mr. Lamberton," and I have to correct him several times. "Just Ken," I say, swallowing the irony. I always wanted my students to call me by my first name. In prison, however, we really are all the same, and distinctions can draw the wrong kind of attention.

Laura Garrison puts me to work on a computer printout of "Inmates by Unit Not Meeting Literacy Standards," identifying and highlighting those men who are not U.S. citizens. There are seventy-two of them at Echo, seventy-two exemptions from education because the department refuses to teach math, reading, and language skills to foreigners—Mexicans, Cubans, a rare Vietnamese. We will lock you up and put you to work dragging a rake in endless transects over the pea gravel, or hoeing weeds, but we will not spend one cent to teach you English.

The department has never paid much regard to education in all the years I've taught here. (I often joke that the administrators know how getting an education in prison diminishes their job security.) The teaching staff gets lip service from lieutenants and captains and deputy wardens and about the same amount of respect as inmates receive. Administrators often see teachers as being on *our* side. Teachers eventually either cow to the department's twin management styles—fear and intimidation—or they step on their peers to rise through the ranks and become what most teachers despise: an education program supervisor. And even with the mandatory literacy laws, education continues to be a litter runt to other programs, particularly prison construction and maintenance and ADOT road crews.

Education costs money; work programs don't. The department saves millions of dollars by employing skilled inmates who, for fifty cents an hour, pour concrete and lay pipe, run electrical wiring, frame up walls and hang plasterboard, operate backhoes and road graders, monitor sewage treatment plants, tape, spackle, and paint, repair and maintain state vehicles, plumbing, and heating and cooling units, even shine boots, cut hair, and wash officers' cars. There would be no prisons without inmates, and not for just the obvious reason. In fact, without inmate labor, the Arizona Department of Corrections couldn't afford to raise its new prisons. If we had any spines at all, inmates would refuse to build and maintain prisons (we string the razor wire that confines us) and push the department's budget up to a billion dollars a year.

Education, particularly college coursework, is a low priority with the prisons because it is low priority with the public. In Arizona, even *public* education ranks lowest in the nation in terms of funding. My own first cousin, a corrections administrator in California (he's one of several of my cousins who works in the California prison system), tells me he has problems with providing education for inmates when "so many [law-abiding citizens] are unable to attend college because of the cost." I hear this argument often. But inmates can't earn college degrees anymore, and haven't for a long time, unless they pay for correspondence courses. Pima College offers only certificates of completion. I understand the argument. Why should criminals be *rewarded* with scholarships, Pell grants, and tuition waivers just because they're in prison? All I know is that for most of the men I teach, our public schools have failed them somewhere along the way. Maybe it was a poor teacher at a critical time, or an overworked one with a large class. Or maybe there were unaddressed problems at home. Or maybe it was something much deeper. The majority of my students have learning problems—dyslexia, attention deficit disorder, hyperactivity—some diagnosed early, some not. These aren't excuses. Most of these men will never make it to college level and they know it, but I would sure like to see them try. There are so few positive goals in prison. And there's this: It is a fact that inmates who go to school, whether to pass a literacy standard or earn a GED or take college classes, are less likely to return to prison. Above all the counseling, job experience, and religious services, school is what works. Education is the single greatest program taxpayers can support to reduce recidivism, to recover lives.

IN THE AFTERNOON Karen visits me alone. She's in a rare mood, kissing me at our meeting—an act even more rare than her pleasant attitude. Before she leaves, she tells me that Jessica dreamed I was home. "You were on your hands and knees, scrubbing the kitchen floor."

Karen has talked with the girls about my return home, explaining to them that we are going to give the marriage another try but that they shouldn't feel left out of the process. She wanted their input, their observations, their praises and complaints. "Dad can act like a fool," she said to them. "That's a guy thing. But I don't want to come home from work and find any girlfriends." Without skipping a beat, Melissa said: "Don't worry, Mom. If that happens, you'll come home and find him in pieces."

How could I ever go wrong with a family that loves me like mine?

TWO DAYS LATER, on July 18, a corrections employee, whose name I won't mention here to protect his job, calls me to his office with some bad news. "You can't tell anyone," he says, extracting a promise from me, one I will begin to break within two minutes of leaving his office. He is disgusted, and it shows. "It looks like we won't be able to continue with our discussions," he says as the blood drains from my face. "You're on a list for transfer to South Unit tomorrow."

He wants to talk, but my mind is reeling. I have ten weeks to go. South Unit is higher custody than Echo, a lockdown, controlled-movement yard seventy-five miles north of Tucson at Florence. A sex offender yard. Does my transfer there mean that the department has determined I'm a violent predator? Will I now be committed to the state hospital upon my release? When I leave his office I walk directly to the phones, hoping to reach my wife before she leaves for work. No answer.

At midmorning, I finally get a hold of Kasondra. I say that I don't want to spoil her vacation, which begins tomorrow. (My family will be flying away from Arizona at the same hour I will be on the road to Florence.) I tell her not to worry about me, that I'll see her again soon. It is a weak, shallow attempt to allay her fears, an attempt cut short when my allotted time runs out and the phone system disconnects us.

Now, the yard is on an early lockdown. I had just talked to Karen. She was upset, crying at times. She made phone calls, but both John Hallahan, the regional director of prisons, and Director Terry Stewart are on vacation. "Maybe it's all just a nasty rumor," I suggested. "Wouldn't be the first time." Neither one of us believed it, but it's all I could think of to say as a voice on the paging system ordered us back to our cells. "You take care of yourself," were Karen's last words to me.

Next door, I hear my neighbor Darrel boxing up his property. He says he's on the movement list, too. I consider pulling down from my bulletin board all the pictures of my family, then change my mind. I can't. It hurts too much.

release day

September 25, 2000, Monday, 6:00 AM, South Unit, Florence complex. I woke four times last night, the first at ten thirty, thinking it was morning, then again at midnight, and at two with the kitchen turnout, then four thirty when a woman on graveyard told me to report to the yard office.

I brushed my teeth, combed my hair, and gave away what little property I still had left to me, feeling like the tooth fairy as I moved among sleeping men in the darkness. I delivered seven origami frogs, colorful paper creations from my last two calendar pages that I folded yesterday. Yazzie, my Native American neighbor, got my pillow, and my wristwatch, which I tucked beneath it. Atop the pillow went a bright green and red frog. Mike got my reading lamp, Coleman cooler, old socks, and coffee mug—frog on the mug. The remaining frogs I placed on various windowsills and shelves.

At 5:00 AM the dorm officer unlocked the door and allowed me to walk over to the yard office and then to breakfast at the dining hall. Half a dozen men joined me, all of them waiting for transportation for legal or medical appointments. I ate a few canned peach slices and drank half my coffee, leaving the bran flakes and French toast untouched. I had no stomach for solid food. Back at the yard office I waited for instructions. The moon, only a curl of silver but fully visible in reflected earth light, hung low and frozen in the eastern sky. When a cop came on day shift, he told me to return to my dorm until transportation arrived. "Really!" I said, thinking I would have to spend hours in the North Gate cage. He said, "No sense in you waiting around here."

So now, I'm sitting on my bare mattress scribbling notes. It's quiet. Through the long, narrow, horizontal window across from me I can see that the sky is bluing, the sun riming the tops of our few pine trees. Soon, if all goes well, I'll see this with new eyes—another sky, other trees—with eyes not narrowed and barred and fenced, eyes not limited by a twelve-year perimeter of consequences. And I will smell the nectar of free air.

The dorm officer says to report to the yard office again. Once there, another officer hands me a chambray shirt and a huge pair of worn blue jeans, "40 x 28" a strip of masking tape reads. Homeless-wear. He's got to be kidding. I have a thirty-one-inch waist, a thirty-six-inch inseam. Why did I bother to give him my size? At North Gate, adjacent to Central Unit's "The Walls" and its towering stone abutments, I change out of my orange clothing and into the blues. A cop gives me a plastic garbage bag for a belt, which I push through my front belt loops and cinch together. I look ridiculous. He then shackles my hands and feet—can't have me escaping fifteen minutes before the department releases me—and takes my ID card. I wish it were as simple to leave behind my inmate number. Or my convict aspect.

I wait alone in one of the cages. Four men in the cage next to me talk about sex offenders. They must be releases from Central Unit. Their conversation ends abruptly when a Pinal County sheriff pulls his vehicle into the sally port. They, too, know what it could mean: new charges, detainers, pending court hearings. I stop breathing. This can also mean a ride to the state hospital. The sheriff has a clipboard and paperwork. He talks with the North Gate officer and points to the name at the top of the page. I can't hear what he says, so I watch his lips . . . Does he say "Lamberton"?

TWO MONTHS EARLIER I had arrived here, at South Unit, with twenty-five other men from Echo Unit, Tucson complex. Yucca dorm, Fox pod, bed nine. Yucca Fox Nine: my housing assignment at the far back wall of the pod, lower bunk. Most of the Echo Unit group were assigned to the same pod, cleared out for us just days before to make room for hundreds of sex offenders coming from minimum-custody units all across the state. Nearly all of South Unit's previous inmates had transferred out—and they weren't happy about it by all the rude messages in permanent marker we found on our mattresses and pillows, those and the broken cable television jacks.

Yucca dorm, one of six dorms circling the perimeter of the main yard, comprises four individual pods—Able, Baker, Fox, and George—with twenty bunks per pod. Except for the twin sets of bunks at the rear of the pod, each bed rests in its own cubicle, a "house" with gray metal shelves and four-foot dividing wall. A central aisle runs between two rows of ten cubicles. At the entrance to the pod a small day room separates the glass-walled control room and the shower room, the latter with its pairs of stain-less steel urinals and toilets, three sinks, and single shower, all in plain view of the cops. I got to know these pods extremely well, since I passed most of my days for the last two months locked down inside one.

OUR TRANSFER BEGAN on the morning of July 19 at 3:00 AM when one of Echo Unit's counselors woke me and ordered me to roll up. Although I had been warned, the reality still sapped the strength from my arms and legs, which trembled with indecision at what to pack first, my books or the photographs on my bulletin board. On the runs I heard the voices of offi-cers and men. I heard someone stripping masking tape from its roll, that wrenching sound of dislocation. I wasn't the only one. The cops were clear-ing Echo of all of its sex offenders: my neighbor Darrel, Bull from down the hallway, Carl, Bruce, Old Man Howard, and many others. By some administrative decision, we no longer deserved to sit in the grass under the cottonwoods, to see swallows and stars, to lay sunlight against our skin. Before I left Echo, before the next twelve hours of packing and hauling property, of inventory and contraband slips, of strip searches and oversized jumpsuits, shackles, bus rides, and waiting in cages began, I stood on the front porch of the housing unit under a black sky. Overhead, somewhere in the north I remembered, comet Linear pointed its dirty finger away from

Tucson, away from my family. July 19. Exactly four years ago to the day since my return to prison.

I KNEW I had come to the end of my minimum-custody status when the transportation officers belly-chained my arms to my waist and shackled my right leg to another man's left. Thirteen pairs of men boarded a steel-cage-reinforced bus while inmates from Echo heckled us with acidic words. I knew I had come to the end of visiting with my wife and daughters as we accelerated along I-10 toward the Casa Grande turnoff to Florence, more than an hour from Tucson. I watched for "A" Mountain through the dirty window grating, and for the giant eucalyptus trees that mark our home. I had told Deputy Warden Heliotes how unhappy Karen would be about this move, that he should expect a call from her. I told him how unnecessary it was, that if he'd waited until the end of the year he would have half as many men to transfer. We would be out of prison by then. He didn't care. "I'd roll you up even if you had only a day to go," he said, puffing out his chest.

When I returned to prison four years ago after the appellate court rescinded my freedom, I surrendered myself to Alhambra, the department's prison-induction facility in Phoenix. When I arrived at South Unit, I thought I had returned to Alhambra. Previously, South Unit had been a semi-open yard with grass and rosebushes and a few trees—but no longer. All rules and policies and procedures changed when the sex offenders showed up. On the main yard plants suddenly became noncompliant. Acres of pea gravel, that ubiquitous landscape surface of lockdown prisons, and empty space replaced the green. Slabs of barren concrete rested where volleyball and basketball courts once held nets and hoops and backboards. The administration had relegated these activities to a fenced section where we could exercise for an hour and a half three times a week. My walking— and my sanity—would suffer. And this was only the beginning. The cops minutely controlled every movement on South Unit's yard. Pod by pod, we marched single file to meals and recreation, both coming and going. We stayed on the sidewalks. (I discovered this was the rule after a cop yelled at me when I stepped into the gravel to get a better look at a dead, bloated gopher.) Officers issued passes for visitation or when we had counselor or medical appointments. In fact, writing an inmate letter was the only way to contact these people. I never saw my "counselor." I wrote letters to request a job, to turn out for the library, to attend church, to make phone calls, to approve visits, and to receive a clothing issue. Many of us still wore the same orange jumpsuit two weeks after our transfer. We had turned in all our clothing at Echo while the inmates at South Unit had kept theirs, leaving us with nothing to wear but our oversized travel suits.

The environment was most severe in the dorms, where petty cops, some worse than others, constantly prowled the runs, searching for reasons to confiscate property and write up anyone for rule violations. These weren't violations for fighting or extortion or stealing or possession of contraband, but for things like unmade (or improperly made) beds, out-of-place shoes, books or papers resting on upper shelves, television viewing without wearing headphones, unemptied trash cans, bare skin, or, the worst crime of all, smoking in the bathroom. All this, for whom even the deputy warden admitted are the "most docile" inmates in the system. South Unit wasn't only a raise in custody level because of the nature of our offenses. It was retribution.

This is how ridiculous it got: One night, two sergeants, a man and a woman, entered our pod to advise us of some policy changes. "You're not going to like it," the woman warned us. "You must be dressed at all times except in the shower." I was already in bed, wearing only my boxer shorts. I asked her, "You mean we have to wear our shirts to bed?" She responded by reading the policy: "Inmates will be fully clothed at all times when outside the cubicle." I pointed out the condition, *when outside the cubicle*, repeating it louder and louder as she continued to ignore me. It was no use; I pulled on my shirt. Later, when another sergeant entered our pod to check on our compliance, I approached him with a new argument. "So, by your interpretation of policy, we have to wear *all* our clothes to bed, not just shirts but pants, socks, boots, and caps?" "No," he said, dismissing my logic. "I don't want you shining up your boots and sleeping on your covers. You can sleep in your Skivvies, but you have to wear a shirt. Use common sense." I said, "Common sense tells me to take off my shirt when I go to bed." By now the sergeant had heard enough. He asked me my number, and learning that it was an old one, told me that I should know better, his implication being that my prison experience should make me more reasonable.

Near midnight, damp in my orange T-shirt, I heard a woman's voice whispering to the men from one dark cubicle to the next. "You can take off your clothes," she said.

I knew that to keep my sanity I would need to get out of the pod for a few hours each day, which meant finding a job. I immediately applied for a position as a teacher's aide. A week later I was walking the yard wearing a lime green vest over my jumpsuit, a plastic bag in hand, scouring the gravel for cigarette butts. Butt patrol. It could have been worse. I could have gotten kitchen duty. Although I don't smoke, and the job only paid ten cents an hour, it allowed me the freedom to explore the perimeter and to photosynthesize. I could be alone, at least within a twenty-foot radius. And, after learning what to look for—someone explained to me that I wouldn't find any discarded filters, that I should search for snipes, the dead ends of "rollies"—I became quite good at it. I started noticing butts everywhere, at all times, on the job and off. It became an obsession, an out-of-control fetish. Like the presence of small feathered bodies, which always got my attention, butts drew my eyes.

I didn't see many birds at South Unit: a few mourning doves and lewd grackles, dozens of obese chowhall pigeons, domesticated beggars that have learned to set their schedule to mealtimes. I could always find a turkey vulture in the sky above the prison. As far as other wildlife, it was pretty bleak. Rattlesnake weed at trackside competed with inmate landscapers who preferred bare ground. It did amuse me upon our arrival to notice a single sturdy jimsonweed growing outside the property office. Someone was obviously caring for it, keeping the plant watered and pruned. Even at the center of this insidious prison city, the drugs sprout wild and free. I couldn't see what thrived in the desert outside the perimeter. A solid, white, six-foot wall, topped with a span of chain link and razor wire, part of a brace of barriers, screened out the cicadas, the cholla and paloverde, and, to the north, the Superstition Mountains. A massive stone barricade shadowed us on the eastern perimeter, the infamous "Walls," home to the Tyson brothers and other notorious felons who never see the sky. Central Unit, one of Arizona's original lockups. There, just beyond our recreation field, a slim ashen pipe rises like a flagless staff above the guard towers, walls, and multitiered cell blocks. I felt its presence on every exercise lap—the exhaust stack of the death chamber, expelling poisonous gases and human lives.

The transfer to South Unit did connect me with people I hadn't seen for ten years: a cellmate from my first years at Santa Rita, friends from our Christian fellowship, students I had taught, and coworkers from my jobs in education. I nearly cheered when Pat, my computer-guru friend, wheeled himself into the dining hall and joined me for lunch. I hadn't seen him since Echo shipped him off to the Lewis complex at Buckeye last January. Pat was brimming with stories, and his movements were flylike as he ate his sandwich and anxiously tried to update me, compressing nine months into our allotted ten minutes. He had just transferred from Florence's medical unit where he needed to recover from complications owing to untreated blood poisoning in one of his legs. "I've had five nurses and a doctor fired," he told me. "They nearly killed me. I'm suing them and now they won't even talk to me without witnesses present." Although the wheelchair and his mistreatment distressed me, it was good to see him again. After I moved to Cactus dorm, I ran into a man who remembered me from Meadows Unit four years ago. He lived in Dorm Five at the time of my attack and saw the whole thing. "That was a wicked place," he said. "Those guys were waiting for you. An officer, he used to be a counselor—he told us what people were in prison for. One guy, they beat him in the head with rocks." David, a friend who was also at Meadows at the time, told me he later met one of the men who assaulted me. "When he came out of lockdown they moved him into my pod. He was proud of what he'd done."

At South Unit I've seen the result of the department's study of ancient history, uncovering men like my former cellmate who, in 1974, at the age of eighteen, received probation for a lewd and lascivious act; or men like Steve, who was cited for indecent exposure when streaking was a fad. Three years ago, when the department started collecting sex offenders at specific units after Arizona passed the sexual predator law, it became necessary to discover and label who was who. A thousand men transferred from Tucson complex alone. And now, hundreds more from all the minimum-custody units statewide—Echo, Apache, Coronado, Cocopah, and others at Globe, Florence, Douglas—have come to South Unit. Together with those men already housed at the Eyman complex a few miles east from here, Florence now holds all of the sex offenders in the state, more than five thousand of us. We should buy homes in town after our release; I'm considering opening a halfway house in Florence.

Among society's worst deviants here, I've seen dozens of men in wheelchairs, some without legs; and with the lame come the blind. These inmates often work out symbiotic relationships—the legless wheeled by the sightless, sometimes in whole trains, a kind of handicap mutualism. Then there are the geriatrics, the elderly and senile and Alzheimer-impaired who've traded nursing homes for prison dorms; and the children, eighteen-year-old girl-faced misfits who haven't yet begun to shave; and the mentally feeble, men who, owing to chronic illnesses such as diabetes, cancer, AIDS, or organ failure, will serve shortened sentences by default; and others, like the emotionally disturbed, the queens, and a four-foot dwarf. Many of us deserve to be here; we readily admit it. But it's hard for me to believe that Arizona couldn't do something a little less insensitive with people like Old Man Howard with his prostate trouble. Do we imprison people simply to punish them? Or to change them? I fear we settle for the former because punishment comes naturally to us, and because we haven't a clue about the latter.

Most of us had striven for years to gain minimum status, nine years in my case. Nine years without disciplinary sanctions. Nine years of "programming," working every day at the same job. I felt I had earned my placement at Echo, and I remained write-up free to keep it. I might as well have trafficked in drugs—at least I'd have money when I left prison. Two weeks after we arrived at South Unit the department reclassified us. A pair of bearded counselors entered the dorm and pushed papers at us one at a time. It was a formality; Central Office had already made its decision. When my turn came, one of the functionaries explained that my public/institutional score would remain unchanged, "However, by the director's order, your custody level is being overridden for South Unit. Do you have any comments?" I had whole paragraphs in my mind, but I said, simply, "I disagree with the move." It was my own formality, and it, too, was meaningless.

Arizona's new retroactive laws not only raised my custody level, but affected me after the fact in other ways. Since I came to prison, the Arizona legislature has added to my sentence: mandatory lifetime registration with the county sheriff requiring a public document for photos and fingerprints, address and vehicle information, and the name of my closest relative; notification of the media with neighborhood fliers upon my release; Internet posting with my face and address; and an annual driver's license/identification card update (ten dollars each time) with the Motor Vehicle Division (MVD). I could go back to prison for failing to do any one of these things, for a "crime" only a specific class of people can commit.

Two weeks ago, after a false start, I fulfilled my now mandatory obligation to MVD. A cop on graveyard shift woke me after midnight to ask me
what size jumpsuit I would need for what she called a "day trip." At 4:00
AM she roused me again, tapping her keys on my bed frame, and told me
to dress and report to the yard office. There, I had some nervous moments
when I overheard another inmate, also wearing a jumpsuit and shower
shoes, talking about transportation to the Pinal County courthouse. Is the
county pursuing civil commitment after all? At breakfast in the Officers'
Dining Room I met Rob, a friend from Echo, who said we were scheduled for pictures at the MVD in Coolidge. It would be a short trip. Only
ten miles from Florence, Coolidge is another small agricultural community whose economy depends upon prison inmates. After our scrambled
eggs and refried beans, eight of us walked up to North Gate under Central
Unit's guard towers to wait, belly-chained and leg-shackled, in the departure cage. Sitting there, while men in other cages shouted obscenities at us,
I wondered if it was a foreshadowing of today, my release day. The cops
had informed the Central Unit arrivals what unit we belonged to. Word
had gotten out. Sex offenders at South Unit. A voice yelled out: "I've seen
your faces. I've got nine days and I'll be out there looking for you in my
stolen car, your MVD pictures on my dashboard." More laughs, screeches.
Not one of us said a word. When the transportation officers were ready, two
men removed our chains, strip-searched us, then replaced the shackles and
loaded us into a cage-upholstered van. At the complex armory both officers
checked out Glock 9mm's and, for the benefit of our eyes, chambered hollow points. At the guard shack near the entrance to the prison complex, our
driver, Officer York, told the uniformed man that we were off to Coolidge.
"They're going to MVD for pictures, he added. "So they can be passed out
to their neighbors. You know, those kind." Fifteen minutes later we sat in the
MVD parking lot while York spoke to a woman employee. After he returned
to the van, both officers buckled up and we drove back to Florence. No pictures. *You idiots*, I thought all the way to the prison. *It's a wonder you can even*

run a prison! I asked York what happened as he uncuffed my legs at North Gate. "We'll have to reschedule you," he said. "There were too many of you and MVD wouldn't take you so close to working hours." Two days later, we repeated the "day trip," that time for pictures. No one saw us.

TODAY, I'm back in the same departure cage at North Gate, sitting in shackles on the same steel bench, waiting for transportation. Only this time it's a one-way trip. Whatever comes next, the Arizona Department of Corrections is done with me now. I hope society got what it paid for. I should wear my blue denim clown pants with their garbage-bag belt proudly. I do have fifty dollars as release money, funds extracted from my own account in the form of a check I can't cash without identification.

I haven't seen Karen since that last Sunday we visited together at Echo Unit more than two months ago. This is what we both wanted, although for different reasons. For Karen, the emotional baggage of coming to Florence to see me was too much. South Unit sits across the highway from the Pinal County courthouse, where it all began fourteen years ago, where she won and then lost my release four years ago. Karen's emotional baggage weighed too much for me as well. Instead of visiting, we wrote each other long, wordy letters full of humor and passion and dull descriptions of our separate lives. And, once I finally received clearance five weeks after arriving here, we spoke on the phone for fifteen-minute blocks every other day. It wasn't anything like our relationship at Echo, but, at least for me, knowing that we had only a short time until my release made it bearable.

I won't see Karen here today either. Family reunions can wait until tonight, at a better time and place—home. Karen decided months ago to ask my attorney Steve Sherick to pick me up, partly, I think, so he might handle anything unexpected—like the county sheriff arriving with wrist bracelets and a trip to the state hospital.

At my request, Steve began looking into the likelihood of my commitment. For security reasons, the department keeps this information to itself, until the day of your release from custody. Court hearings, defense strategies, lawyers, prosecutors, and juries all come later, after the state has had you locked up for months on the mental ward. Steve discovered that the process begins near your release date with a recommendation from a corrections official, at which point county prosecutors decide whether or not to pursue your case with a civil action. Steve told me that he had spoken to Ken Marion at the department who "is in charge of screening all inmates for possible commitment under the Sexually Violent Person statute. . . . Mr. Marion said your evaluation indicated that you were at the lowest risk level, so there would be no referral for commitment."

It was good news, but I still didn't know the position of Pinal County.

At 8:10 AM the sheriff takes someone else, locking him into the back of his vehicle and backing out of the sally port. I begin to breathe again. I'm allowed to leave any time now. My ride must turn off of Butte Avenue onto prison property, park in the visitors lot, walk up to the guard shack in the center of the road (where posted signs read: "Do Not Approach"), and give the officer my name, ADC number, and housing unit. All this I know. What happens next I'm unsure of.

At 8:20 an officer unlocks my cage and removes my shackles. "Time to go," he says. Four other men from the adjacent cage, Central Unit's releases whose rides have already arrived, watch me as I sign some paperwork. They're waiting for me and I'm nervous about it. They know what I am. When the outside gate opens, the sound of its machinery as unfamiliar to me as the sound of my own name, I move to carry my property to a parked truck. One of the men helps me with my boxes. Then, an officer escorts us on foot all the way to the parking lot where my lawyer waits in his car.

It's one of the longest walks of my life.

afterword

When the gulf fritillary emerges from its chrysalis, the first thing the butterfly does as it stretches out its new wings and looks at the world through new eyes is defecate. In one long blood-dark stream, the butterfly expels the metabolized remnants of its former life.

I write this now, seven miraculous years after my release from prison. They began with Madera Canyon.

On Saturday evening, at the end of my first week of freedom, the sky paled in the west where it leaked through the dark juniper and oak. An afternoon thunderstorm slid out of the canyon and onto a shadow-marbled desert, leaving the woodland dripping around my ears. In the post-storm sigh, a Steller's jay called from the trees while a hooded skunk nosed the oak-leaf duff behind the cabin, searching tidbits. The animal was so accustomed to people that it ignored my bare legs and sandaled feet only inches away.

I thought about the last time I sat on that cabin porch: July 16, 1996, only three days away from my return to prison for four years, two months, and some change—exactly what the appellate court ordered me to serve to complete every day of my original twelve-year sentence. My journal entry for that date doesn't betray the anxiety and fear I felt but only records descriptions of the cabin, the birds at the feeder, and a woodland suffering from the worst drought in ninety years. I write: "Interestingly, the pinyon pine have started a fresh, healthy crop of new cones, bright green nodules that decorate the tips of many branches. Is this the pinyon's own response to drought?" I can't escape the symbolism even now. At the bottom of the page I'd penciled: "Last Entry before Return to Prison on July 19, 1996."

When I turn the page, it's two months later and I'm writing about massing barn swallows at the Santa Rita Unit. I don't mention it there, but I was recovering from a pair of broken ribs I had received as a reintroduction to prison life.

Madera Canyon hadn't changed in my four-year absence, and Kubo number four was exactly as I had remembered it: the rough pine molding around the windows and doors, the hand-carved wood-beam furniture, the back porch facing a stream. Karen thought this place appropriate for my reunion with family and friends, and she was right. After my attorney picked me up in Florence and I had a chance to change out of my over-sized prison blues, we met Karen and others from the law office for lunch in downtown Tucson. Karen sat next to me at our outside table, wearing a brown skirt and jacket with a shimmering golden blouse and a dozen golden bracelets she could never have gotten past the metal detectors in prison visitation. We hadn't seen each other in months, and I felt so nervous being close to her that I could hardly eat. Afterward, Karen walked back to work and a friend drove me to Madera Canyon where my daughters were waiting for me. When I found them behind the cabin, they said "Hi Dad" without fanfare as if my presence in their lives were the most natural thing in the world. Karen joined us in the evening.

The next morning, Richard Shelton and Mark Menlove, one of his students and his prison workshop assistant, arrived to take my daughters and me on a wildflower hike to Josephine Saddle. My girls packed my knapsack for me: five pounds of gorp, "gobs of raw protein," Mark called it as he watched me, disbelief on my face, extract the heavy zip-lock freezer bag once we reached the saddle. My daughters thought it was funny. "Didn't you always say," Kasondra explained, "that you should check your pack before going on a hike?" Melissa added: "We could have put rocks in there." We ate cheese and crackers and wonderful dry salami. I passed out oranges to everyone, showing the girls how to remove the peel in one long, curling strip.

This is how my first week outside of prison went: Friends and family arrived at the cabin. We barbecued chicken and ribs, hiked trails, watched birds, and visited with each other. It was as if I had lived in that cabin for twelve years and only recently had begun receiving guests. One friend from church actually thought my family had moved there. My crime and subsequent prison term had become an abstraction.

But prison is never that innocuous; it affects not only prisoners and the prison staff who keep them, but families and friends and relatives associated with both. Prison punches holes in the fabric of society.

By the time I came home, my daughters should have been dropping out of school and getting in trouble with the law, according to the statistical odds against them. The children of prisoners are six times more likely than other children to be incarcerated at some point in their lives. Instead, despite the stigma of welfare and a convict father, my daughters are beating the odds. Jessica, my oldest, graduated from high school fourth in her class and won a $10,000 Baird scholarship, which she has kept for four years, to the University of Arizona, where she is now a senior studying wildlife biology. Kasondra graduated eighth in her class, was president of her high school's National Honor Society, and also received scholarships to the U of A, where she's currently a junior studying community health and psychology. Melissa, my youngest daughter, graduated valedictorian. She was one of nine students in Tucson accepted to Harvard; one of five in the city awarded the prestigious Flinn scholarship. The first year of my release, Melissa won an award at a regional science fair that took the two of us to Washington DC where she won a two-week trip to Hawaii to attend an astronomy camp and had an asteroid named for her.

Shortly after Melissa got her name in the stars, I learned that *Wilderness and Razor Wire* had won the 2002 John Burroughs Medal for outstanding nature writing. In March of that year, during my last semester before receiving my MFA in creative writing at the University of Arizona, Karen and I flew to New York to attend a ceremony at the American Museum of Natural History. Ann Zwinger, my favorite nature writer, conveyed the medal, and I gave a short speech while attempting to recover from the shock of it all. The impossible honor placed me in the company of respected writers like Rachel Carson, Peter Matthiessen, John McPhee, Barry Lopez, David Quammen, Gary Nabhan, and Robert Michael Pyle, a list stretching back to 1926. There is no higher praise, I am told, for nature writing.

Karen still insists my writing is "only a hobby," which is her way of reminding me that I already have a job—taking care of her. Because my role is so clear, we have an amazing relationship. Our marriage has all the sweaty contortionist's passion of a newlywed couple, but it's also tempered by the experience of a quarter century together. Karen likes to say that we're actually into our third marriage (the postprison marriage); I'm expecting a few more marriages to each other yet to come. In fact, just recently, after Karen and I began helping another couple work through the painful consequences that inevitably occur when two separate lives get crammed into one relationship, I suddenly realized that we are going to make it, that we've passed the test, that we're stuck with each other (and probably deserve each other too).

Now, with our daughters moving out and discovering their own lives apart from us (and prison), I bask in the ironies life brings our way. On a Saturday evening last April, Karen and I joined a few hundred people gathered at the posh Arizona Inn to honor Richard Shelton for his several decades of community service in both university and prison classrooms. I was supposed to give a short speech at this black-tie affair, attended by people who, as my daughters reminded me, "have their names on university buildings." They knew I would be way out of my element.

Our three daughters, all UA students, expressed no concerns about their mother's attendance, however. Only mine. Karen had already purchased a new $500 evening gown for the event, while I was considering wearing a green tie decorated with a flock of white sheep, one of which was black. The tie was a gift from my daughters. When we arrived, Karen charmed her way through the crowd while I went straight to the open bar. I later found her discussing with John Lannan, one of the event's sponsors, the benefits of husbands who vacuum floors as a form of foreplay.

After working through a salmon dinner and most of my half-dozen utensils, Gail Browne, director of the University of Arizona's Poetry Center, read a letter from Governor Janet Napolitano proclaiming April 22, 2006, as "Richard Shelton Day."

The speaker program that followed listed ten people, including such dignitaries as John P. Schaefer, UA president emeritus, award-winning poets Alison Hawthorne Deming and Alberto Álvaro Ríos, and the president of the prestigious Lannan Foundation, J. Patrick Lannan. My name fell at number seven; Dr. Schaefer would introduce me. I wondered what he would say. Our only connection was that I had attended the U of A in the late 1970s when he was its president. Under my name, the program said: "Managing Editor, *Walking Rain Review*."

After John Schaefer's very gracious introduction, one in which he did mention the UA biology degree he signed and my John Burroughs Medal for my first book—but not the twelve blank years that separated the two— I took the podium. I said, "Now that you've heard from the ex-president, you get to hear from the ex-con."

I had hoped for laughter, and I got some, but I also sensed a bit of surprise. I continued as I unfolded my prepared speech: "I'll bet Dr. Schaefer didn't know that. He didn't sign my release papers."

I thought about saying more, and I wish now that I had, because I later learned that some people didn't believe me. I should have asked the group, "What? You expected different? Richard Shelton has worked in prisons for thirty years—did you think no one would follow him out?"

Ironies. My life now seems full of them, some completely unbelievable.

A few years ago, Karen and I changed faiths, leaving behind our former Baptist church with its conservatism and joining a more liberal Lutheran congregation—we like to joke with people that we are recovering fundamentalists. While our three daughters found a place with the college ministry, Karen and I enjoyed a period of restful pew-sitting, purposefully remaining uninvolved with church activity. Then, with Karen's urging, I began playing bass guitar—an instrument I hadn't touched since my high school garage-band days—for the Celebrations music team. Its director, I learned, once played keyboards for Oracle, a local rock group I listened to as a teen. I also learned, as we became friends, that he is an appellate court judge, and not just any appellate court judge but one of the three judges—the *presiding* judge—who reversed my release in 1996 and sent me back to prison.

God, indeed, has a sense of humor.

THIS ALL SOUNDS LIKE my family and I are better for the experience—something I may claim as true but to which I would never credit prison. Did prison "fix" me? I don't know. Perhaps this is the wrong question. It certainly punished me. And it certainly punished Karen and my three daughters. Punishment is prison's design, its nature, and at least in our case, prison functioned well. So I suppose in this the public got its money's worth—punishing five people for the price of one.

My family *is* "better" in many ways, but who's to say why. Is character formed from an internal constitution or external events? Or a combination of both? The same fire can either purify or destroy, depending on the substance put to the flame. Crediting prison for who we've become is like praising the furnace for creating the silver. You need pyrargyrite to make silver; the metal is in the ore. I like the illustration of the lapidary. Prison has the power of the rock tumbler; it can take raw stones and produce either gems or worthless sand, depending on the ability of the lapidary.

Currently, prison churns out mostly worthless sand. What's needed is a lapidary who understands that not all stones have the same nature, that not all stones should be polished together because agates will only chip amethysts and neither takes polishing well. What's needed is one who understands the stones, and that polishing the right stones does require abrasive grit, but that timing is critical. Time determines the outcome: the kind of stone prison returns to society. The lapidaries of late haven't cared to learn this skill.

I'm still optimistic, however. In 2003, Governor Janet Napolitano, saying that it's time for change, named the first woman ever to run Arizona's prison system, replacing the latest in a long list of budget-blowing, tough-on-criminals directors. (Terry Stewart retired in 2002 and left for Iraq to use his formidable expertise to begin reforming Iraqi prisons on the American model, prisons like Abu Ghraib.) Dora Schriro revolutionized the operation of prisons in her eight years in the Missouri Department of Corrections, reducing recidivism to 19 percent with a philosophy she calls the "parallel universe." It requires the men to live and work, following the same rules and having the same responsibilities, as they would outside of prison, connecting them to the real world. One result of this change in priority is that by the end of Director Schriro's first year in Arizona, the number of inmates receiving their high school equivalency certificates has doubled. This year, the number has doubled again. Instead of focusing on meaningless punishment, the department is now looking to the future of the inmate who will eventually return to our neighborhoods, giving the men doing time a meaningful life.

I continue to correspond with many of the men I left behind in prison (and occasionally one of them comes walking down my driveway). My address list grows longer every year. For the first time in more than a decade that I've known some of these men, they have real hope.

selected notes

"Monsoon Summer 1998": "The beauty of it is that prisons are a self-adjusting market, Arizona's 'field of dreams.'" *Newsweek*, July 30, 1998.

"Aftersummer 1998": "Representative Henry Hyde, Republican from Illinois, calls it a 'youthful indiscretion.'" *Salon Newsreal*, "This Hypocrite Broke Up My Family," http://www.salon.com/news/1998/09/cov_16newsb.html.

"Winter 1999": "Pass another statute making it illegal to be poor, homeless, or mentally ill.'" "Mental Heath Tab: 356 Million: New Hospital Is Only One of Many Needs," *Arizona Daily Star*, January 5, 2000. Also: "Mentally Ill Get Prison Time, Not Treatment, Advocates Say," *Tucson Citizen*, January 7, 2000.

"Winter 1999": "In Arizona we have an undifferentiated mass, erupting with huge spores and sprawling over the landscape where cities place their landfills." Mark Kimble, *Tucson Citizen*, February 4, 1999.

"Winter 1999": "Prison will never be a solution, particularly the current warehousing without rehabilitation; prison is not even a deterrent to crime." "Study: Drug Use Up Despite Crackdown," *USA Today*, February 4, 1999. Also: "Terms of Imprisonment," *Governing*, April 2000.

"Winter 1999": "There are now more than 1.8 million adults imprisoned in the United States." *USA Today*, March 15, 1999.

"Winter 1999": "Monday's *Tucson Citizen* has an article about a sex offender being touted as the first test of the predator law." *Tucson Citizen*, March 15, 1999. Also: "Cops Hunt Sex Offender Who Failed to Register," *Arizona Daily Star*, November 9, 1999.

"Winter 1999": "While Boggess served another year for parole violation, the result of his registration lapse, a prison 'psychiatrist,' his own therapist 'Doctor' Steve Gray, testified he'd likely reoffend." Personal communication with Willie Boggess, August 29, 2000.

"Spring 1999": "This afternoon I read that the Charles Keating story is in its final episode." "Keating Jumps at 'Justice Lite,' but He's Still a Crook," *Arizona Republic*, April 8, 1999.

"Spring 1999": "The men call her 'Two-clip' Robinson." "Murder Charges Dropped against Florence Woman," *Arizona Daily Star*, July 14, 1991. Case Number S-1100-CR-17536.

"Spring 1999": "In it Terry Stewart discussed the settlement of a lawsuit against ADC concerning the sexual harassment of women prisoners by male officers." *Directions* newsletter, May 1999. Also: "Federal Judge Dismisses Suit against Corrections," *Arizona Republic*, January 13, 2000.

"Spring 1999": "'Court Upholds State Sexual Predator Law,' reads the headline." Associated Press, May 14, 1999.

"Monsoon Summer 1999": "Today, on CNN, Arizona's Maricopa County Sheriff Joe Arpaio is defending his claim as 'the toughest sheriff in the West.'" CNN, July 27, 1999.

"Monsoon Summer 1999": "When I came back to prison in the summer of 1996, his officers killed a man by restraining him and 'cattle-prodding' him to death with electric stun guns." "Simply Stunning," *Phoenix New Times*, July 11, 1996. Also: "Jailers Show a Paraplegic Who's Boss," *Phoenix New Times*, January 23, 1997.

"Monsoon Summer 1999": "Francis Fukuyama, Hirst Professor of Public Policy at George Mason University," *Atlantic Monthly*, May 1999.

"Aftersummer 1999": "Arizona will soon indict seventeen-year-old Jessica Jeffries from Phoenix on eight felony counts for her sexual conduct with two twelve-year-old boys." "Female Teenager Suspected in Molestations Freed on Bail," *Arizona Republic*, December 23, 1999.

"Aftersummer 1999": "Charleen's story, based on the newspaper's investigation, only gets worse." "Corrections Finds No Fault in Death: Prison Nurses Ignored Ill Inmate's Pleas, Records Show," *Arizona Daily Star*, October 24, 1999.

"Aftersummer 1999": "Arizona criminal justice is making national news again." *USA Today*, November 9, 1999.

"Aftersummer 1999": "Here's how fear works." "Imprisonment Prevents Crime," *Arizona Daily Star*, November 7, 1999. Also: "Debate Rages on Value of Incarceration," *Tucson Citizen*, January 7, 2000.

"Fall 1999": "Yesterday, Pima County sheriff's deputy James Tracy Strickler, a twenty-two-year veteran, was arrested for his part in a drug ring." "Deputy Reportedly Part of Ring That Stole Calif. Drugs, Money," *Arizona Daily Star*, December 17, 1999. Also: "Ex-Tucson Cop's Betrayal of Trust in Drug Case Brings Life Sentence," *Arizona Daily Star*, January 21, 2000.

"Fall 1999": "Sergeant Kevin Michael Tennyson collided with a tree and left the scene." "2 Officers Charged in DUI Cases Were Driving Department Cars," *Arizona Daily Star*, November 30, 1999.

"Fall 1999": "Then there's the case of Pima County Court Justice David Mark Anderson, whom officers arrested." "Drug Agency Supervisor, Judge Cited in DUI Cases," *Arizona Daily Star*,

November 28, 1999. Also: "Judge 'Failed Duty,' Official Says," *Arizona Daily Star*, November 30, 1999. "Former Judge Held on DUI, Endangerment Charges," *Arizona Daily Star*, July 4, 2000.

"Winter 2000": "Recently, even America's drug czar has begun to question the effectiveness of prison for drug addicts." "Drug Czar Touting Rehab over Prison," *Tucson Citizen*, January 8, 2000.

"Winter 2000": "Recently, a jury in Tucson decided that Paul Frankovitch, a former offender with a long history of crimes, should be confined because of the likelihood that he would commit another crime." "Predator Law Troubling, but Its Targets Are Hard to Root For," *Tucson Citizen*, January 6, 2000.

"Spring 2000": "For example, in Washington DC, the U.S. Congress—a group of 535 people with an extraordinary number of arrests and indictments for crimes ranging from spousal abuse." "Congress: America's Criminal Class: Part I," *Capitol Hill Blue*, August 16, 1999.

"Monsoon Summer 2000": "This evening, convicted murderer Gary Graham is scheduled to die by lethal injection." CNN: *Larry King Live*, June 22, 2000.

"Monsoon Summer 2000": "The execution will be number 135 for George W. Bush." "The Execution of Youth," *New Yorker*, January 17, 2000. Also: "US Leads the World in Punishment of Juveniles," *Arizona Daily Star*, November 18, 1999.

"Monsoon Summer 2000": "In last Sunday's *New York Times* there's a story by Jennifer Thompson." *New York Times*, June 18, 2000.

"Afterword": "Terry Stewart retired in 2002 and left for Iraq." "Schumer Reveals Fourth Corrections Official with Checkered Record in Power Position at Iraqi Prisons." Senator Charles E. Schumer Web site, June 2, 2004. http://www.senate.gov/~schumer/SchumerWebsite/pressroom/press_releases/2004/PR02662.stewart060204.html.

acknowledgments

I want to begin by acknowledging the men in prison I left behind, many of whom have continued to keep in touch. Without your friendship prison most certainly would have swallowed me alive: Steve Lewandowski, who writes today that I never was a real criminal because I never learned the language, that I never conformed to a prison number, and that this is why he, a career criminal looking for a better way, wanted to be my friend; John Buri, a poet and writer who taught me new ways to see bricks and to see myself; Ken McDonald, storyteller extraordinaire who always pays for his own phone calls from prison (thank you!); Gordon Grilz, another gifted poet who epitomizes a spirit of peace in doing time, even when the time is a life sentence; Mike Lane, composer of hymns; Kim Wilson, avid pen pal to many; and lastly, John Bakke, the best friend I ever had in prison, whose words remain with me though he is gone from this world.

To Richard Shelton and Lois Shelton, my compatriots in crime: you inspire me in so many ways—your marriage of fifty years, your care for our human and natural community, your mentorship to those without mentors.

To my writing compadres, Susan Tweit, Alan Weisman, Alison Deming, Fenton Johnson, Gary Nabhan, Robert Michael Pyle, Scott Slovic, Jimmy Baca, Melanie Bishop, Marcia Bonta, Spring Ulmer, Ariel Marks, Ralph Hager, Tony Luebbermann, Deidre Elliott, Phoenix Psyche Eagleshadow, Steve Gladish, Mac Hudson, Jennifer Schneider: your words and friendship make me believe in a better world, one where prison is an anachronism.

To the Open Society Institute, who saw a glimmer of importance in this book and graciously offered to support it through a Soros Justice Fellowship, and to the Lannan Foundation and its persistent support of the creative writing workshop in prison: through your generosity, grace crosses the razor wire on the wings of swallows. And to Peter Barnes and the Common Council Foundation who gifted me with a second residency at the Mesa Refuge at Point Reyes Station: what a glory it is to write these words in the "South Tower" as Canada geese call from Tomales Bay just outside my window.

To Patti Hartmann, Anne Keyl, Holly Dolan, Christine Szuter, and all the amazing people who make the University of Arizona Press a part of our Southwest community: thank you for indulging me with one more prison book. Maybe it will be my last.

Some of this material first appeared as excerpts in these publications: *Northern Lights*, *Puerto Del Sol*, *South Dakota Review*, and *Walking Rain Review*.

My preference is to use actual names and descriptions where possible; however, I have disguised some people to protect them.

about the author

When Ken Lamberton published his first creative nonfiction book *Wilderness and Razor Wire* (Mercury House, 2000), the *San Francisco Chronicle* called it "entirely original: an edgy, ferocious subtly complex collection of essays. . . . Reading it is like chatting with someone on the street and suddenly noticing there is blood running down his side." The book won the 2002 John Burroughs Medal for outstanding nature writing. He has published more than a hundred nature articles and essays in places like the *Los Angeles Times, Arizona Highways, Bird Watcher's Digest, Manoa, Puerto Del Sol,* the *Gettysburg Review,* and David Quammen's anthology *The Best American Science and Nature Writing 2000.* The University of Arizona Press published *Chiricahua Mountains: Bridging the Borders of Wildness* in October 2003, and his third book, *Beyond Desert Walls: Essays from Prison* in March 2005. Currently, with a grant from the Arizona Commission on the Arts, he's completing a fifth book about hope and redemption on Arizona's Santa Cruz River. He holds degrees in biology and creative writing from the University of Arizona and lives with his wife and daughters in Tucson.